W9-CBP-083

GREGG
SHORTHAND FOR COLLEGES
TRANSCRIPTION

Shorthand written
by Jerome P. Edelman

GREGG

SHORTHAND FOR COLLEGES TRANSCRIPTION

LOUIS A. LESLIE
Coauthor, Gregg Shorthand, Series 90

CHARLES E. ZOUBEK
Coauthor, Gregg Shorthand, Series 90

A. JAMES LEMASTER
Editor in Chief, Gregg Shorthand Publications

KAY MENDENHALL
Instructor, Department of Business Education,
Mountain View High School, Orem, Utah

LORRINE B. SKAFF
Professor of Business,
Southern Oregon State College, Ashland

Gregg Division

McGraw-Hill Book Company

New York / Atlanta / Dallas / St. Louis / San Francisco
Auckland / Bogotá / Guatemala / Hamburg / Johannesburg / Lisbon
London / Madrid / Mexico / Montreal / New Delhi / Panama / Paris
San Juan / São Paulo / Singapore / Sydney / Tokyo / Toronto

This text was prepared by members of the Gregg Shorthand staff:

Editorial: Diana M. Johnson, Albert H. Rihner

Production: Jerome P. Edelman, Mary C. Buchanan, Michael S. Valentine

Art & Design
Coordinator: Karen T. Mino

Designer: A Good Thing Inc.

Cover & interior photos: Martin Bough/Studios Inc.

Library of Congress Cataloging in Publication Data

Main entry under title:

Gregg shorthand for colleges, transcription, series 90.

Includes index.
1. Shorthand–Gregg. I. Leslie, Louis A., date
Z56.2.G7G74 653′.427042′4 79-11916
ISBN 0-07-037760-X

Gregg Shorthand for Colleges, Transcription, Series 90

2 3 4 5 6 7 8 9 0 DODO 8 9 8 7 6 5 4 3 2 1

Gregg Shorthand for Colleges, Transcription, Series 90, is a textbook designed for advanced shorthand students in colleges, universities, community colleges, private schools, and other institutions of higher education. It teaches the students to combine skills already acquired in shorthand and typewriting with a knowledge of the mechanics of English in order to produce mailable correspondence that is accurately transcribed, attractively placed on the page, and free from errors in punctuation, spelling, and grammar. In most cases, *Transcription* will be used after students have completed *Gregg Shorthand for Colleges, Volume Two, Series 90.*

Objectives

Transcription is designed to meet the following objectives:

1 Provide a review of the principles of Gregg Shorthand.
2 Develop further the students' ability to construct outlines for unfamiliar words under the stress of dictation.
3 Develop further the students' command of the mechanics of English.
4 Develop further the students' mastery and understanding of words.
5 Develop further the students' ability to spell and punctuate accurately.
6 Teach the students to place letters attractively on letterheads.
7 Teach the students efficient dictation and transcription techniques.
8 Teach the students to handle the problems of office-style dictation.

Organization

Transcription is organized into 4 parts, 16 chapters, and 80 lessons. Each lesson contains sufficient material for an out-of-class assignment of approximately 40 minutes.

Shorthand Skill Development

The development of the students' shorthand skill continues to receive strong emphasis in *Transcription* through the following features:

BUILDING SHORTHAND SKILL

Each lesson in Part 1 (Lessons 1-20) contains a Theory Recall. The purpose of each recall is to provide a quick, intensive review of brief forms and derivatives, phrases, word beginnings, word endings, and word families.

READING AND WRITING PRACTICE

Each of the 80 lessons contains a Reading and Writing Practice consisting of modern, up-to-date letters and memorandums written in Gregg Shorthand, Series 90. This exercise provides a constant automatic review of the principles of Gregg Shorthand and at the same time develops the students' vocabulary.

The correspondence in each chapter is devoted to a specific business or department of business. The reading level is 9-10.

ACCURACY PRACTICE

A number of lessons contain an Accuracy Practice designed to refine the students' shorthand writing style and thus promote greater fluency and accuracy in writing shorthand.

RECALL DRILLS

In the Appendix a section of Recall Drills provides an intensive review of all the word beginnings, word endings, and phrasing principles of Gregg Shorthand. A few minutes spent on these drills two or three times a week will bring rich dividends.

The Mechanics of English

In *Gregg Shorthand for Colleges, Volumes One* and *Two, Series 90,* much stress is placed on the development of the students' mastery of the mechanics of the English language, an area in which many students entering the stenography course are weak. This emphasis is continued and intensified in *Transcription* through the following features:

PUNCTUATION

In Chapters 1 through 3 the punctuation pointers from the students' early studies in the shorthand course are reviewed. Beginning with Chapter 5, more advanced pointers are introduced.

SPELLING

Marginal Spelling Reminders Words that secretaries frequently misspell are indicated in a second color in the shorthand of each Reading and Writing Practice. The correct longhand spelling and syllabication of these words appear in the margins of the shorthand.

Spelling Families In a number of lessons the students study a Spelling Family, which contains lists of words that have a common spelling problem. Several illustrations from the lists are used in the Reading and Writing Practice of the lesson.

Similar Words A number of lessons contain a Similar-Words Drill. This exercise alerts the students to the need for caution when choosing the correct word from pairs like *week-weak* and *device-devise.*

VOCABULARY DEVELOPMENT

Business Vocabulary Builders Each lesson contains a Business Vocabulary Builder of several words or expressions, selected from the Reading and Writing Practice of that lesson, with which the students may not be familiar. The words and expressions are defined briefly as they are used in the lesson.

Common Prefixes Several lessons contain a drill on common prefixes in the English language. Understanding the meanings of these prefixes will do much to help expand the students' vocabulary.

GRAMMAR

A number of lessons contain drills pinpointing common grammatical errors that secretaries must avoid.

TYPING STYLE

The elements of typing style, presented in *Gregg Shorthand for Colleges, Volume Two, Series 90,* are reviewed in Chapter 4. New, more advanced elements of typing style are introduced, beginning with Chapter 5.

Transcription Techniques

Transcription makes the future secretary aware of many of the problems that are likely to be encountered on the job and shows how to handle them.

CHAPTER OPENINGS

Each chapter of *Transcription* begins with the presentation and discussion of procedures involved in dictation and transcription. Through these chapter openings the students learn how to prepare for dictation, how to take dictation in the employer's office, how to transcribe it, and how to handle other matters related to the business office. Each chapter is beautifully illustrated by photographs especially prepared for *Transcription.*

OFFICE-STYLE DICTATION

In the fourth lesson of each chapter, beginning with Chapter 6, the students are taught how to handle some of the common problems of office-style dictation.

LETTER PLACEMENT BY JUDGMENT

Through a simple but effective device, the students are taught to place letters attractively on a letterhead by judgment.

Other Features

Shortcuts In Chapter 15 the students learn that taking dictation on the job can be made easier if special shortcuts are devised for expressions that are frequently used in certain industries, businesses, or professions.

Model Letters Several model letters are included to show the students the most common letter forms used in business today.

Supporting Materials

STUDENT'S TRANSCRIPT OF GREGG SHORTHAND FOR COLLEGES, TRANSCRIPTION, SERIES 90

The use of this transcript enables the students to complete assignments in the shortest possible time.

WORKBOOK FOR GREGG SHORTHAND FOR COLLEGES, TRANSCRIPTION, SERIES 90

This workbook, correlated lesson by lesson with the text, provides many ways of testing the students' grasp of the nonshorthand elements of *Transcription.*

COLLEGE DICTATION FOR TRANSCRIPTION, SERIES 90

This is a teacher's dictation source book containing several hundred letters correlated lesson by lesson with *Transcription.*

INSTRUCTOR'S HANDBOOK FOR GREGG SHORTHAND FOR COLLEGES, TRANSCRIPTION, SERIES 90

The handbook gives complete information about teaching all phases of transcription. In addition, it includes a course guide and a transcript of the student text.

AUDIOVISUAL AIDS

A number of audiovisual aids are available for use with *Gregg Shorthand for Colleges, Transcription, Series 90*. These include:

College Transcription Tapes, Series 90 These tapes contain the letters from *College Dictation for Transcription, Series 90,* as well as spelling drills and transcription pointers.

Gregg Shorthand Transparencies, Series 90, Set 2, Punctuation; Set 3, Typing Style; Set 4, Spelling.

The publishers are confident that this transcription program will enable teachers to train students to become even more efficient, accurate transcribers than was possible in the past.

The Publishers

Contents

Chapter		Chapter	
1	Employment 17	9	Finance 218
2	Personnel and Training 43	10	Credit 244
3	Energy and Ecology 69	11	Sales 266
4	Motor Vehicles 95	12	Travel and Transportation 290
5	Printed Media 120	13	Recreation and Leisure 316
6	Communications 146	14	Business Equipment 344
7	Homes 170	15	Goodwill and Public Relations 368
8	Agriculture and Food 194	16	General 396

THE SECRETARY ON THE JOB

Part 1

1 Looking for the Job
2 The Interview
3 The First Day
4 Organizing the Work Area

Part 2

5 Taking Dictation
6 Pretranscription Procedures
7 Transcribing
8 Preparing Reports

Part 3

9 Arranging Meetings and Trips
10 Sharpening Skills
11 Composing Letters
12 Accepting More Responsibility

Part 4

13 Moving Up
14 The Replacement
15 Supervising Others
16 Future Advancement

PART

LOOKING FOR THE JOB

Marie Washington was excited about her future. She had recently earned her degree in secretarial administration from a local college, and she was eager to put her skills to use. She felt confident that she would be able to locate a position that would be a challenge and that would be interesting for her—one where her training could be fully utilized.

Marie had had two job interviews, which had been set up by the placement office at her school. Neither of these jobs quite met the standards Marie had set for herself; therefore, she had started looking through the classified ads of her local newspaper for possible job openings. This was where she had found the position for which she would be interviewing tomorrow—secretary to the director of marketing for All-Sports Supply Company. In the event that this interview didn't result in her getting a job, Marie had also made a list of employment agencies she would contact.

However, Marie had good feelings about this interview. She was very much interested in sports in general and was an active participant in several sports. All-Sports was one of the largest distributors of sporting goods in the country and had their headquarters in the city where Marie lived.

Having had two interviews already, Marie knew that pro-

spective employers were looking for more than just good office skills. She knew that her general educational background was an important factor, as were maturity, poise, personality, and good grooming—qualities that would show up during her interview. She also knew that showing a genuine interest in the company would be a plus. Therefore, she had taken the time to find out some general facts about All-Sports from their advertising and from friends who are actively involved in sports.

Marie began preparing for her interview the evening before her appointment. She selected her clothing very carefully, remembering the principles she had learned in her classes at school. She gathered her résumé, her list of references, her shorthand notebook, and two pens. She went to bed early enough to get a good night's rest. She wanted to make the best impression possible during the interview.

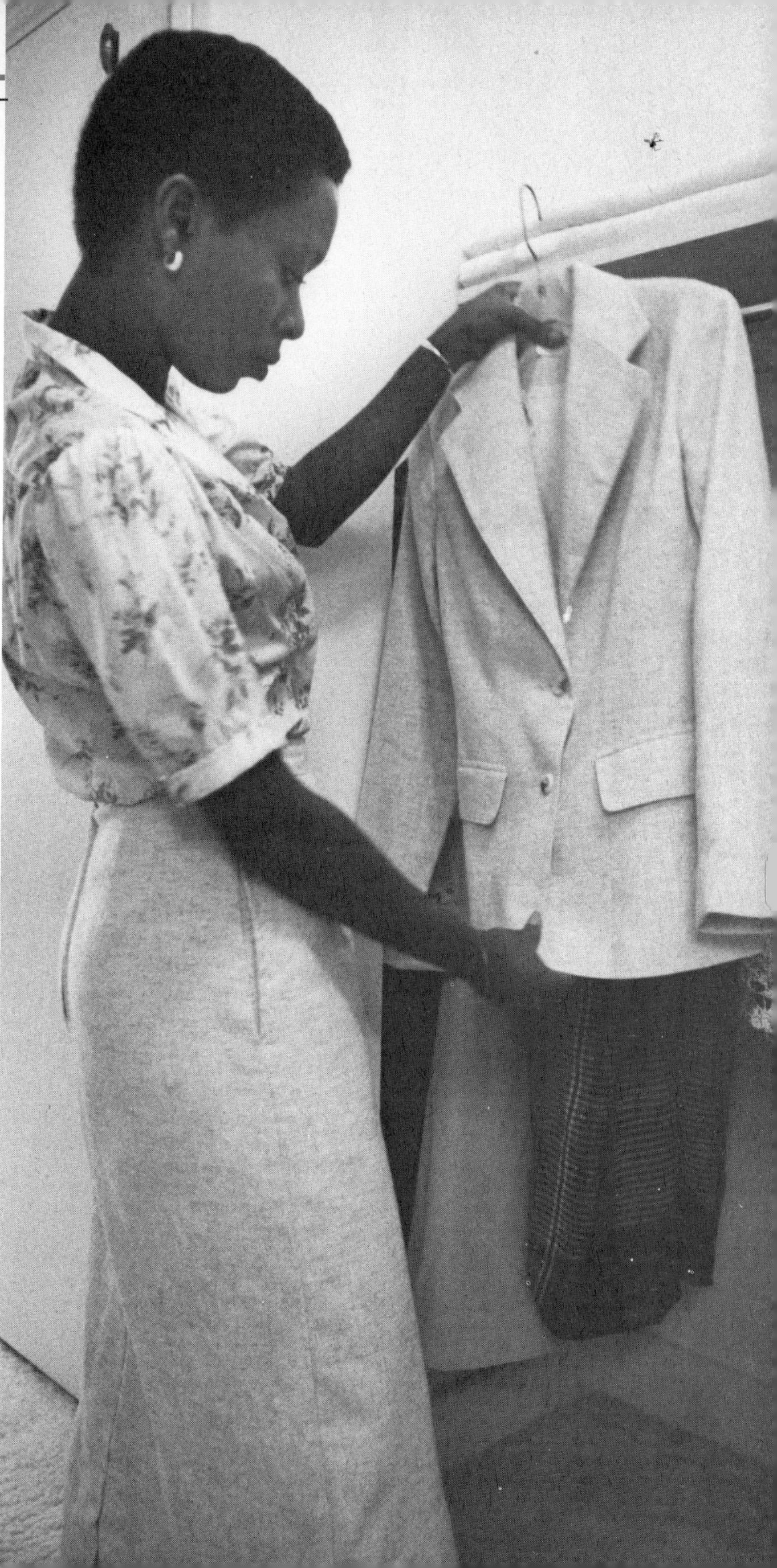

COMMA BRUSHUP

Your major goal in *Gregg Shorthand for Colleges, Transcription, Series 90,* is to further develop your ability to produce mailable copy from dictated material. Mailable copy is defined as any written communication that your employer will sign and mail.

One of the key elements of mailable copy is proper punctuation. For that reason, Volumes One and Two of *Gregg Shorthand for Colleges, Series 90,* contain a systematic presentation of the frequent uses of the comma and other punctuation marks. By following closely the drills in those texts, you should have developed good skills in the proper use of these basic punctuation rules.

In this volume you will continue to build your mastery of punctuation and to improve your ability to spell and to handle the other mechanics of the English language. By faithfully following the drills and activities provided in this text, you will increase your ability to transcribe your shorthand notes into mailable copy.

Chapters 1 through 4 of *Transcription* review the basic punctuation rules that have previously been presented in *Gregg Shorthand for Colleges, Volumes One* and *Two.* Beginning with Chapter 5, you will study additional rules of punctuation.

You will notice that only one punctuation rule is introduced in any one lesson. This will enable you to focus your attention on only one principle at a time. Several examples of the principle will be presented in the lesson in which it is introduced; the principle will then be reviewed in a number of lessons that follow.

In the Reading and Writing Practice of *Transcription* the punctuation marks have been circled and printed in a second color. The reason for the punctuation is indicated directly above the mark.

Words that have been singled out for special attention appear in the margins of the Reading and Writing Practice exercises.

Practice Procedures

The following simple steps will enable you to derive the greatest benefit from the punctuation and spelling pointers in the Reading and Writing Practice exercises:

☐ **1** Carefully read each of the following punctuation rules and examples to be sure that you understand their application.

☐ **2** If possible, read the Reading and Writing Practice exercises aloud. When you encounter a punctuation mark, note the reason for its use, which is indicated directly above it. When you see a shorthand form in a second color, that word appears in the margin correctly spelled and syllabicated. Spell the word aloud, noting the syllable divisions.

☐ **3** Make a shorthand copy of the Reading and Writing Practice exercises; insert and circle the punctuation marks in your notes as you write.

In Chapter 1 you will review the following common uses of the comma:

, parenthetical

A word, a phrase, or a clause that is not essential to the meaning of the sentence should be set off by commas. If the parenthetical expression occurs at the end of the sentence, only one comma is necessary.

You will, however, *be required to furnish all your own tools.*
I hope, Mary, *that you will decide to work with us on this project.*
The chairs are priced separately from the desks, of course.

par

The parenthetical expressions in the Reading and Writing Practice will be indicated in the shorthand as shown in the margin.

, apposition

An expression in apposition is a word, a phrase, or a clause that identifies or explains other terms. When the expression occurs within the sentence, it is set off by commas; when it is at the end of the sentence, only one comma is necessary.

George Brown, our accountant, *will make his presentation next week.*
The trip is scheduled to begin on Saturday, October 14.

ap

The expressions in apposition in the Reading and Writing Practice will be indicated in the shorthand as shown in the margin.

, series

When the last member of a series of three or more items is preceded by *and, or,* or *nor,* a comma is placed before the conjunction as well as between the other items.

Be sure to bring your notebook, a good pen, and a reference manual.
I will be happy to see you on Monday, Tuesday, or Wednesday.

ser

Each time a series occurs in the Reading and Writing Practice, it will be indicated in the shorthand as shown in the margin.

, conjunction

A comma is used to separate two independent clauses that are joined by a conjunction.

I am leaving now, and I will not return until next week.
I will leave early in the morning, but they cannot leave until Friday.

conj

Each time a comma is used to separate independent clauses in the Reading and Writing Practice, it will be indicated in the shorthand as shown in the margin.

, and omitted

When two or more adjectives modify the same noun, they are separated by commas.

Lee is a dependable, efficient *person.*

However, if the first adjective modifies the combined idea of the second adjective plus the noun, the comma is not used.

Joan wore a beautiful blue *suit.*

and o

Each time this use of the comma occurs in the Reading and Writing Practice, it will be indicated in the shorthand as shown in the margin.

Building Shorthand Skill

1 Theory Recall

Each of the first 20 lessons contains a Theory Recall designed to review the major principles of Gregg Shorthand.

You should read each line as rapidly as you can. If you come to an outline you cannot read, spell the shorthand letters in it. This should quickly lead you to the pronunciation of the word. If it does not, refer immediately to the key.

Your reading goal: 1 minute.

Brief Forms and Derivatives

1

Phrases *Be*

2

Word Beginning *Con-*

3

Word Ending *-ble*

4

Word Family *Pro-*

5

1 Advertise, advertisement; regard, regarding; value, values; question, questions.
2 To be, can be, I might be, we will be, I should be, he could be, he will be.
3 Content, contestant, concerned, congratulate, construction, conference.
4 Capable, favorable, likable, trouble, incredible, sensible, possible.
5 Protest, prolong, profound, profit, prominent, provide, pronounce.

Building Transcription Skills

2 **Business Vocabulary Builder** The Business Vocabulary Builders in each lesson will help you continue to increase your vocabulary and your command of the English language.

Each Business Vocabulary Builder consists of several words or expressions that have been selected from the Reading and Writing Practice. You should study these words and expressions together with their definitions to be sure you understand their meaning.

Business Vocabulary Builder

reimburse To pay back.

continental Relating to a continent.

facets The aspects or sides of something.

Reading and Writing Practice

3

prac·ti·cal

par

im·pres·sive

and o

ap

as·sis·tant

conj

dis·cussed

per·son·nel

re·im·burse

mis·cel·la·neous

[181]

4

ap·pli·cant

ser

back·ground

con·ti·nen·tal

dis·cuss

par

great·er

ap·pear

[184]

5

ser

cor·dial

in·for·ma·tive

facets

and o

occupy

solicited

ser

behalf

par

[184]

6

and o

capable

conj

par

[87]

Building Shorthand Skill

1 Theory Recall

Your reading goal: 50 seconds.

Brief Forms and Derivatives

1

Phrases *Been*

2

Word Beginning *In-*

3

Word Ending *-ings*

4

Word Family *-tive*

5

1 Immediate, immediately; value, valuable; responsible, responsibility; particular, particularly.
2 Might have been, should have been, I could have been, has been, it has been, you have been, I have been, I have not been.
3 Infraction, inflation, investments, intentional, indifferent, instant.
4 Recordings, billings, blessings, joinings, meetings, findings, earnings.
5 Initiative, positive, descriptive, alternative, prospective, conservative, cooperative.

982 Underwood Avenue • New Orleans • Louisiana 70101

June 24, 19--

Ms. Nancy Sloan
Sloan and Company
146 West Street
Wilmington, DE 19804

Dear Ms. Sloan:

Thank you for sending me the clipping from the June 18 issue of the Daily Times reporting on my participation in your conference. I appreciate your thoughtfulness.

Please plan to visit me when you are in the area.

Sincerely yours,

Lee Gross

Lee Gross
Director of Marketing

mc

Superior service for generations

Short letter, double spaced, semiblocked style, standard punctuation

Building Transcription Skills

2 Business Vocabulary Builder

expertise The knowledge of an expert.

battery A set or series.

résumé A statement of an applicant's employment experience.

Reading and Writing Practice

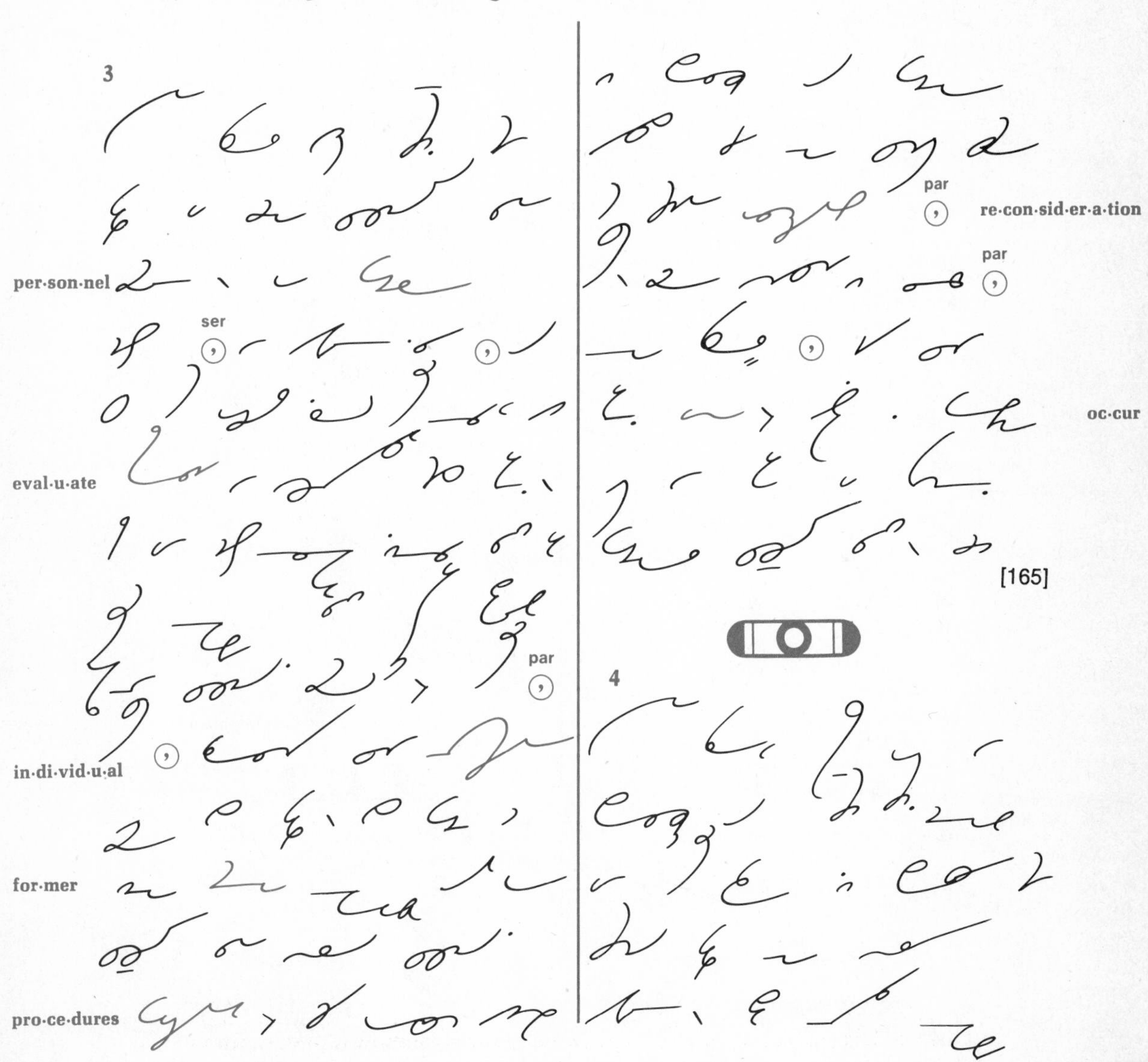

han·dled

par

great·er

com·pen·sa·tion

ap·plied

par

sec·re·tary

ap

de·tails

[138]

5

brief

par

ad·di·tion·al

ser

pur·sue

par

and o

com·pre·hen·sive

[133]

6

ser

NAGENGAST

train·ee

par

ac·cept

ex·cep·tion·al

cal·i·ber

and o

com·pe·tent

[150]

7

par

fluency

par

[121]

Building Shorthand Skill

1 Theory Recall

Your reading goal: 50 seconds.

Brief Forms and Derivatives

1

Phrases *We*

2

Word Beginning *Re-*

3

Word Ending *-ther*

4

Word Family *-ally*

5

1 Under, undergoing; outstanding, outlets; present, representative; correspond-correspondence, corresponds.
2 We have had, we are, we feel, we do not have, we can, we will be glad, we mean, we have.
3 Receive, resign, reason, reasonable, review, replace, refuse, refused.
4 Other, another, together, whether, gathered, neither, further, rather.
5 Personally, originally, incidentally, occasionally, finally, totally.

Building Transcription Skills

2 **Business Vocabulary Builder**

recuperating Recovering; being restored to health.

rehabilitation The process of being restored to a healthy condition.

backlog An accumulation of unfinished work.

clientele Clients; customers.

Reading and Writing Practice

3

ap

ter·ri·to·ry

se·vere·ly

ther·a·py

par

par

par

as·sign

ap

and o

en·thu·si·as·tic

in·dus·tri·ous

oc·ca·sions

[209]

4

en·gi·neers

ap

ac·cept

par

de·pend·able

and o

cre·ative

par

some·one

ap·prised

[148]

5

ap

par

guar·an·tee

par

cli·en·tele

in·cur

[159]

6

ap

quite

par

[108]

PLACING SHORT LETTERS BY JUDGMENT

When you are transcribing a letter, you should, of course, transcribe it accurately and rapidly. You should spell all words correctly and supply the proper punctuation.

In addition, you should place each letter attractively on the letterhead so that it will make a good impression.

Experienced secretaries learn to place letters by judgment; they do not use a placement scale. They simply glance at their shorthand notes and decide what the margins should be.

Much of the dictation you will take will consist of short letters—letters that contain approximately 100 words. The suggestions given below will help you acquire the skill of placing short letters by judgment.

On page 31 you will find Letter 6 from Lesson 3 of *Transcription*—a short letter—as it was written in shorthand by an experienced stenographer and the transcript that was typed. Notice that this letter required a little more than half a column in the notebook.

Make a shorthand copy of this short letter in your notebook and determine how much space it requires in *your* shorthand notebook. If your notes are small, they may require less space than the notes in the illustration; if they are large, they may require more space.

Whenever your notes for a dictated letter require approximately the same space in your notebook that they require for the illustration, here is what you should do to place the letter attractively on the letterhead (assuming your machine has elite—small—type):

☐ **1** Set your margin stops about 2 inches at the left and 2 inches at the right.

☐ **2** Insert your letterhead and type the date on the third line below the last line of the letterhead.

☐ **3** Start the inside address about ten lines below the date (about eight lines if your machine has pica—large—type).

By following these suggestions for placing short letters, you should be able to produce letters that will make a very good impression.

10 MAGNOLIA STREET • LOUISVILLE • KENTUCKY • 40205

April 1, 19--

Mr. Charles Jacobs
Jacobs Associates, Inc.
150 King Street
Atlanta, GA 30331

Dear Mr. Jacobs:

I just received a letter from one of our former employees, Miss Mary Green, telling me that she is applying for the position as your secretary and asking permission to use my name as a reference. I am quite happy to give her permission to do so.

Miss Green was my secretary for several years. She is a good shorthand writer and an accurate transcriber. She also gets along well with people.

I am confident that she will do an excellent job for you if you decide to hire her as your secretary, Mr. Jacobs.

Yours very truly,

Marilyn Washington

Marilyn Washington
Marketing Director

dmj

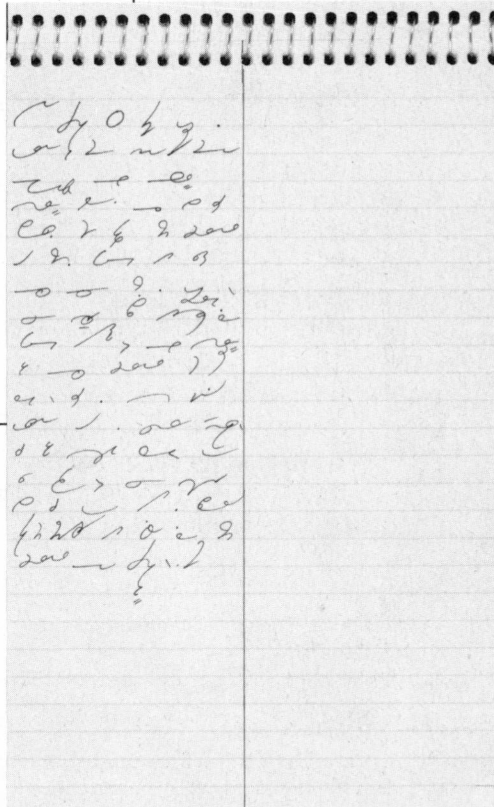

Building Shorthand Skill

1 Theory Recall

Your reading goal: 50 seconds.

Brief Forms and Derivatives

1

Phrases *Special*

2

Word Beginning *Re-*

3

Word Ending *-ful*

4

Word Family *-dent*

5

1 Speak, speakers; request, requesting; regular, regularly; satisfy-satisfactory, satisfaction.
2 We hope that, I hope that, of course, let us know, to do, as soon as, as soon as possible, to us.
3 Respond, receive, reference, resign, reasonable, referred, reported, irreplaceable.
4 Careful, faithful, meaningful, wasteful, hopeful, helpfulness, delightfully, grateful.
5 Evident, accident, superintendent, student, president, resident.

Building Transcription Skills

2 **Business Vocabulary Builder**

clearinghouse A central office.

simulations Imitations.

fundamental (*adjective*) Basic.

Reading and Writing Practice

3

Mary·land

eval·u·ate

ser

suit·ed

sem·i·nars

ser

help·ful

sim·u·la·tions

ac·quaint

[148]

4

re·gard·ing

for·mer

ap

ter·mi·nat·ed

re·hired

ab·sen·tee

con·sci·en·tious

ser

faith·ful

ser

sole·ly

dis·ap·point·ed

par

[182]

5

de·vel·oped

ser

ob·serve

prin·ci·ples

ser

[183]

6

com·pe·tent

ser

ser

and o

re·cep·tion·ists

par

[139]

Building Shorthand Skill

1 Theory Recall

Your reading goal: 50 seconds.

Brief Forms and Derivatives

1

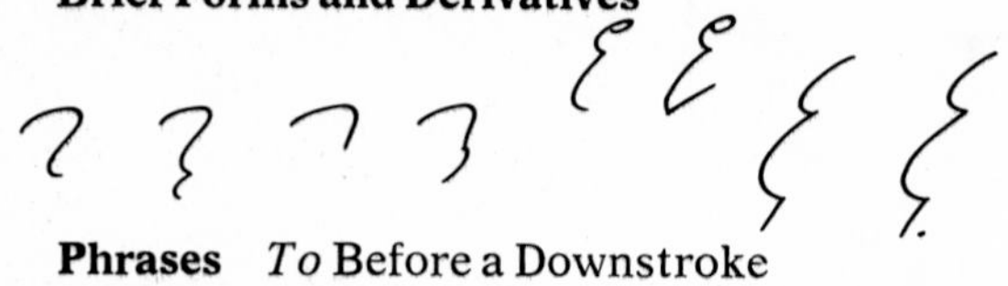

Phrases *To* Before a Downstroke

2

Word Beginning *Dis-*

3

Word Ending *-ment*

4

Word Family *-er*

5

1 Company, companies; question, questions; experience, experienced; publish-publication, publishing.
2 To be, to have, to permit, to plan, to produce, to see.
3 District, distinguished, disbursement, disapprove, discharge, discipline.
4 Department, elementary, fundamental, improvement, requirement.
5 Consider, writer, dinner, owner, water, alter, center, better.

Building Transcription Skills

2 Business Vocabulary Builder

roster A list.

elect To choose; to decide.

oversight An unintended omission or error.

Reading and Writing Practice

3

eval·u·at·ed

ap·ti·tude

conj

par

cat·e·go·ries

re·gard·ing

1973 1975

omit·ted

conj

over·sight

com·plete

[137]

4

col·lege

conj

an·tic·i·pat·ing

grad·u·ates

as·signed

conj

ros·ter

ben·e·fits

[165]

5

par

par

par

mean·time

par

elim·i·nate

conj

par

dis·con·tin·ued

pay·roll

conj

[150]

6

ap

con·trol·ler

par

nu·mer·ous
dis·tinc·tive

and o

conj

hon·or·ing

oc·ca·sion

and o

mem·o·ra·ble

[109]

7

conj

par

ser

[104]

THE INTERVIEW

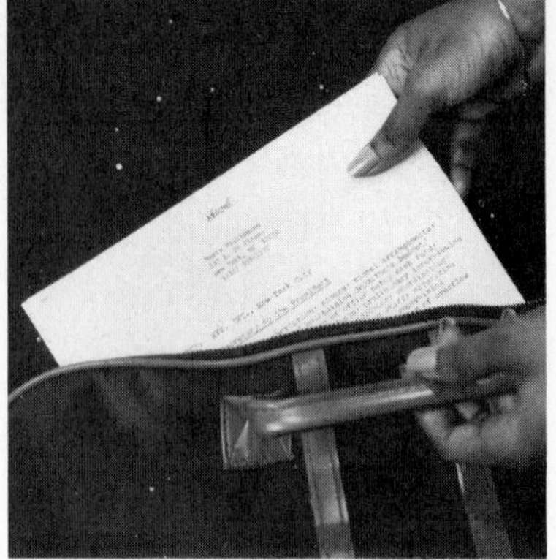

Before leaving for her appointment, Marie checked her appearance carefully and made sure she had all the materials she wanted to take with her. She arrived at All-Sports fifteen minutes before her scheduled appointment. The receptionist gave Marie an application form and asked her to complete it. At 10 o'clock Marie was introduced to Mrs. Joan Stanley, personnel director of the company.

Mrs. Stanley briefly explained the duties of the secretary to the director of marketing and how this position related to the company as a whole. She then asked Marie several questions—questions that would help her determine whether Marie had the necessary qualifications for the job. Many of the questions were prompted by what Marie had written on her application and résumé. Marie was then encouraged to ask any questions she might have about the job or about the company. She was then given shorthand and typing tests—both of which she completed more than satisfactorily.

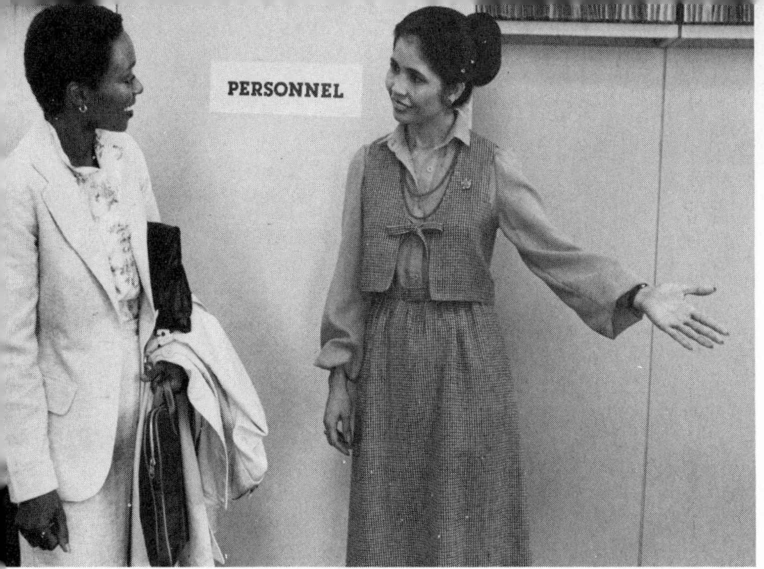

Mrs. Stanley then took Marie to meet Mr. Peter Franklin, the director of marketing. He was interested in why Marie thought she would be interested in working for this particular company and what her long-term employment goals were. Marie learned that her job would involve performing all routine secretarial duties as well as special tasks such as compiling monthly sales reports. Marie indicated that she would be willing to work overtime if necessary.

Having done well on the tests and feeling that both interviews had gone very well, she left All-Sports with a feeling of self-confidence. When she returned home, Marie wrote short thank-you notes to Mrs. Stanley and Mr. Franklin.

Four days later, Mrs. Stanley called Marie and offered her the position of secretary to Mr. Franklin. Marie happily accepted because she felt that this was the right job for her. She assured Mrs. Stanley that she would be at the office at 9 o'clock sharp the following Monday.

COMMA BRUSHUP (CONCLUDED)

In the lessons of Chapter 2 you will review the use of commas with introductory expressions, nonrestrictive clauses, and geographical terms.

Introductory commas will be treated under the four headings listed below. Next to each of these headings is the indication that will appear in the Reading and Writing Practice exercises for that use of the comma.

, when — when (,)   , as clause — as (,)   , if clause — if (,)   , introductory — intro (,)

All introductory dependent clauses beginning with words other than *when, as,* and *if* will be classified as "introductory."

When you have made your decision, *please notify the board.*
As we discussed, *we must finish the next project.*
If you are willing to make a few changes, *we can sign the contract now.*
Because you are typing the agenda, *I hope you will duplicate and distribute it.*

No comma is used between the main clause and the dependent clause when the main clause comes first.

We will attend the meeting *if it is held on Wednesday.*
The report will be presented *whether or not we approve it.*

A comma is also required after introductory words and explanatory expressions such as *frankly, consequently, on the contrary,* and *for instance.*

Frankly, *our sales record was not too impressive.*
For instance, *those who pay early should receive the greatest discount.*

, nonrestrictive

Nonrestrictive, or nonessential, clauses or phrases are set off by commas. A nonrestrictive clause or phrase may be omitted without changing the meaning of the sentence.

restrictive—no commas All persons who are old enough to vote should register.
nonrestrictive—commas George Adams, who is old enough to vote, should register.

Each time the nonrestrictive use of the comma occurs in the Reading and Writing Practice, it will be indicated in the shorthand as shown in the margin.

nonr (,)

, geographical

A comma is used to separate a city and state. If the name of the state does not end the sentence, a comma is placed after the state also.

We sent the report to Salem, Oregon.
Our itinerary includes a stop at Dallas, Texas, *on December 10.*

Whenever this use of the comma appears in the Reading and Writing Practice, it will be indicated in the shorthand as shown in the margin.

geo (,)

Building Shorthand Skill

1 Theory Recall

Your reading goal: 55 seconds.

Brief Forms and Derivatives

1

Phrases *Words Omitted*

2

Word Beginning *Ex-*

3

Word Ending *-lity*

4

Compounds

5

Word Family *Man-*

6

1 Enclose, enclosed; work, worked; manufacture, manufacturing; suggest, suggestion.
2 In the past, some of the, one of the, one of the most, some of our, in the future.
3 Example, extra, excessive, examination, explained, exercise, experiment.
4 Ability, possibility, vitality, reliability, capability, facility, flexibility.
5 Anyhow, anywhere, someone, thereupon, within, somewhere, however.
6 Manager, management, manifest, mandate, manipulate.

Building Transcription Skills

2 Business Vocabulary Builder

adhering Following; observing.

reconcile To bring into harmony; to agree.

exhilarating Refreshing; stimulating.

Reading and Writing Practice

3

in·quired

ap

en·able

ex·ist·ing

conj

when

re·ceive

siz·able

intro

choose

[157]

4

when

griev·ances

em·ploy·ees

ap

conj

in·ten·tion

intro

ap·pears

ad·her·ing

rec·on·cile

when

ar·range·ments

[155]

5

geo

nonr

con·sul·tant

and o

in·no·va·tive

de·vel·oped

and o

cir·cuit

conj

de·tails

as

ex·hil·a·rat·ing

[154]

6

when

intro

touch

ser

prompt·ly

[83]

7

en·ti·tled

when

if

as·sis·tant

ap

[123]

Building Shorthand Skill

1 Theory Recall

Your reading goal: 50 seconds.

Brief Forms and Derivatives

Phrases *Be able*

Word Beginning *Inter-*

Word Ending *-ual*

Word Family *-come*

1 Recognize, recognized; probable, improbable; progress, progressive; from.
2 Be able, they would be able, I will be able, you should be able, he might be able, could be able, may not be able.
3 Interest, interview, intercept, interdependent, interpose, interfere, international, interaction.
4 Actual, intellectual, contractual, individual.
5 Come, income, become, outcome, oncoming, welcome.

Building Transcription Skills

2 Business Vocabulary Builder

precautionary Care taken in advance; foresight.

confided Told confidentially and trustingly.

negotiated Conferred with others to arrive at an agreement.

Reading and Writing Practice

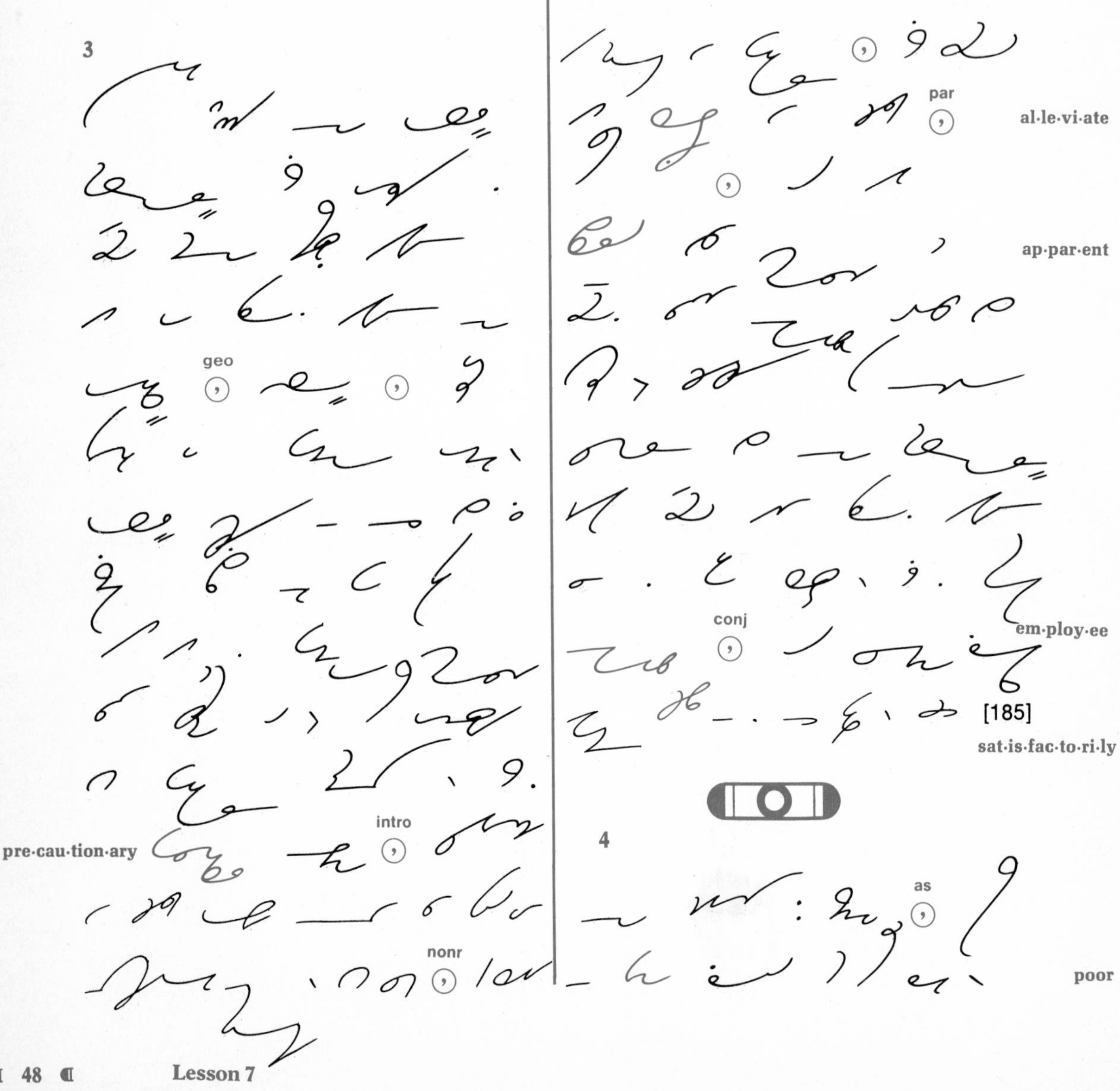

de·te·ri·o·rat·ed

conj

im·prob·a·ble
be·yond

ne·go·ti·at·ed

[145]

5

geo

as

pro·gres·sive

sur·vive

enor·mous

intro

Con·se·quent·ly
de·vel·oped

de·scribed

if

conj

work·shop

[157]

6

ap

intro

pay·roll

intro

[87]

7

pro·found

and o

course

per·suade

as

conj

en·roll·ment

en·rich

[131]

Building Shorthand Skill

1 Theory Recall

Your reading goal: 50 seconds.

Brief Forms and Derivatives

1

Phrases *Ago*

2

Word Beginning *For-*

3

Word Ending *-ingly*

4

Word Family *-rial*

5

1 Difficult, difficulties; part, department; organize, organization; acknowledge, acknowledged.
2 Years ago, several months ago, minutes ago, weeks ago, months ago.
3 Formal, fortunate, formulate, inform, reform, performance, forgive, forward.
4 Willingly, accordingly, surprisingly, convincingly, seemingly, increasingly, sparingly.
5 Editorial, territorial, managerial, serial, memorial.

Building Transcription Skills

2 Business Vocabulary Builder

imprinted Marked by pressure.
encounter (*verb*) To come upon unexpectedly.
optimistic Expecting the best possible outcome.

Reading and Writing Practice

3

rec·re·ation

geo

va·ri·ety

Mere·ly

conj bro·chure

op·ti·mis·tic

intro

if un·usu·al

[157]

4

de·cid·ed
ex·er·cise

geo

nonr

lo·cat·ed

re·al

prem·ises

[115]

5

gov·ern·ment

re·leased

vi·tal

intro

if

geo

oc·cu·pa·tions

ex·ceed

un·filled

con·se·quences

ser

steno·graph·ic

[170]

6

geo

ex·cel·lent

nonr

if

add

zest

and o

[155]

7

geo

dis·played

par

intro

[97]

con·sid·er·ation

Building Shorthand Skill

1 Theory Recall

Your reading goal: 50 seconds.

Brief Forms and Derivatives

1

Phrases *Hope*

2

Word Beginning *Un-*

3

Word Ending *-tial*

4

Word Family *-port*

5

1 Usual, unusually; success, successful; be, before; their, theirs; you, yours.
2 We hope, I hope, I hope you will, we hope you can, we hope you will, we hope you will be able.
3 Unless, unfortunate, until, uncertain, unfamiliar.
4 Substantial, especially, potential, impartial, residential, commercial, financial.
5 Transport, passport, importation, report, import, transportation, export, exported.

2 Business Vocabulary Builder

lucrative Profitable.

reprimands (*noun*) Formal reproofs.

preclude To make impossible; to prevent.

Reading and Writing Practice

3

geo

In·di·a·nap·o·lis

intro

rep·re·sen·ta·tive

geo

im·port

lu·cra·tive

intro

sab·bat·i·cal

cal·en·dar

pro·vi·sions

conj

ap·pears

[168]

4

intro

com·piled
sta·tis·ti·cal

ra·tios

al·low·ance

nonr

sub·stan·tial·ly

[162]

5

intro

eval·u·a·tion

ab·sen·tee·ism

rep·ri·mands

intro

ap·par·ent

intro

Con·fi·den·tial·ly

intro

ter·mi·nate

pre·clude

[109]

6

me·chan·i·cal

ap

in·tri·cate

intro

intro

en·able

geo

[120]

7

conj

pay·roll

re·ceive

conj

spec·i·fy

intro

[113]

Building Shorthand Skill

1 Theory Recall

Your reading goal: 45 seconds.

Brief Forms and Derivatives

Phrases *Want*

Word Beginning *Trans-*

Word Ending *-rity*

Word Family *Form*

1 Govern, government; out, outlined; advantage, advantages; ordinary, ordinarily; short, shortly.
2 I want, you want, who wants, he wanted, we want, do you want, if you want.
3 Transaction, transcribe, transmission, transplant, transparent, translation, transfer.
4 Prosperity, maturity, priority, celebrity, familiarity, authority, regularity.
5 Formal, information, formula, formation, formerly, formidable, inform.

Building Transcription Skills

2 Business Vocabulary Builder

transmission The passage of radio waves through space.

components Parts; ingredients.

transistors Electronic devices.

Reading and Writing Practice

3

spon·sor·ing

in·vit·ed

geo

trans·mis·sion

po·ten·tial

[125]

4

as

geo

au·thor·i·ty

conj

ini·ti·ate

grad·u·al·ly

conj

pro·pose

5:30

lunch

nonr

am·ple

trans·fer

if

su·per·vi·sor

par

[162]

5

for·mer·ly

nonr

geo

intro

sub·ject

intro

pri·or·i·ties

[146]

6

tech·ni·cal

ac·quaint·ed

par

geo

per·son·nel

nonr

ap·pear

suc·cess·ful

nonr

agen·cies

ex·haust

[156]

7

nonr

en·gi·neer·ing

par

geo

thought·ful·ness

[125]

8

ad·mis·sion

conj

intro

conj

par

va·can·cies

nonr

when

[94]

9

if

weap·on

nonr

em·ploy·able

ac·quire

when

[118]

THE FIRST DAY

On Monday Marie reported to the personnel department. Her first hour was spent at an orientation session with a member of the personnel staff. During this session, Marie was told about general company policies and procedures and about the benefits offered by the company—including employee discounts on sports equipment! She was given several forms to fill out—payroll forms, insurance and medical forms, and tax forms. After she had been given the opportunity to ask questions, Marie reported to Mr. Franklin's office.

Mr. Franklin welcomed Marie to the company and then took her on a brief tour of the office, pointing out the files and the supply room. He introduced her to some of the people with whom she would be working, including his boss, Ms. Carmen Valdez. When they returned to his office, Mr. Franklin explained that he would be out of the office that afternoon, so Marie would have plenty of time to get things organized and become familiar with her surroundings.

Mr. Franklin indicated that he would like to have his mail opened and on his desk the first thing every day. After he had had time to read this correspondence, he would call her in for dictation. The rest of the day would be devoted to whatever other work they had at a particular time. Marie was told that a very important matter that would have to be taken care of the first of every month was issuing the previous month's sales report—this was always a difficult task and Marie should be prepared for it.

As he was leaving for the afternoon, Mr. Franklin wished her luck on her new job. He told her to use the rest of the day for becoming acquainted with the office and if she had any questions, any of the other secretaries would be happy to help her. Since it was now noon, Marie decided that she would get to work right after lunch. Two of the other secretaries came over and invited Marie to join them for lunch—and she accepted gladly.

After a very pleasant lunch, Marie was ready to get to work. She knew that she had to do a great many things during the afternoon. She wanted to get her desk organized, and, if time permitted, she wanted to review the office procedures manual and become familiar with some of the files. She wanted to be ready for her first full day of work the next day.

PUNCTUATION BRUSHUP

In Chapter 3 you will review the following: the use of the period to indicate a courteous request, the hyphen, the apostrophe, and one use of the semicolon.

. courteous request

If one person wished to persuade another to take some definite action, a request for direct action could be made with a statement such as:

Send your answer as soon as possible.

A direct statement of this type, however, might antagonize the reader. The writer, therefore, may prefer to make such a request in the form of a question.

Will you please send your answer as soon as possible.

When a request for definite action is put in the form of a question, a period is used at the end of the sentence.

This is how you can decide whether to use a question mark or a period:

☐ **1** If the question calls for an answer in the form of action, use a period.

☐ **2** If the question calls for a yes-or-no answer, use a question mark.

Whenever the period is used in this situation in the Reading and Writing Practice, it will be indicated in the shorthand as shown in the margin.

cr ⊙

The hyphen

To decide whether to use a hyphen in compound expressions like *past due* or *well known,* observe these rules:

☐ 1 If a noun follows the expression, use a hyphen.

Your past-due *account (noun) has come to my attention.*

Whenever a hyphenated expression occurs in the Reading and Writing Practice, it will be called to your attention in the margin thus:

past-due
hyphenated
before noun

☐ 2 If no noun follows the compound expression, do not use a hyphen.

Our company is up to date.

Occasionally, these expressions in which a hyphen is not used will be called to your attention thus:

up to date
no noun,
no hyphen

☐ 3 No hyphen is used in a compound modifier where the first part of the expression is an adverb ending in *ly.*

It is a beautifully decorated *room.*

To be sure that you do not put a hyphen in expressions of this type, your attention will occasionally be called to them in the Reading and Writing Practice thus:

beau·ti·ful·ly dec·o·rat·ed
no hyphen
after ly

The apostrophe

☐ 1 A noun that ends in an *s* sound and is followed by another noun is usually a possessive, calling for an apostrophe before the *s* when the word is singular.

Our company's *transfer policy will be revised soon.*

☐ 2 A plural noun ending in *s* calls for an apostrophe after the *s* to form the possessive.

Several students' *grades are very high.*

☐ 3 An irregular plural calls for an apostrophe before the *s* to form the possessive.

Our men's *department has been discontinued.*

☐ 4 The possessive forms of pronouns do not require an apostrophe.
The papers are ours, *not* theirs.

; no conjunction

A semicolon is used to separate two independent but closely related clauses when no conjunction is used to connect the clauses.

We will travel to California this year; we will make our trip to Florida later.

The above sentence could be written as two sentences.

We will travel to California this year. We will make our trip to Florida later.

Because the two thoughts are closely related, however, the use of the semicolon seems more appropriate.

Each time this use of the semicolon occurs in the Reading and Writing Practice, it will be indicated in the shorthand as shown in the margin. **nc** (;)

Building Shorthand Skill

1 Theory Recall

Your reading goal: 45 seconds.

Brief Forms and Derivatives

1

Phrases *Special*

2

Word Beginning *Em-, Im-*

3

Word Ending *-tain*

4

Word Family *-peration*

5

1 Where, whereby; never, nevertheless; for, therefore; with, without.
2 To make, to me, to know, let us, let us know, to us, your order, more than.
3 Employ, embrace, embellish, empire, improbable, impartial, impossible, impatient.
4 Obtain, fountain, certainly, maintain, containing, sustain, attain, obtaining.
5 Operation, cooperation, expiration, asperation, inspiration, desperation.

Building Transcription Skills

2 Business Vocabulary Builder

empowered Gave power or authority to.

grievous Causing grief or distress.

scrutinize To examine closely.

conspicuous Easy to see; obvious.

Reading and Writing Practice

3

pol·lu·tion

else·where

par

yours

griev·ous

intro

haze
lin·ger

ban·ning

vi·tal

[161]

4

as

un·usu·al·ly heavy
no hyphen
after ly

pre·mi·um

ser

un·lead·ed

intro

less·en

conj

emer·gen·cy

cus·tom·ers'

se·ri·ous

cr

[159]

5

intro

scru·ti·nize

gro·cery

adopt·ed

intro

intro

af·ter-tax hyphenated before noun

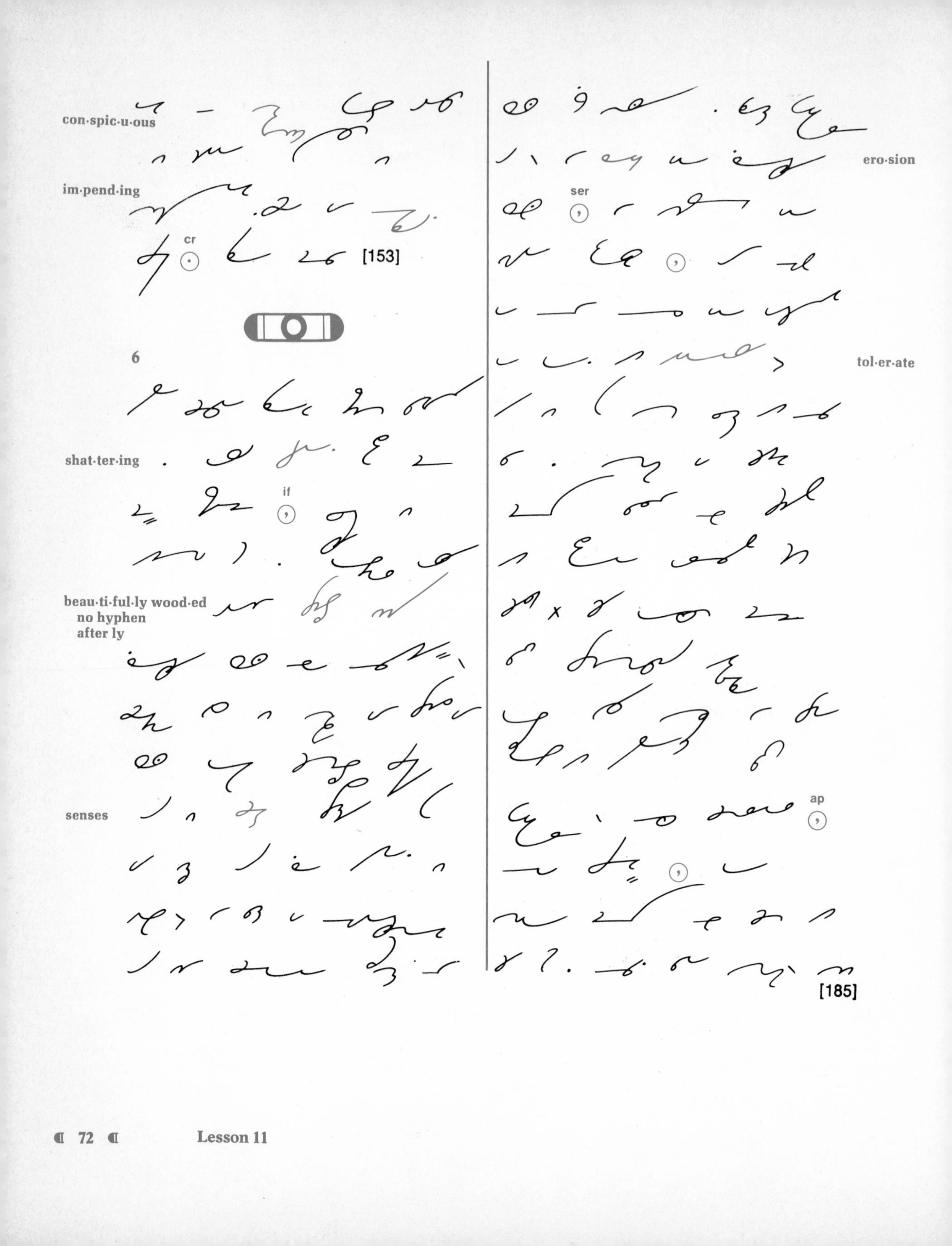

con·spic·u·ous

im·pend·ing

cr

[153]

6

shat·ter·ing

if

beau·ti·ful·ly wood·ed
no hyphen
after ly

senses

ero·sion

ser

tol·er·ate

ap

[185]

Building Shorthand Skill

1 Theory Recall

Your reading goal: 45 seconds.

Brief Forms and Derivatives

1

Phrases *Will*

2

Word Beginning *En-*

3

Word Ending *-ification*

4

Word Family *-tive*

5

1 Every, everyone; work, working; your, yourself; time, meantime.
2 You will, you will be, I will have, we will not be, it will be, there will be.
3 Enrolling, enthusiasm, enjoy, enrich, environment, enforcement.
4 Specification, justification, verification, modifications, gratification, certification, notification.
5 Creative, native, imaginative, relative, relatives, positive.

Building Transcription Skills

2 Business Vocabulary Builder

compliance Following or adhering to a request or order.

diminished Decreased; reduced.

monitoring Checking; observing.

Reading and Writing Practice

3

safe·ty

nc

ev·ery·one's

ser

streams

pure

ours

conj

theirs

par

new·ly en·act·ed no hyphen after ly

cr

[174]

4

air·craft

and o

in·no·va·tive

hy·dro·gen

intro

intro

well-known hyphenated before noun

cr

ad·di·tion·al

[157]

5

yes·ter·day's

ref·er·ences

conj

first-rate

ex·ceed

intro

as

mon·i·tor·ing

bi·o·log·i·cal

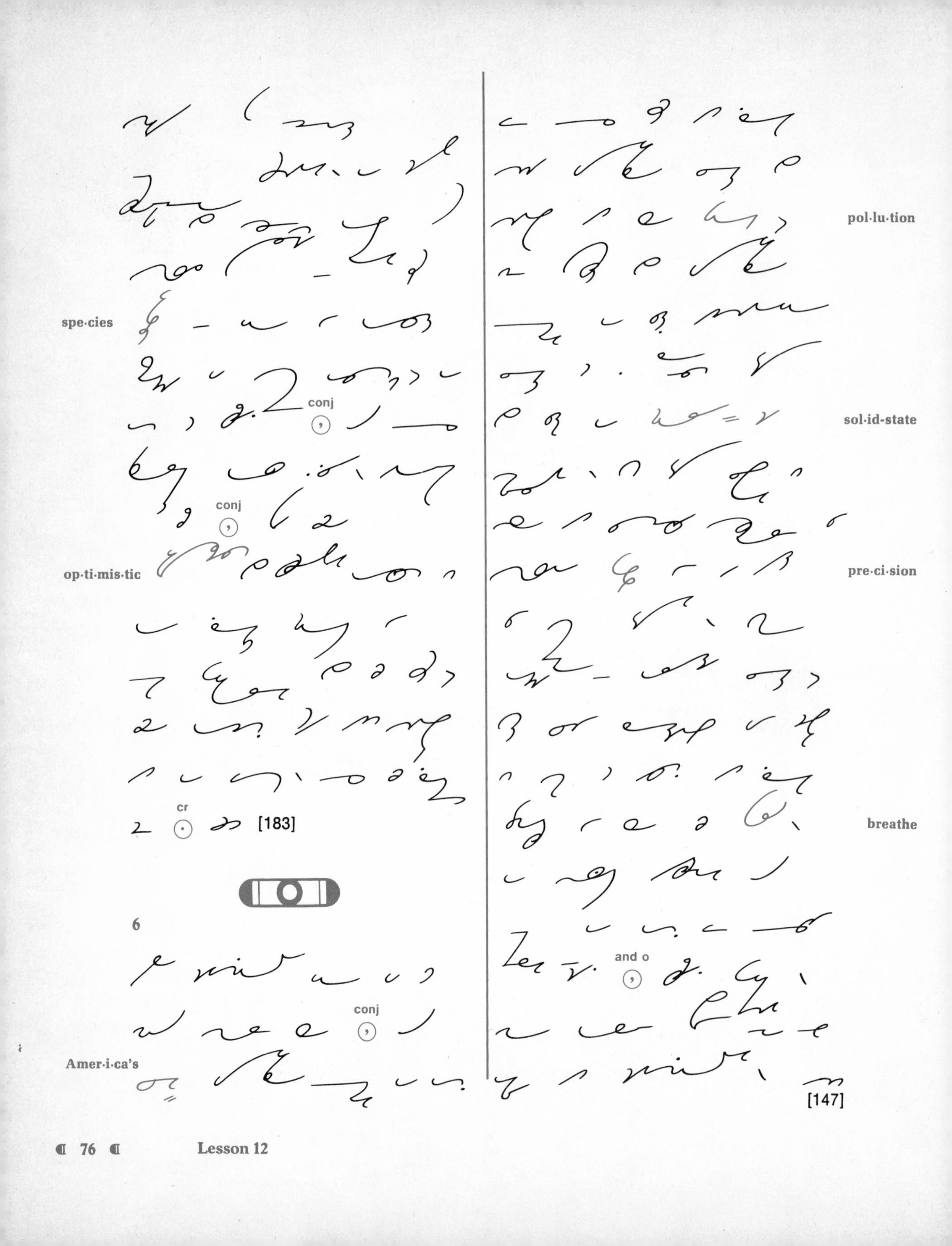

spe·cies

conj

conj

op·ti·mis·tic

cr [183]

6

conj

Amer·i·ca's

pol·lu·tion

sol·id-state

pre·ci·sion

breathe

and o

[147]

Building Shorthand Skill

1 Theory Recall

Your reading goal: 45 seconds.

Brief Forms and Derivatives

1

Phrases *Words Omitted*

2

Word Beginning *Sub-*

3

Word Ending *-ure*

4

Word Family *Point*

5

1 For, before; glad, gladly; when, whenever; out, without.
2 One of our, two or three, as a result, in the past, one of the most, some of them, one of the.
3 Submit, submitted, submission, substantial, substitute, subscribe, subdivide.
4 Furniture, lecture, future, natural, picture, miniature.
5 Point, appoint, appointment, disappointed, reappoint, standpoint.

Building Transcription Skills

2 Business Vocabulary Builder

ingenious Clever; resourceful; original.

credentials Items that establish one's confidence in a person's abilities.

subcommittee A part of a committee organized for a specific purpose.

Reading and Writing Practice

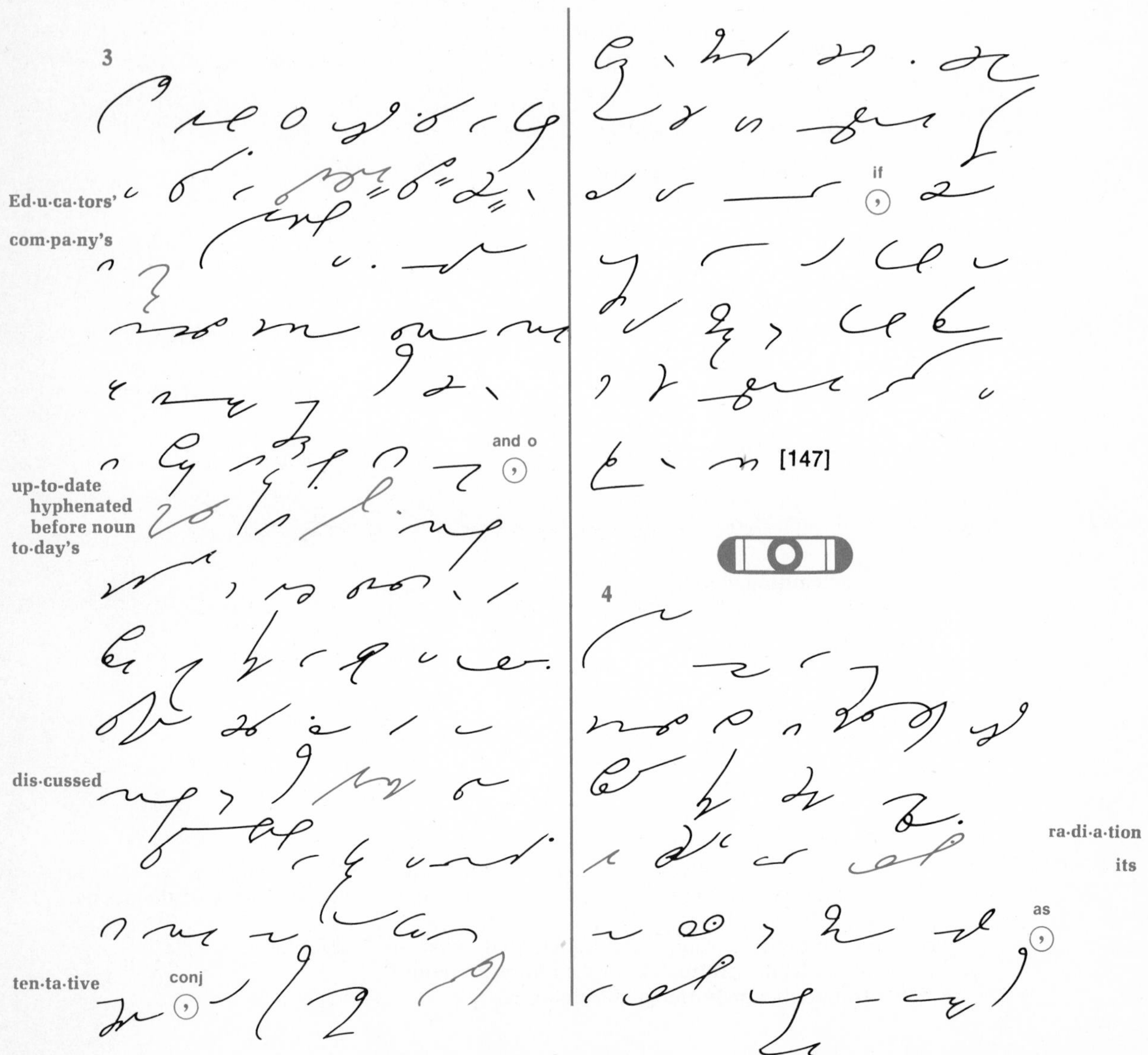

ex·ceed

intro

sub·soil

evac·u·a·tion

intro

com·plete

nonr

weeks'

as·sis·tance

if

[158]

5

par

long-range hyphenated before noun

well-qual·i·fied hyphenated before noun

conj

[128]

6

intro

yours

re·al·i·ty

if

ev·ery·one's

well-known
hyphenated
before noun

intro

nc

na·tion's

crit·i·cal·ly short
no hyphen
after ly

[136]

7

as

well pre·pared
no noun,
no hyphen

par

cus·tom·ers'

intro

agen·cies'

days'

[130]

Building Shorthand Skill

1 Theory Recall

Your reading goal: 45 seconds.

Brief Forms and Derivatives

1

Phrases *Able*

2

Word Beginning *Super-*

3

Word Ending *-ily*

4

Word Family *-ct*

5

1 Idea, ideas; time, timed; part, depart; street, streets.
2 Will be able, we have been able, we may be able, we should be able, to be able, I should be able, we will not be able.
3 Superior, supervision, supervisory, superintendent, superficial, superimpose, supersede, superstitious.
4 Easily, steadily, necessarily, families, primarily, customarily, heavily.
5 Effect, prospect, reject, perfect, reflect, neglect, inspect.

Building Transcription Skills

2 **Business Vocabulary Builder**

contaminants Substances that produce an impure or unclean condition.

supersede To make way for another.

compromise To settle by concessions from both sides.

Reading and Writing Practice

3

can·cer

cit·ed

de·vel·op

intro

can·cer-caus·ing

intro

com·pa·ny's

harm·ful

and o

po·ten·tial·ly dan·ger·ous no hyphen after ly

intro

[180]

4

gov·ern·ment's

su·per·sede

if

an·a·lysts

elim·i·nat·ed

new·ly con·struct·ed
no hyphen
after ly

nc

com·pro·mise

some·time

cr

[178]

sit·u·a·tion

5

morn·ing's

nc

col·umns

near·by

and o

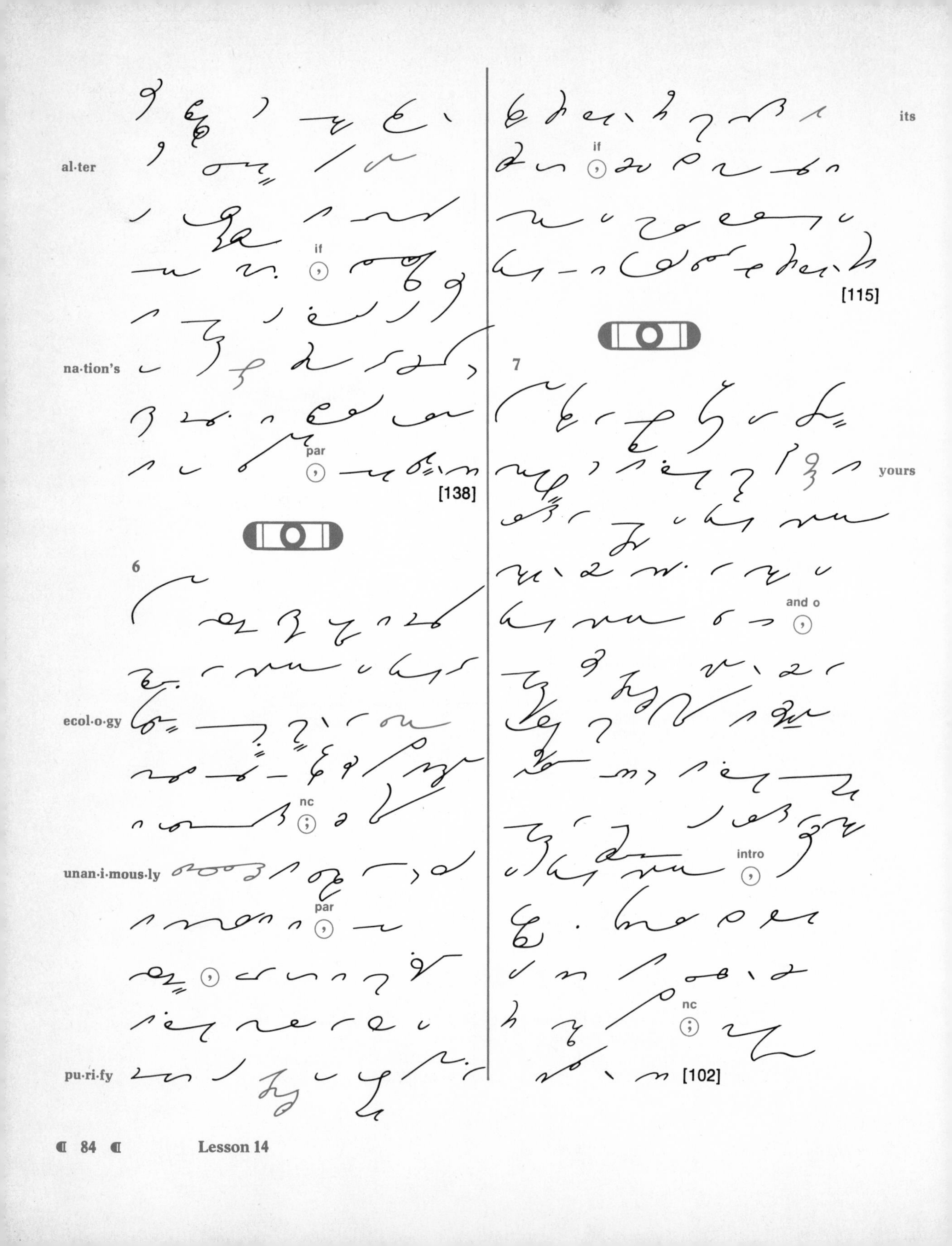

al·ter

if

na·tion's

par

[138]

6

ecol·o·gy

nc

unan·i·mous·ly

par

pu·ri·fy

its

if

[115]

7

yours

and o

intro

nc

[102]

Building Shorthand Skill

1 Theory Recall

Your reading goal: 45 seconds.

Brief Forms and Derivatives

1

Phrases *Glad*

2

Word Beginning *Al-*

3

Word Ending *-cal*

4

Word Family *-sure*

5

1 Under, understand; general, generally; with, without; thing, something; what, whatever.
2 Would be glad, we will be glad, I am glad, will be glad, he will be glad.
3 Almost, although, alteration, alternative, altogether, already.
4 Medical, surgical, practically, articles, periodical, economical.
5 Measure, pressure, ensure, leisure, disclosure, exposure, reassure.

Building Transcription Skills

2 Business Vocabulary Builder

blatant Outright; obvious; brazen.

habitat Environment.

respiratory Pertaining to breathing.

Reading and Writing Practice

3

or·ga·ni·za·tion's

oc·cur·ring

week's

wide·ly re·spect·ed no hyphen after ly

intro

en·vi·able

[120]

4

ex·ists

ours

an·i·mals'

par

se·vere·ly

and o

wild·life

if

di·vi·sion

big-game hyphenated before noun

ap

[168]

5

nc

par

intro

re·ac·tion

fil·tra·tion

intro

ser

res·tau·rants

intro

jeop·ar·dize

re·spi·ra·to·ry

en·dorse

cr

[166]

6

mon·i·tor·ing

air-pol·lu·tion hyphenated before noun

bad·ly need·ed no hyphen after ly

as·sign·ment

if

op·er·a·tion's

[97]

7

conj

intro

rec·la·ma·tion

geo

nonr

nom·i·nal

par

com·pa·ny's

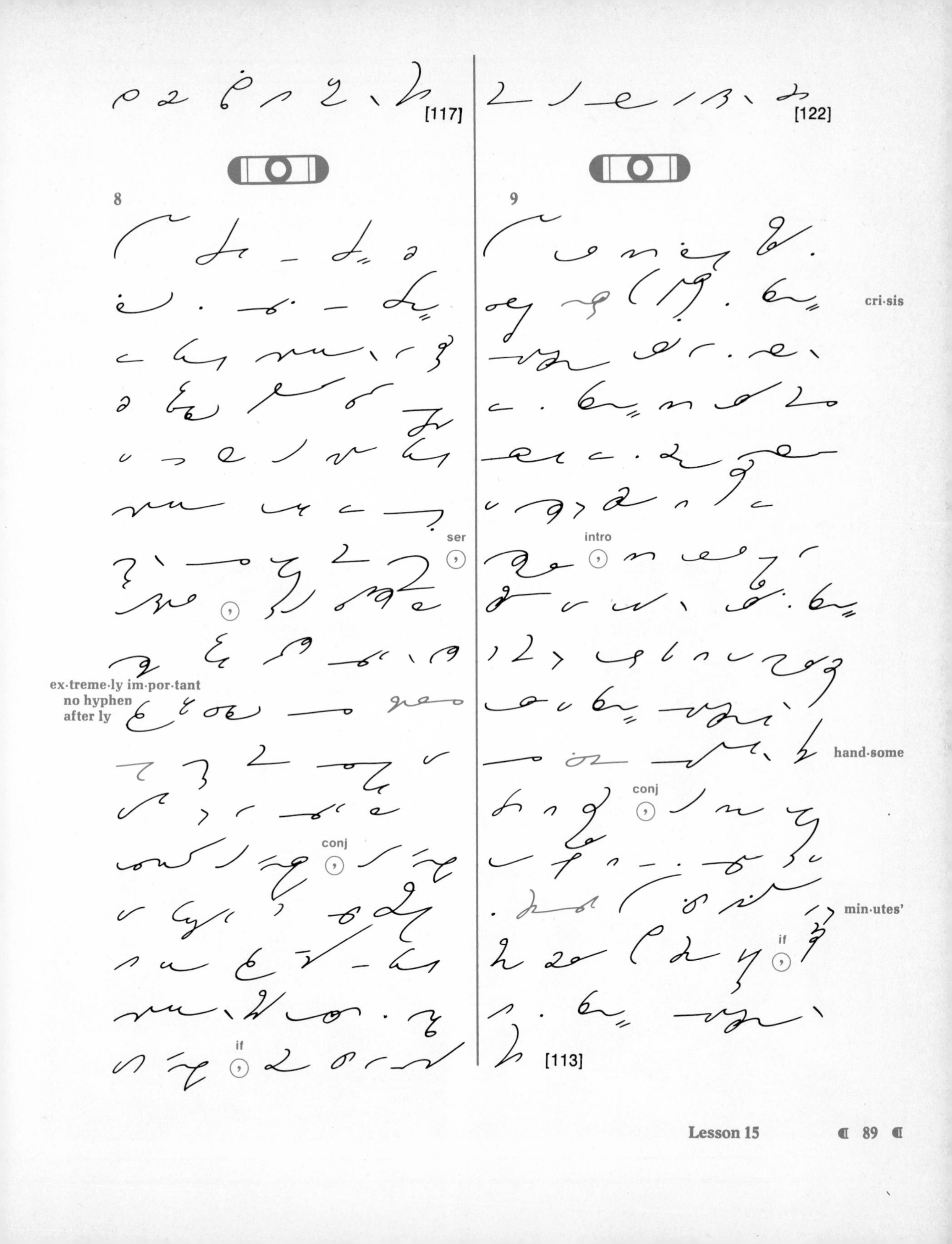

[117]

[122]

8

ser

ex·treme·ly im·por·tant
no hyphen
after ly

conj

if

9

cri·sis

intro

hand·some

conj

min·utes'

if

[113]

ORGANIZING THE WORK AREA

Marie started organizing by taking inventory of the general supplies in her desk. She made a list of those supplies she felt she would need and made a trip to the supply room to get them. She first organized the top right-hand drawer, putting all stationery supplies in a logical order from back to front: interoffice stationery, letterhead, carbon paper and carbon packs, second sheets, onionskin for additional copies, plain bond, and envelopes. Marie put all the standardized company forms she found in the lower right-hand drawer—she would be using them frequently.

All extra supplies—staples, paper clips, rubber bands, erasers, correction materials, scissors, a ruler, extra pens and pencils, and a letter opener—were arranged neatly in the middle drawer. Since her typewriter was to the left of the desk, the bottom drawer on that side of the desk would be used for files or materials that were not needed often.

In order to keep the top of her desk as clear as possible, Marie limited desk-top items: "in" and "out" boxes, a copyholder, a calendar, a stapler, a tape dispenser, a date stamp, a notebook (opened and ready for dictation), a pen and pencil

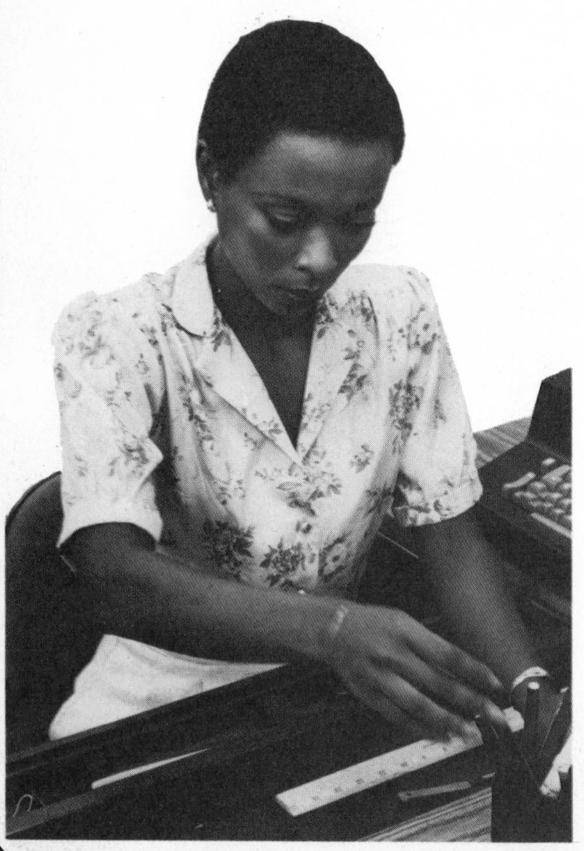

holder, and two or three reference books.

The reference books that Marie felt should be most handy were a dictionary, *The Gregg Reference Manual, 20,000 Words,* and the company's office procedures manual. She had used the first three books in her secretarial training classes and knew how valuable they were. Telephone directories, a National ZIP Code Directory, an airline guide, a hotel guide, and an almanac were located in a central area for use by all the secretaries in the office.

Next, Marie decided to do a maintenance check on her typewriter. She checked and cleaned the type element to be sure it was in good working order. She put a new ribbon in the machine and cleaned the typewriter by brushing away dust and eraser particles.

Finally, Marie started to familiarize herself with the business of the office. She reviewed the basic procedures outlined in the office manual and looked through the files to see how they were organized. By doing this, she was able to see the type of

correspondence and forms she would be working with and exactly where they were located.

By the end of the first day, Marie knew that she was well organized and ready for whatever tasks she was assigned.

TYPING STYLE BRUSHUP

In Chapter 4 you will review the correct ways of typing numbers, percents, addresses, amounts of money, dates, and expressions of time. In addition, you will review several rules for capitalization.

Addresses

☐ **1** Always use figures to designate house numbers.

Our address is 800 (*not* eight hundred) *Baker Drive.*

☐ **2** Spell out numbers below 11 in street names.

Mario lives at 450 Third *Avenue.*

☐ **3** Use figures in street names of 11 and above. Omit *th, st,* or *d* if a word such as *West* precedes the street number.

I own a store at 35 West 75 *Street.*

When street addresses occur in the Reading and Writing Practice, they will occasionally be called to your attention in the margin of the shorthand thus:

Transcribe:
345 West 21 Street

Amounts of Money

☐ **1** When transcribing whole amounts of dollars in business letters, do not add a decimal point or zeros.

He paid his bill of $355 (*not* $355.00).

☐ **2** In business letters, use the word *cents* for amounts under $1.

The pencil cost only 15 cents (*not* $.15).

☐ **3** Even millions, billions, and higher may be transcribed in figures and words for easier reading.

The value of the land was $5 million.

When amounts such as the above appear in the Reading and Writing Practice, they will occasionally be called to your attention in the margin of the shorthand thus: **Transcribe:** **$355** **Transcribe:** **15 cents**

Time

☐ **1** Use figures in expressing time with *o'clock*. (Remember the apostrophe!)

We must finish by 10 o'clock (*not* ten o'clock).

☐ **2** Use figures in expressing time with *a.m.* and *p.m.*

The plane will arrive at 10:25 a.m. *and depart at* 1 p.m.
The meeting is from 8 *to* 9 a.m.

Note: Type *a.m.* and *p.m.* with small letters and no space after the first period.

☐ **3** Spell out time if *a.m., p.m.,* or *o'clock* is not used.

The store is open from ten *until* six.

Occasionally these expressions of time will be called to your attention in the margins of the shorthand thus:

Transcribe:
10 o'clock
ten

Transcribe:
9 a.m.
10:25 a.m.

Dates

☐ **1** If the name of the month precedes the day, do not use *th, st,* or *d* after the number. This is the way dates are most frequently expressed in business letters.

On November 25, 1987, *he will retire.*

☐ **2** If the day precedes the month, *th, st,* or *d* should be included.

On the 13th of May, *we leave for vacation.*

When dates appear in the Reading and Writing Practice, they will occasionally be called to your attention in the margin thus:

Transcribe:
April 5, 1960,

Transcribe:
13th

Numbers

☐ **1** Spell out numbers 1 through 10.

We attended three *times.*

☐ **2** Use figures for numbers above 10.

There are 26 *students here.*

☐ **3** If several related numbers appear in the same sentence, some of which are above 10 and some below, use figures for all.

The vote was 3 *for Kay,* 5 *for Lee, and* 21 *for Gail.*

☐ **4** Spell out a number that begins a sentence.

Twenty *people attended the meeting.*

For consistency, spell out related numbers.

Twenty *or* thirty *people were there.*

□ **5** Express percentages in figures and spell out the word *percent.*

We pay 10 percent *interest.*

□ **6** When a number contains four or more digits, a comma is used to separate thousands, millions, billions, and so on.

3,000 *246,489* *1,356,000* *4,300,700,000*

□ **7** Commas, however, are not used in serial numbers, house or street numbers, ZIP Codes, telephone numbers, page numbers, and between digits of a year.

No. 34538	*3532 Third Street*	*Houston, TX 77004*
page 1950	*the year 1987*	*telephone number 555-1902*

These correct uses of numbers will occasionally be called to your attention in the margin of the Reading and Writing Practice thus: **Transcribe:**
5,000
ten

Capitalization

□ **1** Capitalize company names. Capitalize the word *the* only if it is actually part of the company name. Such words as *of* or *and* are not capitalized within a company name.

We work for the National Department Store.

□ **2** Common organizational terms, such as *advertising department* or *finance committee,* are not ordinarily capitalized.

I will serve on the budget committee.

□ **3** Capitalize *east, west,* and so on, only when these words designate definite regions or when they are part of a proper name.

We drove east.
We live in the West.
They live in South Carolina.

Building Shorthand Skill

1 Theory Recall

Your reading goal: 40 seconds.

Brief Forms and Derivatives

1

Phrases *Contractions*

2

Word Beginning *Fur-*

3

Word Ending *-ulate, -ulation*

4

Word Family *Stand*

5

1 What, somewhat; thing, nothing; not, notwithstanding; public, publicly.
2 Wasn't, shouldn't, haven't, couldn't, doesn't, isn't, won't.
3 Furnish, furnishings, furniture, further, furthermore, furnace.
4 Congratulate, tabulation, circulate, accumulation, stipulate, population.
5 Stand, stands, understanding, misunderstanding, standpoint, standard.

Building Transcription Skills

2 Business Vocabulary Builder

unblemished Unspoiled.
inevitable Certain to happen.
restraints Things that limit or restrict.

Reading and Writing Practice

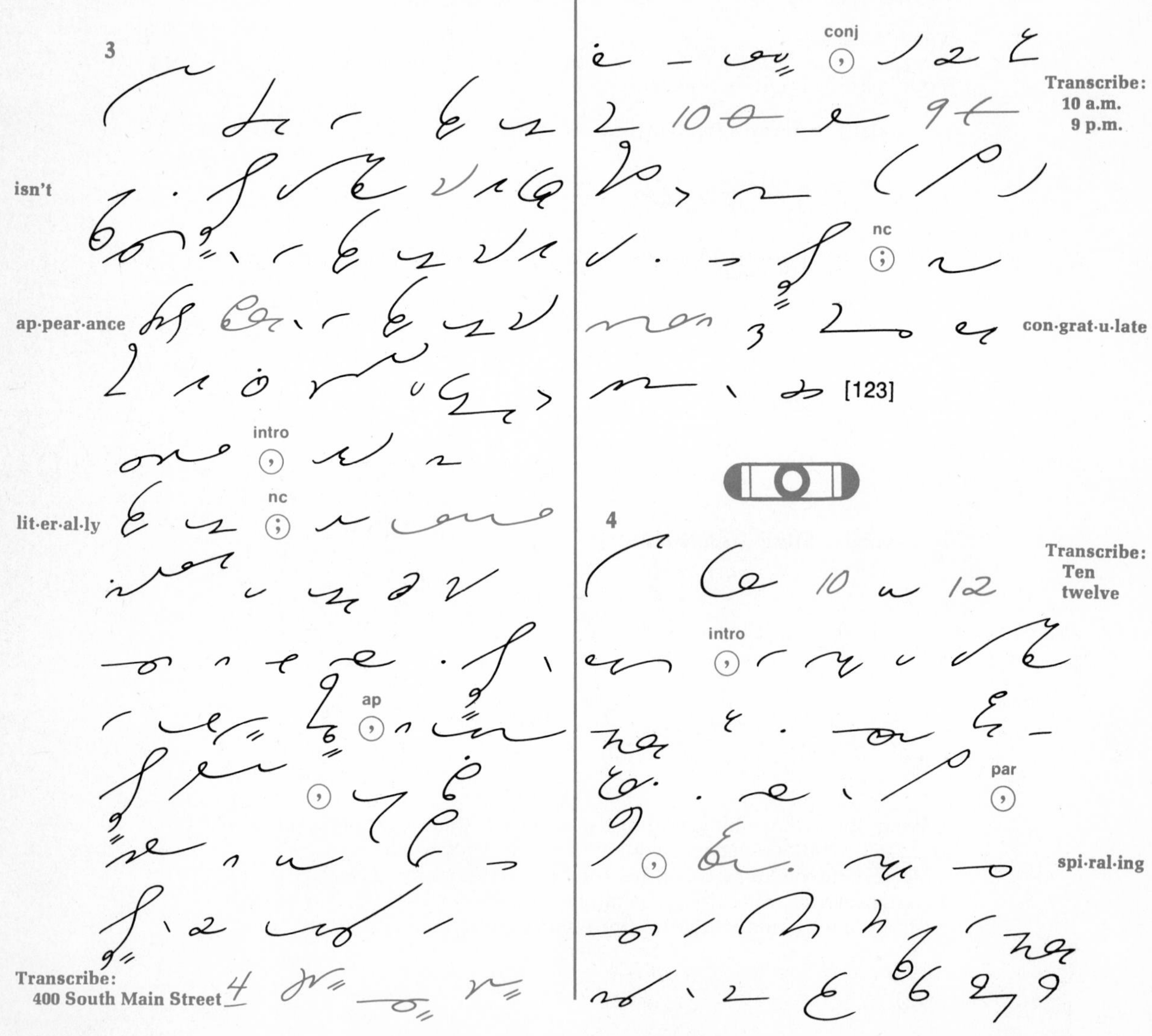

Transcribe: $1,000

Not·with·stand·ing

intro

com·pre·hen·sive

par

low-risk hyphenated before noun

Fur·ther·more pol·i·cy·hold·er's

intro

Transcribe: five

Transcribe: nine six

conj

[188]

5

and o

in·for·ma·tive poll

Transcribe: 75 percent

intro

75

intro

some·times

ac·cep·tance

Transcribe: $1,000

intro

in·ev·i·ta·ble

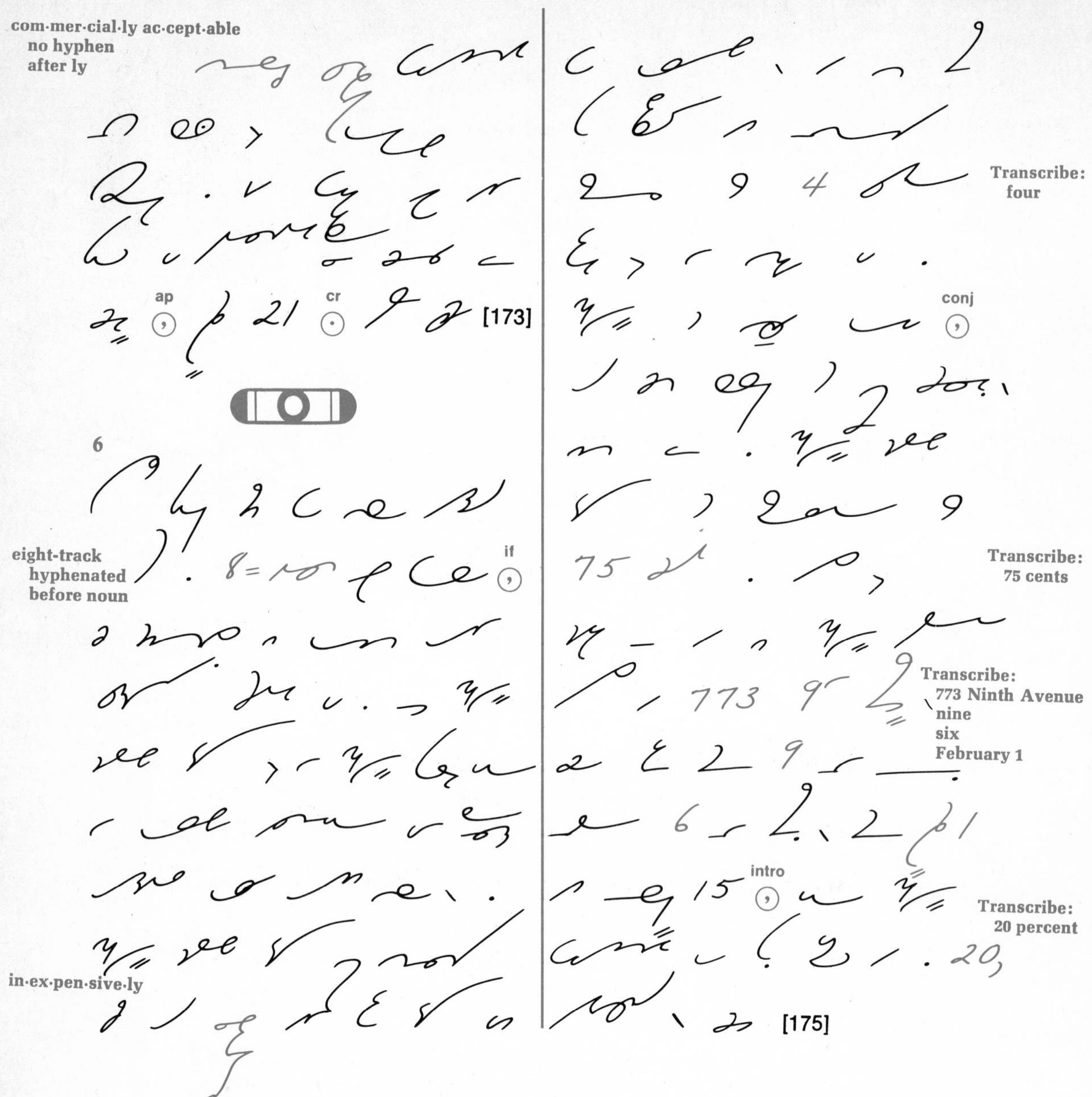

Everyone makes errors. However, good secretaries learn from their mistakes and avoid making the same mistake twice.

Building Shorthand Skill

1 Theory Recall

Your reading goal: 40 seconds.

Brief Forms and Derivatives

1

Phrases *Words Omitted*

2

Word Beginning *Inter-, Intr-, Enter-, Entr-*

3

Word Ending *-gram*

4

Word Family *-sive*

5

1 Out, without; for, before; executive, executives; regular, regularly.
2 Men and women, up to date, many of the, many of them, in a few minutes.
3 Interest, interaction, introduce, introduction, entering, entertain, entrance.
4 Program, telegram, radiogram, monogram, diagram.
5 Expensive, intensive, extensive, comprehensive, defensive, permissive, impressive.

Building Transcription Skills

2 **Business Vocabulary Builder**

declining Decreasing; lowering.

book value The value of something as shown on account books.

levy (*verb*) To require; to charge.

Reading and Writing Practice

3

un·der·stand·able

nc

par

Transcribe: $176

176

ex·ces·sive

levy

com·pre·hen·sive

and o

up-to-date hyphenated before noun

conj

fair

Transcribe: January 10, 1978,

10 1978

if

[185]

4

Transcribe: two

brakes

life-or-death hyphenated before noun

peace

to·day's

best-sell·ing steel-belt·ed hyphenated before noun

ra·di·al

smooth·est

and o

Transcribe: 1 million

turn·pikes

ser

Transcribe: 12 percent

[140]

5

man·age·ment

nonr

pur·chased

stan·dard-size hyphenated before noun

Transcribe: 28 cents

ve·hi·cle

if

de·creases

ser

if

Transcribe: 10,000 20,000

and o

[147]

6

ex·cept

intro

car's

if

per·ma·nent·ly

intro

its

nc

Transcribe:
$35

[139]

7

dis·sat·is·fied

ap

geo

par

[97]

Building Shorthand Skill

1 Theory Recall

Your reading goal: 40 seconds.

Brief Forms and Derivatives

1

Phrases *If*

2

Word Beginning *Mis-*

3

Word Ending *-ship*

4

Word Family *-est*

5

1 Business, businesses; one, once; work, working; character, characteristics.
2 If you, if you need, if you can be, if you wish, if you know, if you have, if you would.
3 Mistake, misplace, misunderstanding, misconception, misfortune, misgivings.
4 Hardship, steamship, relationship, scholarship, dealership, ownership.
5 Hardest, finest, nearest, broadest, typist, dentist.

Building Transcription Skills

2 Business Vocabulary Builder

exhibit (*verb*) To show; to demonstrate.

liberal (*adjective*) Generous.

condensers Devices used for receiving and storing electrical charges.

Reading and Writing Practice

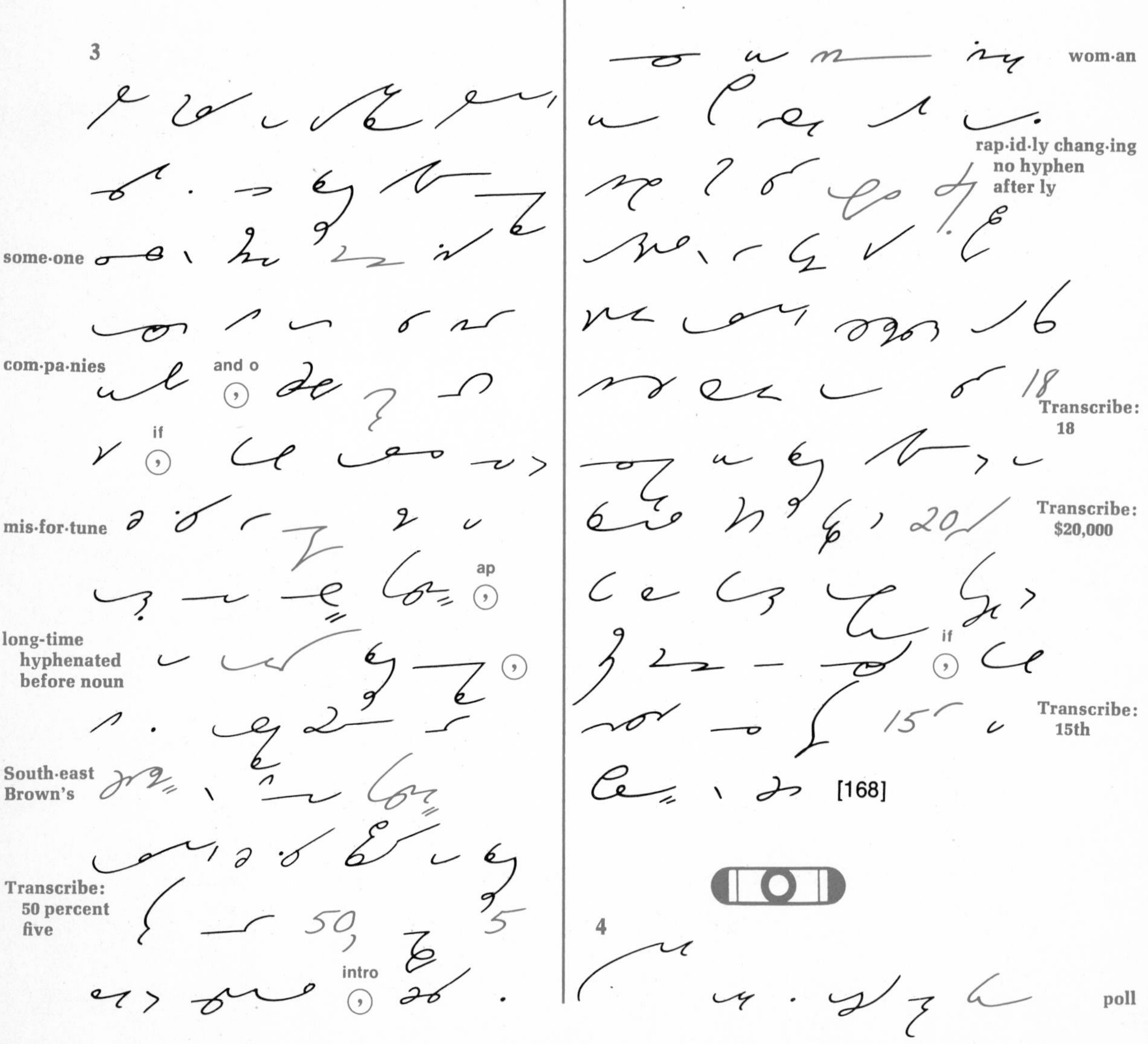

be·lieve

hon·est
es·ti·mate

fee
mis·cal·cu·late

Transcribe:
10 percent

intro

ser

if

10,

if

ap·peal

nc

ac·quaint·ed

[167]

Transcribe:
8 o'clock

5

ap

Transcribe:
7:30 p.m.

7:30

Transcribe:
21 East Main Street

21

ap

ser

de·signed

intro

mi·nor

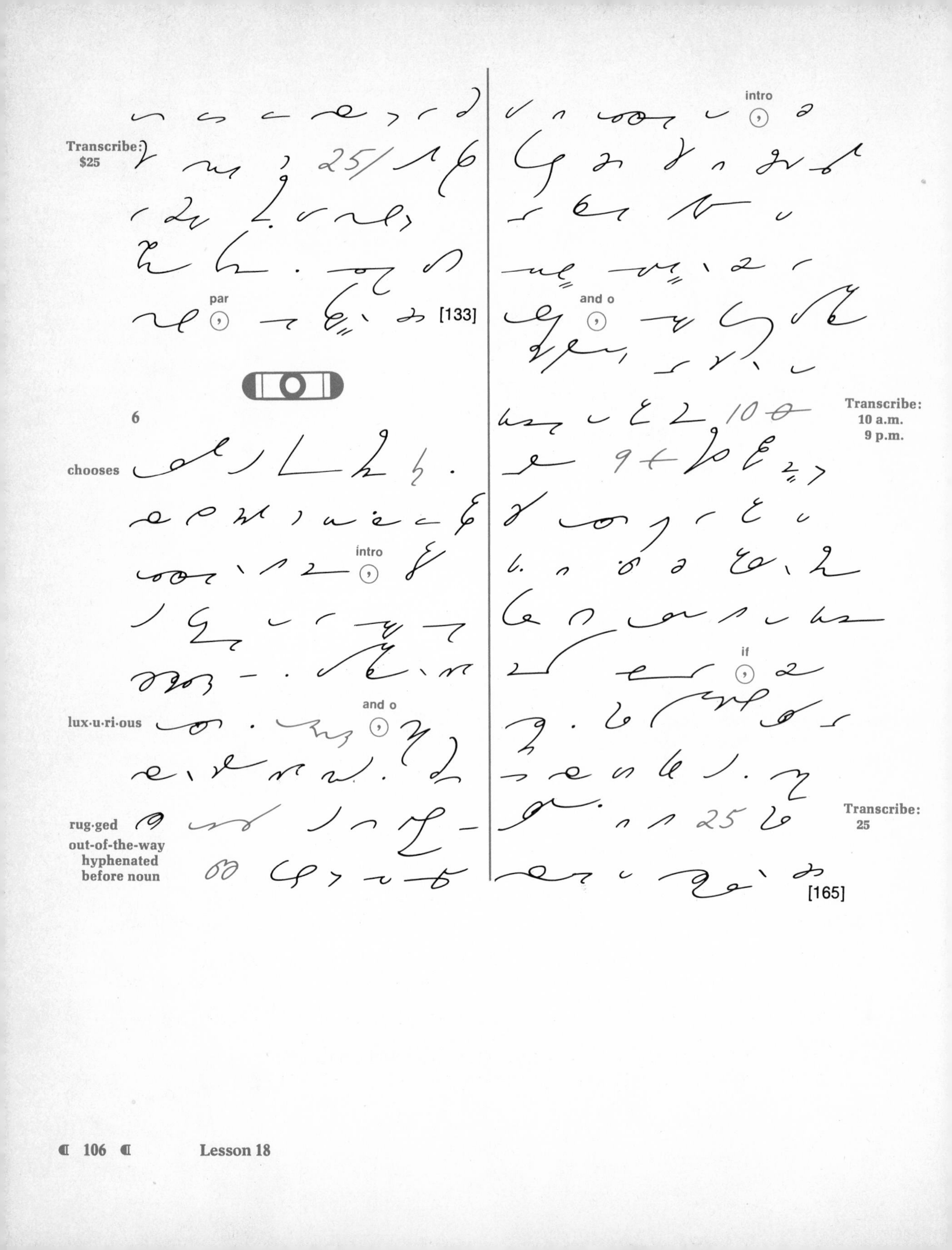

Transcribe: $25

par [133]

6

chooses

intro

lux·u·ri·ous

and o

rug·ged

out-of-the-way hyphenated before noun

intro

and o

Transcribe: 10 a.m. 9 p.m.

if

Transcribe: 25

[165]

Building Shorthand Skill

1 Theory Recall

Your reading goal: 40 seconds.

Brief Forms and Derivatives

1

Phrases *Thank*

2

Word Beginning *Circum-*

3

Word Ending *-tern, -term*

4 

Word Family *-stant*

5 

1 Probable, probably; over, overdue, overtime; subject, subjected, subjects.
2 Thank you for, thank you for the, thank you for your, I thank you for the, to thank you, thank you for your order.
3 Circumstance, circumstances, circumstantial, circumvent, circumnavigate, circumscribe.
4 Turn, western, eastern, return, term, terminal, termination.
5 Assistant, assistants, consistent, consistently, insistent, resistant.

Building Transcription Skills

2 Business Vocabulary Builder

lease (*verb*) To rent.

patronage Support; business.

constant Unchanging; regular.

Reading and Writing Practice

3

lease

intro

prob·a·bly

par

cir·cum·stances

conj

Transcribe: $7,000

long-term hyphenated before noun

intro

[141]

4

pa·tron·age

conj

as

to·day's

year's

nonr

liq·ui·dat·ed

Transcribe:
200
203 Fifth Avenue

203

conj

ap·prox·i·mate·ly
Transcribe:
$1,000

par

intro

[138]

5

qual·i·ty

ap

intro

nonr

east·ern

cus·tom-paint·ing
hyphenated
before noun

Tren·ton's

conj

ful·ly

if

dec·o·ra·tive

3725

Transcribe:
3725 East Baker Street
8 a.m.
5 p.m.

[137]

6

when

ser

in·ac·ces·si·ble

trail·er

intro

12-acre hyphenated before noun

12

when

[150]

7

intro

good-driv·er hyphenated before noun

Transcribe: Eight ten

8 10

intro

intro

Transcribe: 10,000

10

full-time hyphenated before noun

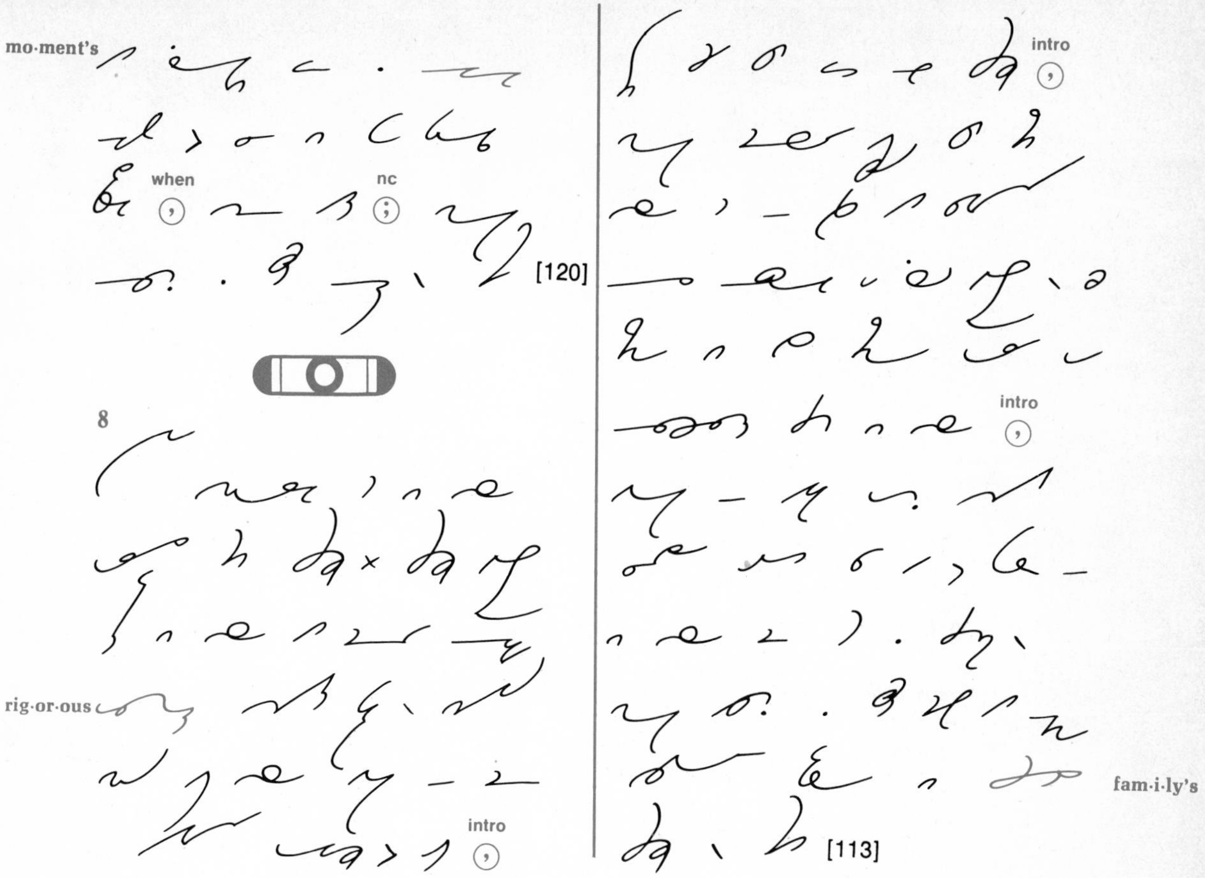

mo·ment's

when nc

[120]

8

rig·or·ous

intro

intro

intro

fam·i·ly's

[113]

Does it make sense? After typing every letter, the experienced secretary checks not only to be sure that the letter looks good and contains no typographical errors but also to be sure that the letter makes good sense. Sometimes just one wrong word can change the entire meaning of a letter.

Building Shorthand Skill

1 Theory Recall

Your reading goal: 40 seconds.

Brief Forms and Derivatives

1

Phrases *Special*

2

Word Beginning *Electric, Electr-*

3

Word Ending *-self, -selves*

4

Word Family *-eously, -iously*

5

1 State, states; recognize, recognized; manufacture; manufactured; our, ours.
2 To know, to make, to me, as soon as, as soon as possible, let us, your order, of course.
3 Electric, electric wire, electrical, electrically, electronic, electronics.
4 Myself, yourself, himself, herself, themselves, ourselves, itself, oneself.
5 Seriously, courteously, previously, obviously, tediously, furiously.

Building Transcription Skills

2 Business Vocabulary Builder

citation A summons to appear before a court of law.

revoked Withdrawn; taken away.

revolutionary Resulting in new, radical changes.

Reading and Writing Practice

3

harsh·est

ex·te·ri·or

cor·ro·sion

nc

and o

intro

intro

brakes

ser

Transcribe: $25

nc

[128]

fa·vor

4

ci·ta·tion

Transcribe: 18 20

as

max·i·mum

re·voked

intro

Transcribe: two

conj

ad·min·is·ter

[128]

5

intro

rev·o·lu·tion·ary

intro

intro

and o

ef·fi·cient ac·ces·so·ries

to·day's

pi·o·neer

com·po·nents

intro

[157]

6

re·sale

Transcribe: $2,000

conj

Transcribe: $1,800

conj

Transcribe: 34,000

if

[103]

7

ne·go·ti·at·ing

if

ef·fect

conj

intro

paid

as

[97]

8

when

ser

intro

Con·se·quent·ly

easy-to-reach hyphenated before noun

ser

and o

and o

intro

guar·an·tee

nc

[103]

9

se·ri·ous·ly

when

ap

[151]

PART

TAKING DICTATION

The next morning, after Mr. Franklin had read through the mail, Marie was called in to take dictation—and she was well prepared.

She had placed a rubber band around her notebook cover so that later she could fasten the used pages under it and always have a blank page ready for dictation. Although she was starting out with a new, blank notebook, Marie knew that the time would come when she would have to have two notebooks ready to be sure she didn't run out of pages during dictation. Marie had also dated several blank pages at the bottom. She was sure to attach several paper clips to the cover for use in flagging important or rush items. Two ball-point pens and a colored pencil for special notations were located next to her notebook on her desk.

The dictation session lasted for over an hour because Mr. Franklin's correspondence had backed up while he was without a secretary. Marie numbered each letter as it was dictated, and she numbered any pieces of related correspondence Mr. Franklin handed her in the same sequence. She also left several blank lines between letters for any special notes or insertions Mr. Franklin might give her during and after the dictation. Marie was sure to ask questions immediately after each letter was dictated so that she would not have to disturb Mr. Franklin later.

During the hour, Mr. Franklin received two telephone calls and one co-worker stopped in. These interruptions were short, but Marie made good use of the time. She inserted punctuation in her notes, inserted any words she had omitted, improved some of her outlines, and marked words that she felt she might have difficulty spelling. If Marie had felt that a particular interruption would be a lengthy one, she would have returned to her desk and worked until Mr. Franklin was ready to continue dictating.

Several minutes after Marie had returned to her desk, Mr. Franklin came out to tell her that the third letter he had dictated had to go out that day and that it should be sent special delivery. Marie quickly found the letter in her notebook and made the special notations on the blank lines she had left for just this purpose. She also marked the letter with a colored pencil and folded the page diagonally across the notebook so that it extended beyond the cover. She would have no trouble finding this rush item.

Even though Marie was confident about her skills, she was glad she had learned these important organizational techniques.

Building Transcription Skills

1 **TYPING STYLE STUDY ● titles of separate publications**

Underscore titles of books, booklets, magazines, and newspapers. Underscore the title as a unit with a continuous line.

My book, Home Repair Made Easy, will be published soon.

The booklet, Finance: Some New Ideas, will be distributed free of charge.

The article will appear in the January issue of Business World.

I read an interesting column in the Morning Register.

The first word and all the other main words in a title are capitalized. Words such as *and, in, the, of,* and *a* in the body of the title are not capitalized.

Note: This style is suggested for general business letters; it is the one followed in this book. However, some publishers prefer to have titles of their publications typed in all caps; others prefer to have them quoted. If you should work for a publisher, be sure to inquire about the style the company prefers.

2 **Business Vocabulary Builder**

depreciation Decrease in value.

capital gains Profits gained from the sale of assets.

deductible *(adjective)* Able to be subtracted.

Reading and Writing Practice

3

too

de·pre·ci·a·tion
cap·i·tal

ser

par

sit·u·a·tion
mil·lions

if

com·plete

ap

en·able

step-by-step
hyphenated
before noun

nonr

par

in·ci·den·tal·ly
de·duct·ible

nc

[153]

4

suc·cess·ful

def·i·nite
prin·ci·ples

when

po·ten·tial

if

for·ward
Transcribe:
$15

if

[175]

5

car·ri·ers

ca·su·al·ly

intro

par

al·ready

par

conj

its

fac·ets

re·al
Transcribe:
$10

ap

[154]

6

ap

Madison College

256 Jefferson Street   Baltimore, MD 21213

July 1, 19--

The General Publishing Company
800 Main Street
Boston, MA 02601

ATTENTION MS. MARTHA SWOPE

Ladies and Gentlemen:

Next fall I will be teaching a beginning accounting class in our continuing education program. There will be between 20 and 30 students in the class. Some of them will be recent high school graduates; others will be adults who are returning to school after a number of years. Most of them will have had no accounting instruction.

I want a text that will allow the students with some background in the subject to progress at a very fast rate but one that will allow the students with no background to take as long as is necessary to complete the course. Do you have such a book on the market at the present time? I am currently using Basic Accounting by Smith. However, I am afraid this text is not appropriate for this particular class.

If you have a book that you feel would be appropriate for this class, I hope you will let me know immediately. I would also appreciate receiving a complimentary copy of the text and any teaching materials that accompany it.

I will be looking forward to hearing from you.

Very sincerely yours,

Ellen Swanson

Ellen Swanson
Assistant Professor

lj

Average-length letter, semiblocked style, with attention line, standard punctuation

Transcribe: 15th

ap

To·mor·row's

and o

nc

af·fect

if

conj

req·ui·si·tion

per·ti·nent

and o

Transcribe: $25

[164]

7

Transcribe: December 10

intro

and o

ar·ti·cle

conj

conj

per·mis·sion

ser

par

[117]

Building Transcription Skills

1 **TYPING STYLE STUDY ● titles of sections of published works**

The sections of complete published words, such as articles and chapters, are enclosed in quotation marks.

"New Trends in Recreation" is the title of the article we read.

"Principles of Sound Investing" is the last chapter in the text.

The titles of complete but unpublished works, such as manuscripts and reports, are also enclosed in quotation marks.

I sent my report entitled "International Law" to the committee.

Your manuscript entitled "Energy Sources" arrived in this morning's mail.

2 Business Vocabulary Builder

prestige Status; prominence.

bibliography A list of publications.

guidelines Statements of policy.

Reading and Writing Practice

3

Fo·rum

as

sum

conj

pres·tige
dead·line

ap

ex·ceed
Transcribe:
10,000

re·ceiv·ing
manu·script

cr

[134]

4

ap

Per·son·al

Groom·ing

de·vot·ed
dis·cus·sion

its

bib·li·og·ra·phy

Transcribe:
50

if

fur·ther

[98]

5

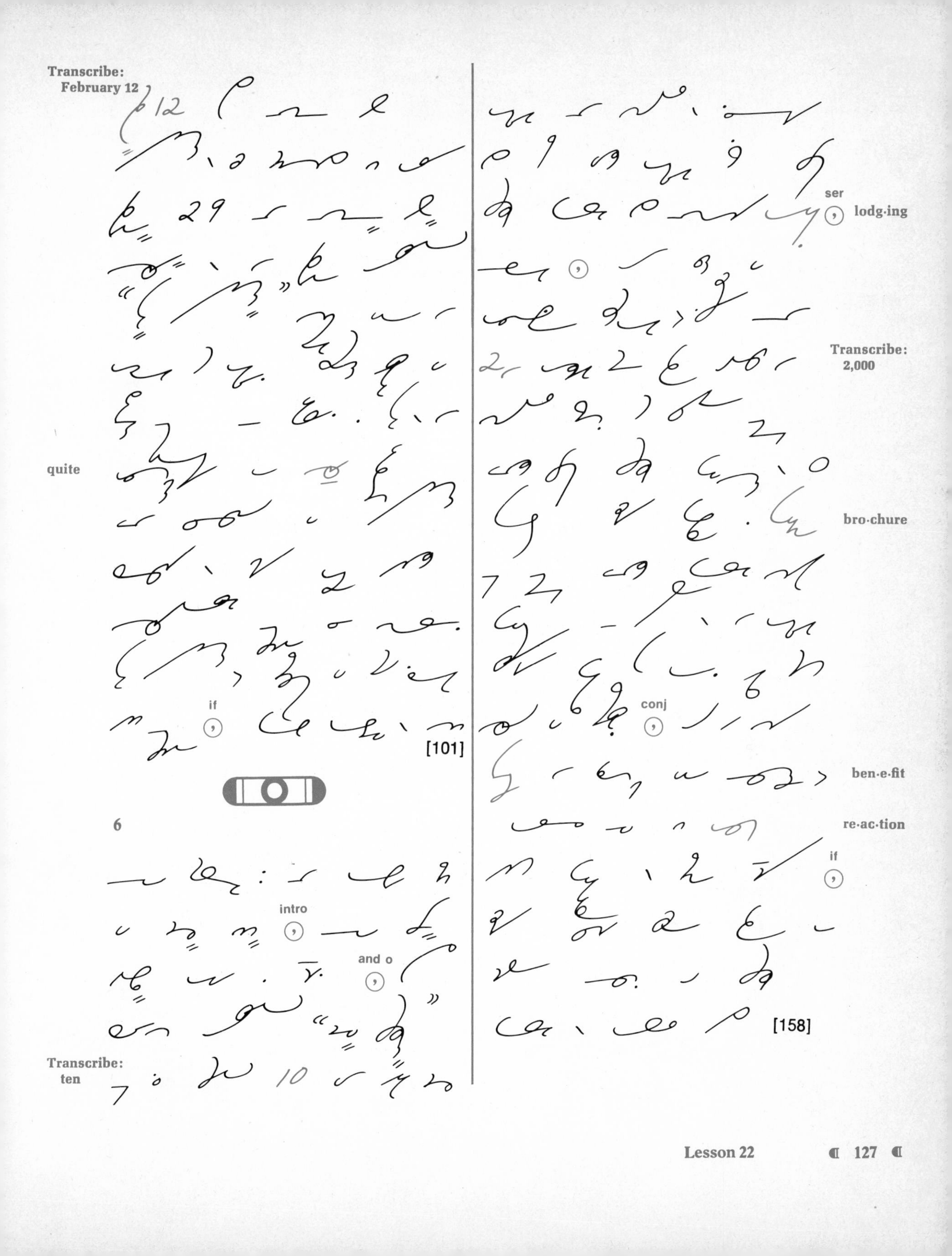

Transcribe: February 12

quite

if

[101]

6

intro

and o

Transcribe: ten

ser

lodg·ing

Transcribe: 2,000

bro·chure

conj

ben·e·fit

re·ac·tion

if

[158]

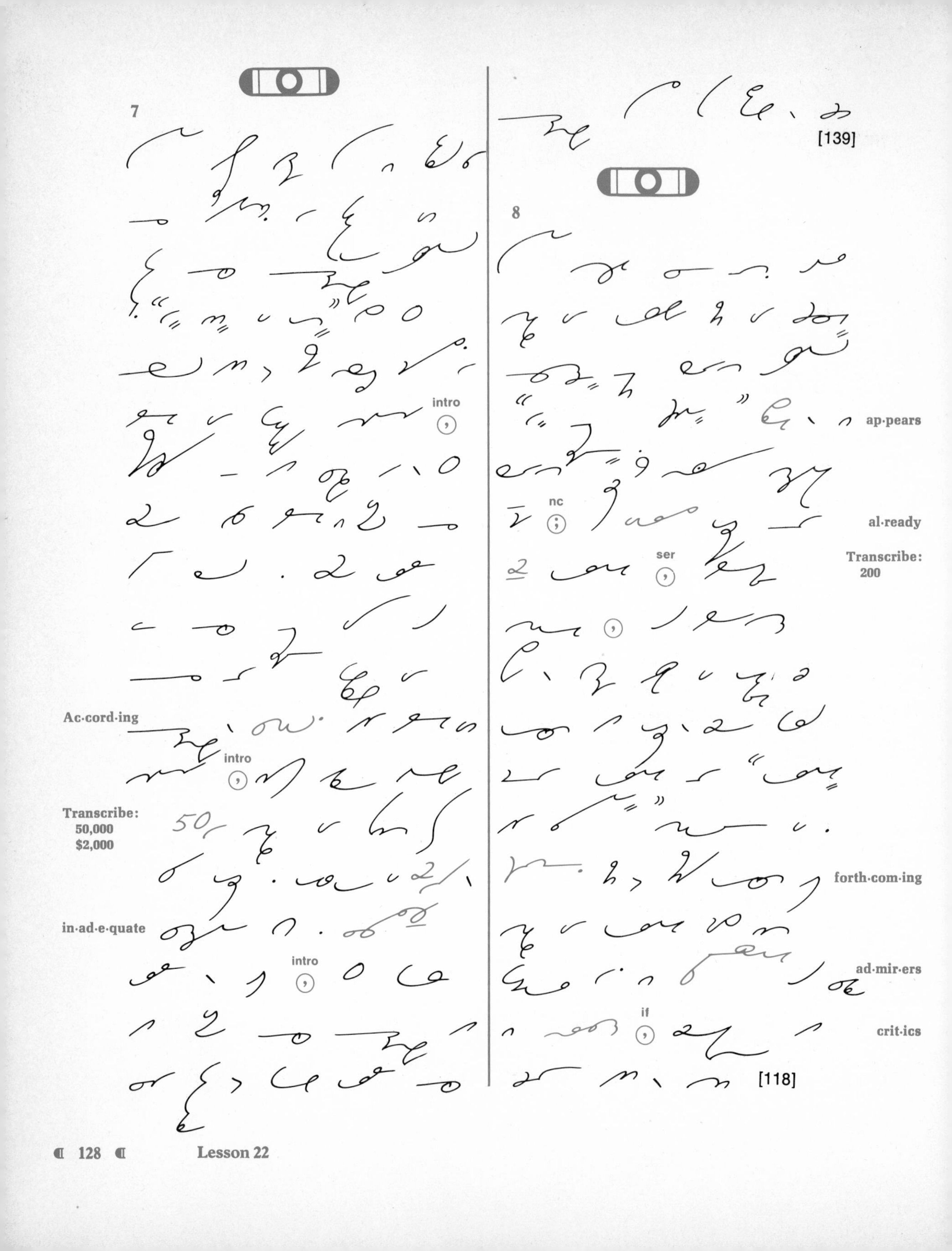

7

intro

intro

Ac·cord·ing

Transcribe:
50,000
$2,000

in·ad·e·quate

intro

[139]

8

ap·pears

nc

al·ready

ser

Transcribe:
200

if

forth·com·ing

ad·mir·ers

crit·ics

[118]

Building Transcription Skills

1 **PUNCTUATION PRACTICE ●: enumeration**

A colon is used after an expression that introduces some following material such as a list or an enumeration.

I think we should invite the following people: Mary Adams, George Savoy, and Lee Hernandez.

In my next report to the board I will discuss the following items:

1. *Our present financial condition*
2. *Recommendations for increasing production*
3. *The outlook for future sales*

Each time this use of the colon occurs in the Reading and Writing Practice, it will be indicated in the shorthand thus: enu (:)

2 **Business Vocabulary Builder**

critique *(verb)* To review; to evaluate.

nationally syndicated Associated with a firm that sells material for publication throughout the country.

practicality Usefulness.

Reading and Writing Practice

3

par (,)

de·cide

whose

cri·tique

enu

prac·ti·cal·i·ty

as·sis·tance

par

[118]

and o

com·pre·hen·sive

coun·try's

na·tion·al·ly syn·di·cat·ed
no hyphen
after ly

if

three-month
hyphenated
before noun

Transcribe:
40 percent

[132]

4

Transcribe:
four
five

gained

sur·vey

enu

5

ar·ti·cle

achieve

enu

care·ful·ly

com·plete·ly

thor·ough·ly

if

[162]

6

dis·con·tin·ue

enu

intro

Transcribe: two

too gloomy

[147]

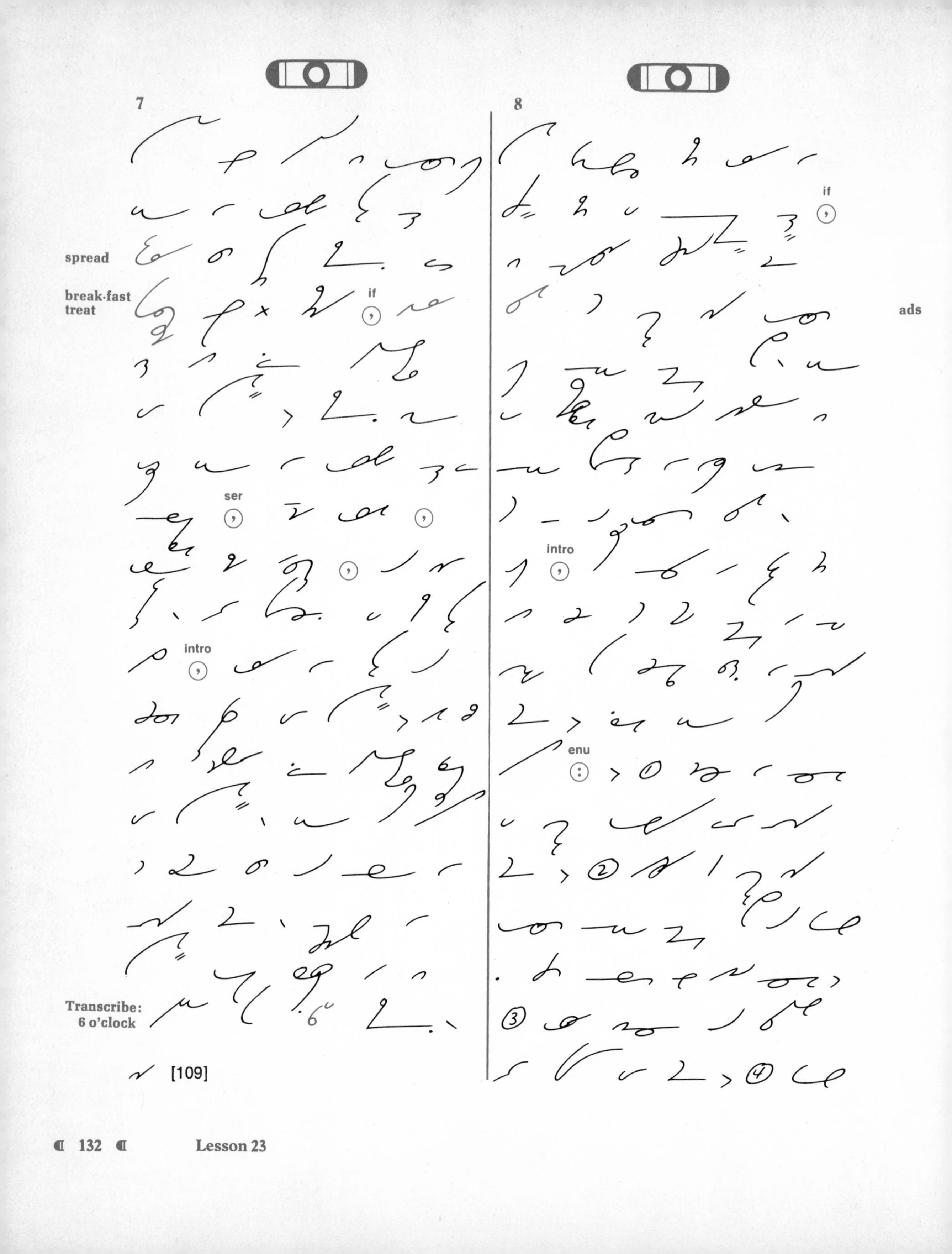

7

spread

break·fast
treat

if

ser

intro

Transcribe:
6 o'clock

[109]

8

if

ads

intro

enu

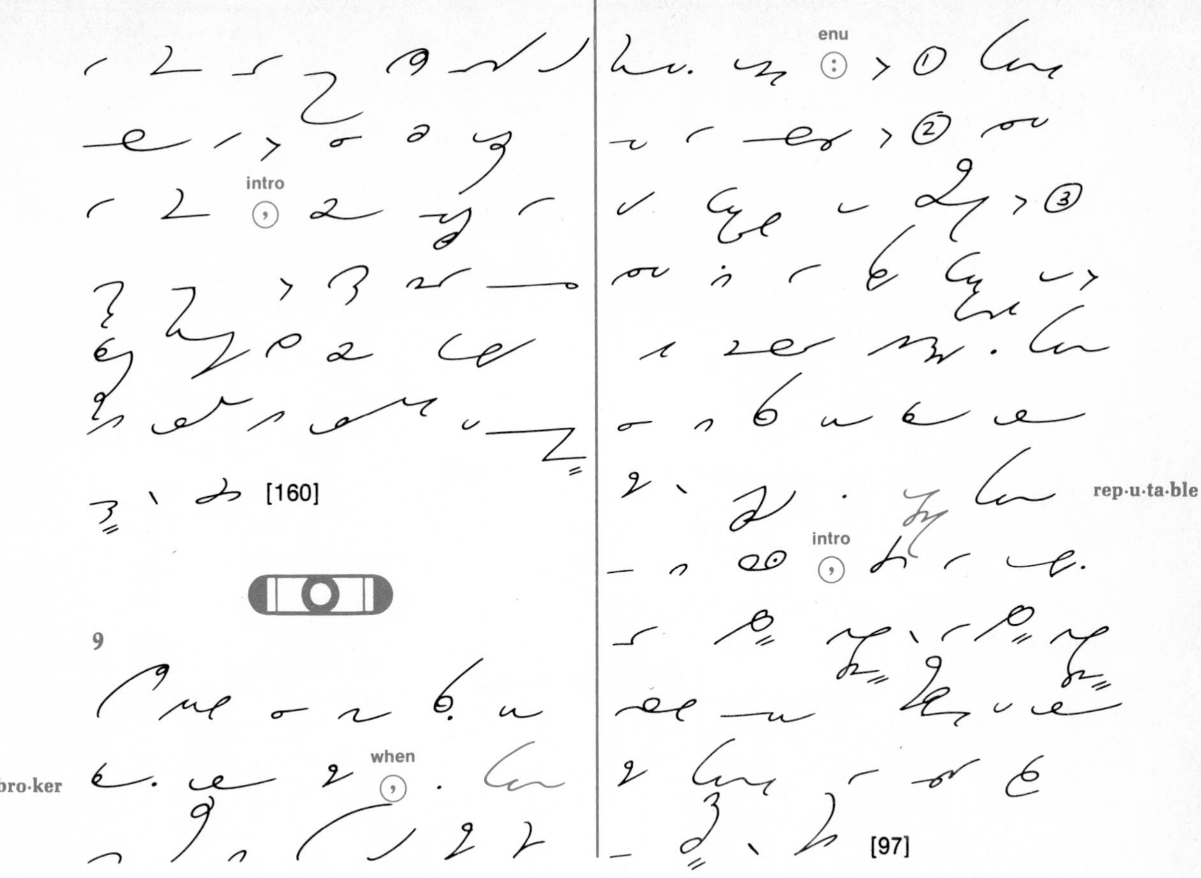

The person who is satisfied with the way things are today will probably be in the same job year after year. The person who constantly looks for a better way to do a job is the one who will be recognized—and rewarded—in the long run.

Earlier you learned how to place a short letter (one that contains up to approximately 100 words) by judgment. In this lesson you will take up the placement of an average-length letter (one that contains about 150 words). On page 135 you will find Letter 8 from Lesson 23 of *Transcription* as it was written in shorthand. About one column in the shorthand notebook was required for this letter.

Make a shorthand copy of this average-length letter to determine how much space it requires in your notebook. You may require more space if your notes are large or less space if your notes are small. Try to fix in your mind the space you require in your notebook for your notes for an average-length letter.

Whenever your notes for a dictated letter require approximately the same space in your notebook that they require for Letter 8, here is what you should do to place the letter attractively on a letterhead (assuming your typewriter has elite type):

☐ **1** Set your margin stops for about 1½-inch margins at the left and at the right.

☐ **2** Insert your paper and type the date on the third line below the last line of the letterhead.

☐ **3** Start the inside address about eight lines below the date.

☐ **4** Then transcribe the body of the letter.

Caution: When you are taking dictation on the job, you will, of course, have to take into consideration any insertions or deletions that your employer has made before you place the letter on the letterhead. Even though a dictated letter may fill up the amount of space in your notebook required for an average-length letter, it may still be a "short" letter because of deletions.

J. Robert Johnson Publishing Co.

8992 Belvedere Drive Seattle, WA 98117

July 15, 19--

Ms. Margaret Pulaski
234 West 45 Street
New York, NY 10020

Dear Ms. Pulaski:

If you read the January issue of Management News, you no doubt found some ads for companies you would like to have more information about. All our advertisers want to tell you more about themselves than they have room for in their regular ads. Therefore, we have made it possible for you to send for further information at no cost by simply using the enclosed form.

Here is all you have to do:

1. Scan the names of companies listed on the enclosed form.

2. Decide which companies you would like more information about and place a check mark next to their names.

3. Write your name and address at the bottom of the form.

4. Place the form in the envelope that is enclosed and mail it.

When we receive the form, we will notify the companies involved.

This is one of the many services that we are pleased to render to readers of Management News.

Sincerely yours,

William T. Adams

William T. Adams
Advertising Manager

bh
Enclosure

Building Transcription Skills

1 **PUNCTUATION PRACTICE ●, introducing short quote**

Short quotations are introduced by a comma.

She said, "Your work must be completed by next Monday."

Each time this use of the comma occurs in the Reading and Writing Practice, it will be indicated in the shorthand thus: isq (,)

, inside quote
. inside quote
? inside quote

Commas and periods are typed inside the final quotation mark.

My article, "Secretarial Tips," will be published soon.
He said, "Let the meeting begin at once."

Question marks are placed inside or outside the final quotation mark according to the sense of the sentence.

She asked, "In which drawer did you place the report?"
Why did he say, "Monday is not a good day for the meeting"?

Notice that there is no end punctuation mark immediately after the word *meeting.*

Semicolons and colons are placed outside the final quotation mark.

Mark the letter "Special Delivery"; then deliver it to the post office.
The following items should be marked "Handle With Care": plates, cups, and saucers.

When punctuation is placed inside the quotation marks in the Reading and Writing Practice, it will be indicated in the following ways: iq (,) iq (.) iq (?)

2 **Business Vocabulary Builder**

currently Now; at this time.
fascinating Interesting; exciting.
significance Importance.

Reading and Writing Practice

3

tru·ly — isq

iq — if

ar·ea

en·joy·able — and o — intro

fas·ci·nat·ing

ser

de·sign·ers

re·al·ly

if

nc

[108]

4

Transcribe: January 15, 1950,

15 1950

His·to·ry

fourth

vol·ume

oc·curred

ap

geo

isq

iq

ref·er·ence li·brary

grasp

writ·ten

if

[154]

5

as

ar·ti·cle

sched·uled

iq

Transcribe:
June 15

cel·e·brate

Wil·son's

intro

plan·ning

Transcribe:
703 East 23 Street
5 to 7 p.m.

[137]

6

ap

ac·quain·tances

isq

ser

iq

and o

best-known
hyphenated
before noun

if

if

[113]

7

ap

press·room

isq

ad·e·quate

high-qual·i·ty hyphenated before noun

intro

iq

intro

conj

cr

dwin·dling

intro

[125]

8

as

ap·peal·ing

conj

heart·en·ing

par

grate·ful

if

[103]

Building Transcription Skills

1 **PUNCTUATION PRACTICE ● : introducing long quote**

Long quotations are introduced by a colon.

The report stated: "In the future there will be less reliance on fossil fuels for heating our homes and driving our automobiles. It is quite obvious that more research must be done to discover alternate energy sources that are clean, efficient, and economical."

Each time a long quotation is introduced by a colon in the Reading and Writing Practice, it will be indicated in the shorthand thus: ilq (:)

2 **Business Vocabulary Builder**

low ebb Declining.

primary First.

objective *(noun)* Goal.

Reading and Writing Practice

3

manu·script

Sur·viv·al

ac·cept

ap iq enu intro

ebb

too

ex·am·ined

eval·u·a·tion

po·ten·tial

re·con·sid·er
lat·er

sub·mit·ting

ilq

intro

iq

if

[173]

4

as·sis·tant

Transcribe:
seven

7

tru·ly

ef·fi·cien·cy

ini·tia·tive

ser

ilq

intro

iq

when

nc

ad·vice

re·ceive

ex·cel·lent

[133]

5

Transcribe:
Twenty

20

tech·ni·cal

first-class

ilq

in·ten·tion

spare

iq

Transcribe: 2,000

intro

dai·ly

ex·ceed·ed

South's

conj

ac·quaint·ed

intro

[172]

6

mill

its

ilq

intro

par

Transcribe: 15 percent July 1

iq

conj

re·course

par

Transcribe: 25 cents

and o

[153]

7

iq

ilq

al·ready

conj

Transcribe: ten

10

iq

intro

thought·ful·ness

[110]

8

Transcribe: June 18

18

ap

intro

geo

nc

intro

when

nonr

[112]

PRETRANSCRIPTION PROCEDURES

The first thing Marie did when she returned to her desk was to read through her notes. Not only did she read for continuity and for sense, but she also inserted punctuation and words she had omitted; verified days, dates, and amounts of money; and looked up the spelling of words and points of grammar in her dictionary and in her reference manual respectively.

Marie also made sure that she had a complete address, including the ZIP Code, for each letter, and she looked for special instructions given by Mr. Franklin about checking the files or with other persons for special information. By noting these things now, she could avoid having to get up each time she started to transcribe a letter; she could make one trip to the files and one trip to the other reference books in the office to gather all the information she needed.

In addition, Marie checked to see how many copies she would need of each letter. This helped her decide which type of copies she would make—carbon copies or photocopies.

One very important thing that Marie looked for in her notes was implied instructions—statements indicating that she would have to take certain actions. In an interoffice memorandum he had dictated, Mr. Franklin indicated that he was enclosing copies of sales reports, and it would be up to Marie to obtain these reports without specifically being told to do so. In a letter, Mr. Franklin indicated that he would make hotel reservations for a customer, and he assumed that Marie would follow through with the arrangements, using the information given in the letter. Marie flagged these notes with paper clips so that she would be sure to remember to do them.

Finally, reviewing her notes gave Marie the opportunity to set priorities as to which correspondence should be transcribed first. She was able to determine this by the instructions Mr. Franklin gave her and by the content of the dictated material.

Since Marie had already checked her typewriter and stocked her desk with all the supplies she would need, she was ready to start transcribing in an orderly, efficient manner.

Building Transcription Skills

1 TYPING STYLE STUDY ● capitalization

Days, etc.

Always capitalize the names of the days of the week, months of the year, and holidays.

The report is due Monday.
Your peach trees should blossom in April.
Workers will be paid overtime on Christmas Day.

The names of the seasons are not usually capitalized.

The leaves turn brown in the fall.
The summer *weather is welcome.*

---

2 Business Vocabulary Builder

incurred Became liable for.
prospective Expected; likely to become.
pinpoint *(verb)* To locate; to identify.

Reading and Writing Practice

3

Cor·po·ra·tion

ap 13 ap

Wednes·day
Feb·ru·ary

dis·cuss

it·self

in·curred

intro

res·i·den·tial

Transcribe: 18 percent

18,

rec·om·mend·ed

[140]

4

po·ten·tial

if

lo·cal·i·ty

yours

555-2121.

and o

help·ful

in·ex·pen·sive·ly

Transcribe: 4 million

4

spring

intro

ap

10. [153]

5

Christ·mas Day

nonr

al·most

conj

dis·patched

intro

pin·point

conj

days'

conj

dis·cov·er·ing

cr

[118]

6

conj

ex·haust·ed

day's

as

di·lem·ma

cr

in·no·va·tive

[125]

7

con·sent

for·bid

yours

touch

intro ,

taped

na·tion's

[161]

8

pro·ce·dures

sim·i·lar

ser ,

,

off-cam·pus hyphenated before noun

intro ,

[118]

Building Transcription Skills

1 **SPELLING FAMILIES ● -an, -on, -en**

A good way to improve your ability to spell is to study words in related groups, or spelling families. In this lesson you will study words that end with *-an, -on,* and *-en.* These words are often a source of spelling difficulty.

To derive the greatest benefit from these spelling families, observe the following procedure:

- ☐ **1** Pronounce the word.
- ☐ **2** Spell the word aloud.
- ☐ **3** Write or type the word.

Words Ending in -an

met-ro-pol-i-tan	**par-ti-san**	**vet-er-an**
sub-ur-ban	**slo-gan**	**or-gan**

Words Ending in -on

but-ton	**lun-cheon**	**sea-son**
cot-ton	**par-don**	**sur-geon**
les-son	**per-son**	**wag-on**

Words Ending in -en

broad-en	**giv-en**	**less-en**
bur-den	**hid-den**	**spo-ken**
cit-i-zen	**kitch-en**	**writ-ten**

---

2 **Business Vocabulary Builder**

conversing Talking.

insight The ability to see the true nature of something.

metropolitan *(adjective)* Pertaining to a major region.

Reading and Writing Practice

3

up to date no noun, no hyphen

col·leagues

hours'

pre·ced·ing

Amer·i·can

writ·ten per·son

broad·en

ser

as·so·ci·ates

per·son·al

Transcribe: $35

ap

conj

Transcribe: October 1

[230]

4

Met·ro·pol·i·tan

conj

well or·ga·nized
well pre·pared
no noun,
no hyphen

par

lun·cheon
speech

prin·ci·ples

[110]

5

hand·writ·ten

ser

type·writ·ten

intro

in·ter·pret

ap

12

con·sist
les·sons

20

nonr

ap

White's

ilq

re·ceived

praise

iq

conj

[186]

6

conj

Sub·ur·ban

conj

Transcribe: 10 million

long-term hyphenated before noun

Transcribe: 10 percent

Transcribe: $14 million

intro

nonr

wel·come

[141]

Building Transcription Skills

1 **GRAMMAR CHECKUP ● one word or two?**

Your employer will occasionally make an error in grammar during dictation. It is your job to see that any grammatical errors are corrected before the letter is typed. Even the most experienced secretary will need to refer to a reference book in order to be sure that no grammatical errors appear in the transcript.

In this Grammar Checkup, and in those that appear in later lessons, you will study errors in grammar that both secretaries and dictators often make.

The following expressions are sometimes written as one word, sometimes as two.

everyone, every one

everyone Everybody; all people.

Everyone (everybody) *enjoys a relaxing holiday.*

every one Each one.

Every one (each one) *of the telephone calls is necessary.*

sometime, some time

sometime At an unspecified time.

They will be here sometime (an unspecified time) *soon.*

some time A period of time.

It will be some time (a period of time) *before we are ready.*

Hint: If the word *little* can be mentally inserted between *some* and *time,* the two-word phrase is correct.

2 **Business Vocabulary Builder**

retained Kept.

rendering Delivering; performing.

broadcast *(verb)* To make public by means of radio or television.

Reading and Writing Practice

3

ap ap

course

Ev·ery·one ap

conj

Transcribe: 20

ex·cel·lent

ev·ery one

par

enu

re·tained

weeks'

some·time

cr [124]

4

ap

Transcribe: October 26

intro

Con·se·quent·ly

some time

its

conj

fans'

intro

some·time

[110]

5

ev·ery one

24

par

intro

par

ev·ery one

mes·sages

ser

con·ve·nience

when

friend·ly

po·ten·tial

some·time

[157]

6

am·pli·fi·ca·tion

intro

call·ers'

ser

5

Transcribe:
5
10
20

10

20

conj

par intro

al·most suf·fered

ex·hib·it

some·time some time

some time

[141]

ser

7

man·ners

intro if some·time

[157]

Building Transcription Skills

1 OFFICE-STYLE DICTATION

Routine letters will often be dictated without any changes or insertions. When dictating important letters, however, your employer may change words, transpose sentences, and even revise entire paragraphs. It will be your job to make all these changes in your notes in such a way that you will be able to transcribe the letter correctly.

If you have good shorthand speed, you will have no difficulty making the transition from the timed dictation that you have been taking in class to the dictation of your employer. The more shorthand speed you possess, the easier this type of dictation will be for you.

In this chapter, and in each chapter hereafter, you will take up one of the common problems of office-style dictation. Here is what you are to do:

- ☐ **1** Read the explanation of the problem.
- ☐ **2** Study the illustration that accompanies it.
- ☐ **3** Read the shorthand letter to see how the problem would be handled in your shorthand notes.

OFFICE-STYLE DICTATION ● deletions

A dictator will occasionally decide to delete—take out—a word or a phrase or even a sentence that has been dictated. For example:

The four-page brochure has been sent to you—take out **four-page.**

To indicate this deletion, you would simply strike a heavy downward line through the expression *four-page* thus:

Sometimes the dictator may simply repeat the sentence without the word or phrase to be deleted.

Please explain the most effective and timely course to follow—make that **Please**

explain the most effective course to follow.

To indicate this deletion, you would mark out in your notes the words *and timely.*

When only a short word or phrase is to be deleted, use a heavy downward line; when several words are to be deleted, use a wavy line.

If you should change your mind on submitting the report—scratch out that phrase.

In your notes, you would show the deletion thus:

Illustration of Office-Style Dictation

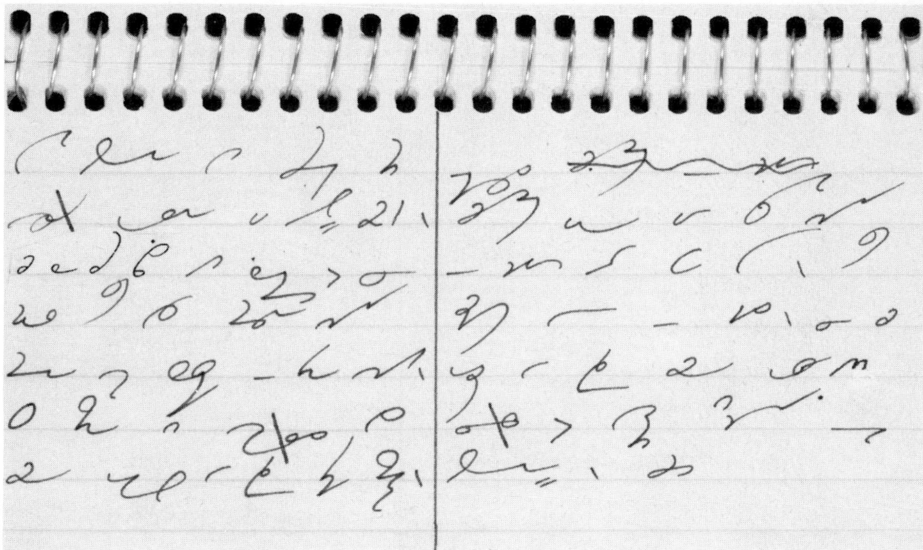

2 Business Vocabulary Builder

activates Starts.

audible Able to be heard.

transacted Conducted; carried on; completed.

Reading and Writing Practice

3

an·swer
so·lu·tion

if

when

fre·quen·cy

de·vice

re·ceiv·er

au·di·ble

Transcribe:
$1
131 East Main Street

geo

dem·on·stra·tion

mod·el

par

[178]

4

quote

ilq

intro

trans·act·ed

un·an·swered

nonr

if

long-dis·tance

conj

Transcribe: five

Transcribe: $87

iq

and o

well-trained hyphenated before noun

intro

re·ceive

ser

screen

[151]

conj

hard·ly

5

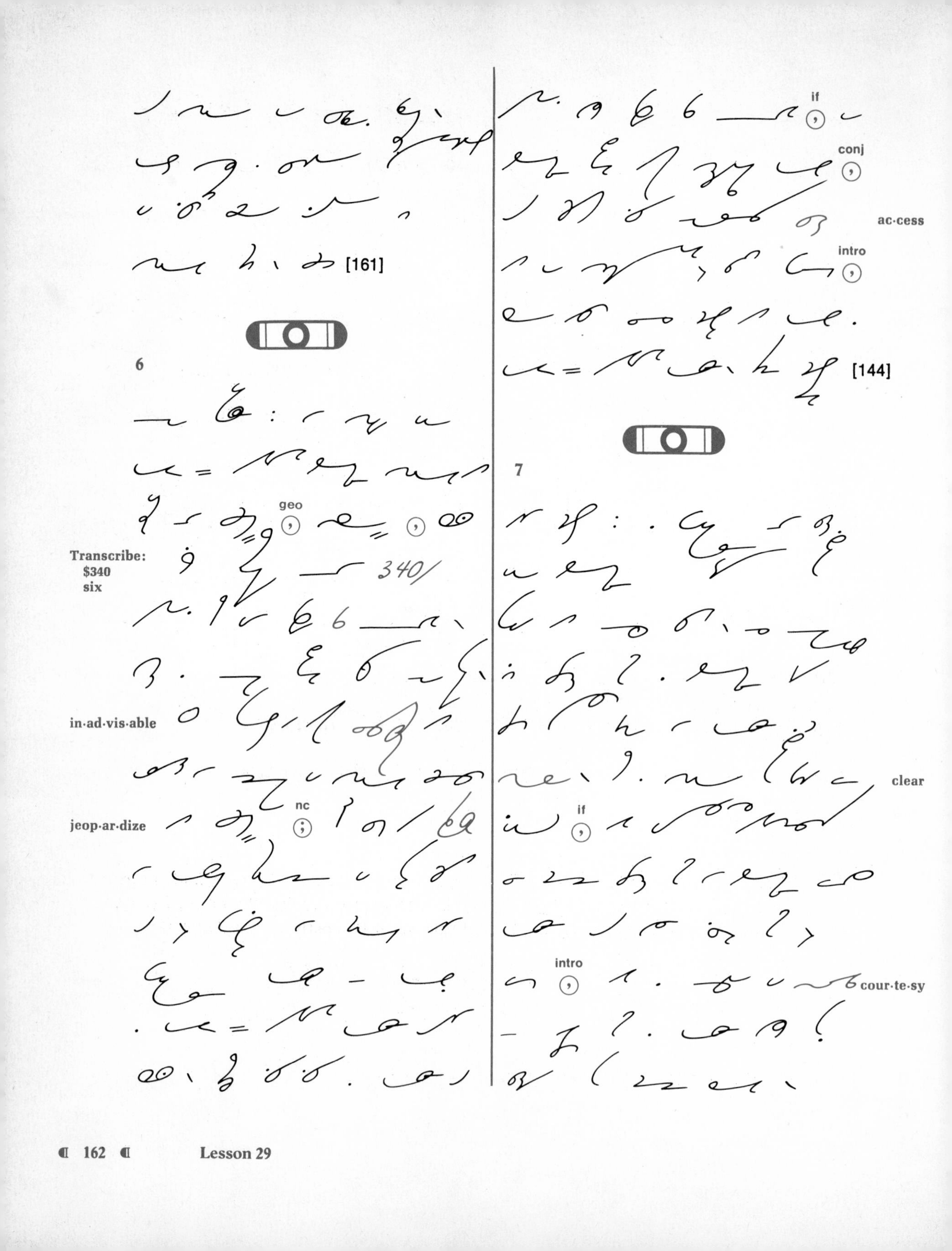

[161]

6

geo

Transcribe:
$340
six

340/

6

in·ad·vis·able

nc

jeop·ar·dize

if

conj

ac·cess

intro

[144]

7

clear

if

intro

cour·te·sy

[92]

8

as

isq

iq

cr

Com·pa·ny's

out-of-state hyphenated before noun

thank-you hyphenated before noun

if

intro

[145]

Company business is just that—company business! A secretary should never discuss matters relating to office work with people outside the office. Even a casual remark innocently made could prove to be costly to the company.

Building Transcription Skills

1 COMMON PREFIXES

Another effective way to build your vocabulary is to learn the meaning of common English prefixes. In earlier volumes of Gregg Shorthand, Series 90, you studied a number of them. In this volume you will study several more.

COMMON PREFIXES ● mis-

mis- The prefix *mis-* means *wrong, erroneous,* or *incorrect.*
mistaken In error.
misplace To put in the wrong place; to lose.
mistreat To handle roughly or wrongly; to abuse.
misunderstand To interpret incorrectly.
misinform To give incorrect information.

2 Business Vocabulary Builder

brokerage A firm that handles the buying and selling of property for others.
modest Moderate; not extreme.
device A piece of equipment.

Reading and Writing Practice

3

bro·ker·age

460 ... 14 ... 90

ap

role

ap

sec·re·tary

Mis·takes

pub·li·ca·tions

ap

ac·quaint

if

[131]

4

when

de·vice

de·vel·oped

re·li·able

ser

con·ver·sion

Transcribe: $1 million

intro

com·plet·ed

intro

mis·un·der·stand·ing

ap

if

[182]

5

col·lege

mis·in·formed

ours

intro

Transcribe: $50

ter·mi·nate

par

[176]

6

as

faith·ful Gray's

cr

Transcribe: $300

nonr

some·time

[123]

7

Transcribe:
ten
three

intro

par

mis·con·cep·tion

conj

intro

intro

con·cur

[138]

8

intro

Transcribe:
$82.40
$25

conj

if

[101]

TRANSCRIBING

Now that Marie had taken care of the preliminary tasks involved in transcribing, she began typing the correspondence Mr. Franklin had dictated. However, she knew transcribing her notes would not be the final step. Proofreading, making corrections, and making copies are all part of the transcription process.

Even though she tried to catch and correct errors while she was transcribing, Marie might still overlook some mistakes, and she knew that it was the responsibility of a good secretary to find and correct these mistakes. She proofread each page while it was still in the typewriter. It would be easier and quicker to correct errors in this manner rather than to reinsert the page and try to line it up. She was especially careful to check any figures in the transcripts because such an error could prove costly and embarrassing to the company. She read each page character by character to be sure to catch any errors. As she became more adept at proofreading, she would be able to read word by word, but she would never just skim a page. Marie marked each error with a light pencil mark in the margin so that she could make all her corrections at once.

There would be occasions when Marie would not be able to proofread a transcript while the page was in the typewriter. If a report contained a great many statistics, Marie would proofread with another person who would read aloud what she had typed as she followed silently in her notes. This was the most effective way to proofread this type of material.

As she read her transcripts, Marie took special care to check for transpositions, similar-word errors, double-letter errors, and errors in numbers.

Marie's typewriter was a self-correcting model with a backspace correction key and a special cartridge containing a correcting ribbon. However, she had been well trained and was able to make corrections using different materials—correction fluid, correction paper, a typewriter eraser, a razor blade, and correction tape when she knew that only photocopies of her transcript would be distributed. Even with the specially equipped typewriter, Marie had to correct carbon copies. She did this with a soft pencil eraser and used an eraser guard between multiple carbon copies.

Before she began transcribing each letter, Marie noted the

number of copies she would need. Usually she needed to make only one carbon copy for the files. If two or three copies were to be sent to other persons, she was able to use a carbon pack. But if more than two or three copies were needed, she made photocopies. When the time came for Marie to prepare lengthy reports for a large distribution, she intended to have them duplicated by the company's duplicating department or have them prepared on an automatic typewriter.

As she completed each letter, Marie drew a line through her notes, including any special notations or instructions accompanying them, and typed an envelope.

Finally, Marie gathered all the letters, made sure she had typed all the envelopes and attached all enclosures, and submitted them to Mr. Franklin in a folder labeled "For Your Signature."

Building Transcription Skills

1 SIMILAR-WORDS DRILL

Words that sound alike, such as *week-weak,* and words that sound almost alike, such as *device-devise,* are the cause of many transcription errors. Often secretaries know which word in a similar-sounding pair is the correct one to use in a sentence, but because of carelessness they transcribe the wrong one.

In the lessons ahead you will study a number of Similar-Words Drills that will call your attention to pairs of words that may lead to transcription errors if you are not careful.

Read the definition of each word carefully to be sure you understand it. The words in each Similar-Words Drill are used in the Reading and Writing Practice. Watch for them.

SIMILAR-WORDS DRILL ● residents, residence

residents People who make their homes in a particular place; those who live in homes.

The *residents* of Washington County voted for a new state senator.

residence The place in which one lives.

My *residence* is not for sale.

---

2 Business Vocabulary Builder

leisure time Time free from work or duties.

periodically At fixed or regular intervals of time.

drudgery Dull, unpleasant work.

Reading and Writing Practice

3

in·di·vid·u·al

ten·nis

lei·sure

and o

if

main·te·nance

Acres

in·sects

intro

week·ly

res·i·dents

Transcribe: 402 East State Street

drudg·ery

res·i·dence

[165]

4

Transcribe: 347 West 23 Street

es·ti·mate

enu

Trim·ming

con·tact

Feb·ru·ary

ap

nc

ar·range·ments

[98]

5

men·tioned

seek·ing

iq

De·stroy

at·tack

treat·ment

conj

care·ful·ly

if

Transcribe:
$9.50
April 15

if

nc

res·i·dents

[154]

6

res·i·dents

at·trac·tive·ly land·scaped
no hyphen
after ly

stra·te·gi·cal·ly lo·cat·ed
no hyphen
after ly

res·i·dence

intro

in·su·lat·ing

conj

555-9625

[139]

7

if

your·self

intro

chem·i·cals

ser

intro

roll

res·i·dents

if

and o

well-trained
hyphenated
before noun

[114]

Building Transcription Skills

1 **SPELLING FAMILIES ● -cal, -cle**

Whenever you hear the ending that is pronounced "kle," be careful; it may be spelled *cal* or *cle*. Here are examples of each ending.

Words Ending in -cal

med-i-cal	**rad-i-cal**	**po-lit-i-cal**
log-i-cal	**phys-i-cal**	**crit-i-cal**
sur-gi-cal	**mu-si-cal**	**chem-i-cal**
iden-ti-cal	**ver-ti-cal**	**op-ti-cal**

Words Ending in -cle

ve-hi-cle	**mir-a-cle**	**bi-cy-cle**
par-ti-cle	**ar-ti-cle**	**spec-ta-cle**
ob-sta-cle	**re-cep-ta-cle**	**ici-cle**

2 **Business Vocabulary Builder**

assess To determine; to evaluate.

random Without definite direction or method.

ceramic Made of earthenware, porcelain, brick, etc.

venture *(noun)* An undertaking involving risk or chance.

Reading and Writing Practice

3

and o

harsh

as·sess

home's
en·er·gy·sav·ing
hyphenated
before noun

enu

drafts

mois·ture

freeze

if

weath·er strip·ping

nc

conj

eco·nom·i·cal

intro

[158]

4

ran·dom
Transcribe:
100

sin·gle-fam·i·ly
hyphenated
before noun

ce·ram·ic

Transcribe:
23 percent

nonr

ve·hi·cles

cap·tured

if

ven·ture

[145]

5

ar·ti·cle

pe·ri·od·i·cal

ap

to·day's

isq

vir·tu·al·ly

iq

quar·rel

ar·ray

crit·i·cal

when

and o

[149]

6

if

intro

un·com·fort·able

es·ca·lat·ing

intro

sense

years'

alu·mi·num

[140]

7

enu

of·ten

bur·glary
Transcribe:
9 a.m.
5 p.m.

crit·i·cal

if

skill·ful

van·dals

intro

Transcribe:
555-9206

and o

well-trained
hyphenated
before noun

[134]

Building Transcription Skills

1 ACCURACY PRACTICE

When you are writing rapidly, you will occasionally write an outline that is out of proportion. In most cases, the context of the sentence will tell you the meaning of the outline. There are only a few outlines in which exact proportion is critical because the sense of the sentence will not help you to read the outline.

In this Accuracy Practice, and in several others in this text, a few such outlines will be called to your attention. When you write these outlines, take special care to write them using correct proportion.

Here is the way to handle each Accuracy Practice:

- □ **1** Write the words in Group 1 slowly, paying attention to proper proportion.
- □ **2** Write these words once again as rapidly as you can while maintaining proper proportion.
- □ **3** Read and copy the sentences for Group 1 in the Practice Drill.
- □ **4** Repeat the procedure for the other groups.

Group 1	**Group 2**	**Group 3**
fear	in the	order
feel	at the	audit

practice drill

1

2

1 *I* fear *we are late.*
I feel *we are late.*

2 *I will meet you* in the *bus terminal.*
I will meet you at the *bus terminal.*

3 *We will* order *the books tomorrow.*
We will audit *the books tomorrow.*

---

2 Business Vocabulary Builder

retail store A store that sells goods directly to consumers.
chandeliers Branched lighting fixtures suspended from the ceiling.
surveyed Examined as to condition or value.

Reading and Writing Practice

3

par

and o

el·e·gant

par

house·ful

high-qual·i·ty hyphenated before noun

Transcribe: $10,000

Transcribe: 340 State Street

ap

best-known hyphenated before noun

your·self

and o

conj

re·lax·ing

en·joy·able

Transcribe: 50 percent

Transcribe: 20

ac·com·mo·date

reg·is·tra·tion

[201]

4

chan·de·liers

fix·tures

geo

conj

la·bor

tem·po·rar·i·ly

intro

conj

fear

pur·sue

if

nc

[108]

5

in·te·ri·or

high-qual·i·ty hyphenated before noun

sur·veyed

geo

theirs

Transcribe: 23 percent

intro

com·pet·i·tor

ours

when

[154]

6

intro

intro

ser

au·dit·ing

as·sis·tance

hes·i·tate

[121]

Building Transcription Skills

1 **OFFICE-STYLE DICTATION ● substitutions**

Occasionally an executive will dictate a word or phrase but then decide to substitute another word or phrase. The dictator might say:
Your concern for my safety—make that **welfare**—*is appreciated.*

In your notebook you would simply place a heavy downward line through the word *safety* and write *welfare* next to the outline you crossed out thus:

Sometimes the dictator may decide on a change after completing the sentence. The dictator might say:
You should receive our check for $25 tomorrow—make that **$35.**
You would indicate the change in this way:

35

restorations

There will be times when the dictator will use a word or phrase, decide to substitute another word or phrase, and then, on further reflection, decide that the first word or phrase was better. The dictator might say:

We will send you a bill—make that **a statement;** *oh, perhaps we should leave it* **bill.**

When the dictator says, "Make that *a statement*," strike a heavy downward line through *bill* and write *statement*. Then, when the dictator says, "Oh, perhaps we should leave it *bill*," write the word *bill* again. This is the way it would look in your notes.

Do not try to indicate that the original outline for the word *bill* is to be restored. This may take you longer than writing the word a second time. In addition, it may lead to confusion when you are transcribing.

Illustration of Office-Style Dictation

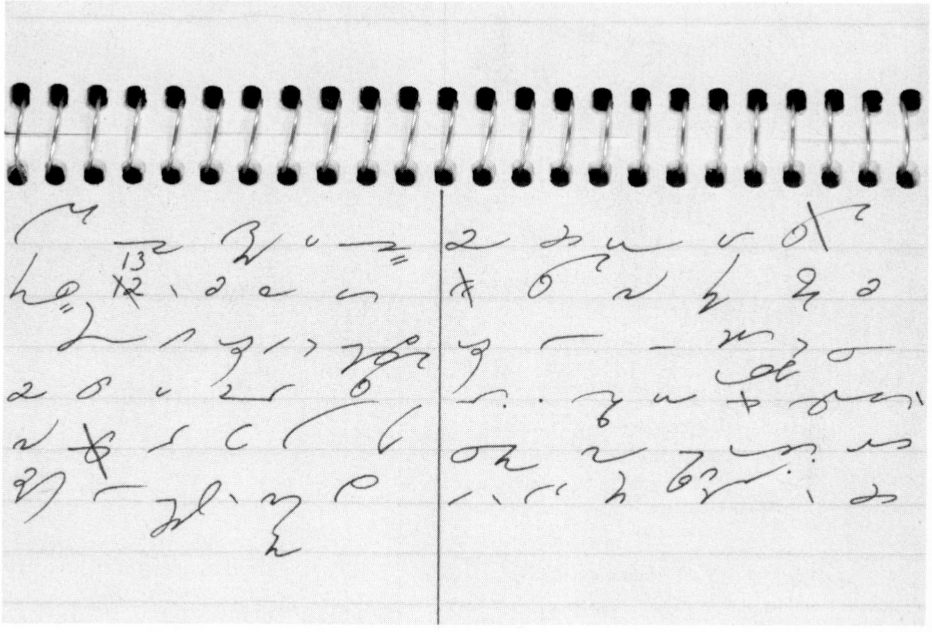

2 Business Vocabulary Builder

proceed To begin; to continue.

sketch *(noun)* A rough drawing.

insulation Material that prevents the loss of heat from a building.

locality Area.

Reading and Writing Practice

3

year's

conj

Transcribe: 9 a.m. May 15

some time

Transcribe: Four·teen

and o

theme

iq

so·lar

sen·si·ble
de·sign

ser

ap

nc

some·time

nc

[164]

4

conj

vi·tal

pro·ceed
shop·ping

ben·e·fits

par

puz·zled

and o

eco·nom·i·cal

pre·lim·i·nary

enu ser

intro

intro

re·ly

as·sis·tance

par

[178]

5

de·vot·ed

de·signed

geo

in·su·la·tion

two-sto·ry hyphenated before noun

beau·ti·ful·ly de·signed no hyphen after ly

Brown's

ex·cit·ed

conj

lo·cal·i·ty

con·cepts

con·ve·nient

cr

[185]

6

ser

ser

nonr

alarm

ser

nc

roomy

nc

[89]

7

Transcribe: 15 percent

chim·ney

pre·vent

sense

enu

[124]

Building Transcription Skills

1 SPELLING FAMILIES ● -ize, -ise, -yze

Be very careful when you transcribe a word ending with the sound *iz*. The ending may be spelled *-ize, -ise,* or *-yze.*

Words Ending in -ize

apol-o-gize	**rec-og-nize**	**spe-cial-ize**
re-al-ize	**or-ga-nize**	**uti-lize**

Words Ending in -ise

rise	**ad-vise**	**com-pro-mise**
ad-ver-tise	**en-ter-prise**	**com-prise**

Words Ending in -yze

an-a-lyze	**par-a-lyze**

2 Business Vocabulary Builder

patios Paved areas adjoining houses.

municipalities Self-governing communities such as cities and towns.

dimension Quality; aspect.

Reading and Writing Practice

3

dis·like

if

ap

com·plete

rec·re·ation·al

up-to-date hyphenated before noun

and o

intro

pa·ti·os

swim·ming

ser

dis·plac·ing

an·a·lyz·ing

par

self-ad·dressed

if

[164]

4

fast·est-grow·ing hyphenated before noun

Mu·nic·i·pal·i·ties

and o

intro

and o

suc·cess·ful

prof·it·able

intro

pro·spec·tive

dis·il·lu·sioned

if

intro

di·men·sion

ap

ser

com·prised

cas·sette

nonr

choose

ap

[194]

[125]

5

6

when

dis·re·gard

nc

re·duced

Transcribe:
50 percent

high-qual·i·ty
built-in
hyphenated
before noun

ser

ceil·ing

nonr

Transcribe: $1,000

ap

conj

intro

conj

dis·cour·aged

cr

[130]

7

base·ment

musty

ser

dis·agree·able

and o

en·joy·able

if

ap

uti·liz·ing

conj

nc

par

[125]

8

ap

Re·mod·el·ing

Transcribe:
416 West 42 Street

416 42

rec·om·mend conj

dis·ap·point·ed

conj

[143]

9

cab·i·net

isq

if

piece

step by step
no noun,
no hyphen

Transcribe:
50

50

nc

[117]

PREPARING REPORTS

One morning, after Marie had been on the job two weeks, Mr. Franklin reminded her that it was the first of the month and they would have to work on the previous month's sales report. He told her that they would set aside the daily routine and work only on the report because it would probably take all day to complete. Mr. Franklin gave Marie detailed instructions about doing the work, which she jotted down in her shorthand notebook, and she returned to her desk and started working.

The first thing Marie had to do was to compile all the figures from the reports sent in by the sales representatives from all over the country—there were 50 individual reports. Using an electronic calculator, she added the various columns of sales figures and penciled them in on the report form Mr. Franklin had given her. She wanted to be absolutely sure that the totals were accurate, so she added the figures a second time.

With the figures Marie had prepared for him, Mr. Franklin was able to dictate an analysis and summary of the report. When he had finished dictating, he asked Marie to read her notes to him so that he could double-check all the figures with those on the sales report forms. When they were satisfied that all the figures were accurate,

Marie transcribed her notes and made a typewritten copy of the sales report forms. Since accuracy was so important, Marie asked one of the other secretaries to proofread with her. Marie read her notes and the rough copy of the sales form silently while the other secretary read aloud what Marie had typed. After Marie had made one or two corrections and Mr. Franklin had approved the report, Marie realized that she would have to work rapidly—but carefully—if the report was to be finished on time.

Since this was a rush project, Mr. Franklin told Marie that she would have to do the duplicating and collating herself rather than sending the report to the duplicating department. Marie photocopied 12 sets of her typewritten material as well as each sales representative's report. She then 3-hole punched all the pages and, using a collator, assembled the report. Before inserting the pages into binders, she checked them to be sure that all the pages were there and in proper sequence. Marie had used her time efficiently by preparing labels for the binders while Mr. Franklin was reading the final copy of the report.

At 4:45 p.m., Marie realized that Mr. Franklin had been right—preparing the report had taken all day. She would distribute the copies of the report first thing tomorrow morning.

Building Transcription Skills

1 SIMILAR-WORDS DRILL ● adopt, adapt, adept

adopt To take as one's own; to accept.

You will increase your sales if you *adopt* the plan.

adapt To make fit; to make suitable.

We will *adapt* our procedures to the new circumstances.

adept Thoroughly proficient; expert.

They conducted the business in an *adept* manner.

---

2 Business Vocabulary Builder

culinary Relating to cooking.

unqualified Without reservations, restrictions, or exceptions.

strict Inflexible; not subject to change.

Reading and Writing Practice

3

in·qui·ry

ap

for·mer

Cu·li·nary

un·qual·i·fied

Transcribe:
September 1, 1977,

quite
ad·ept

intro

ser

conj

adopt·ed

intro

[138]

4

com·ments

en·joyed

conj

be·lieve

intro

adopt

intro

bud·get

adapt

if

[122]

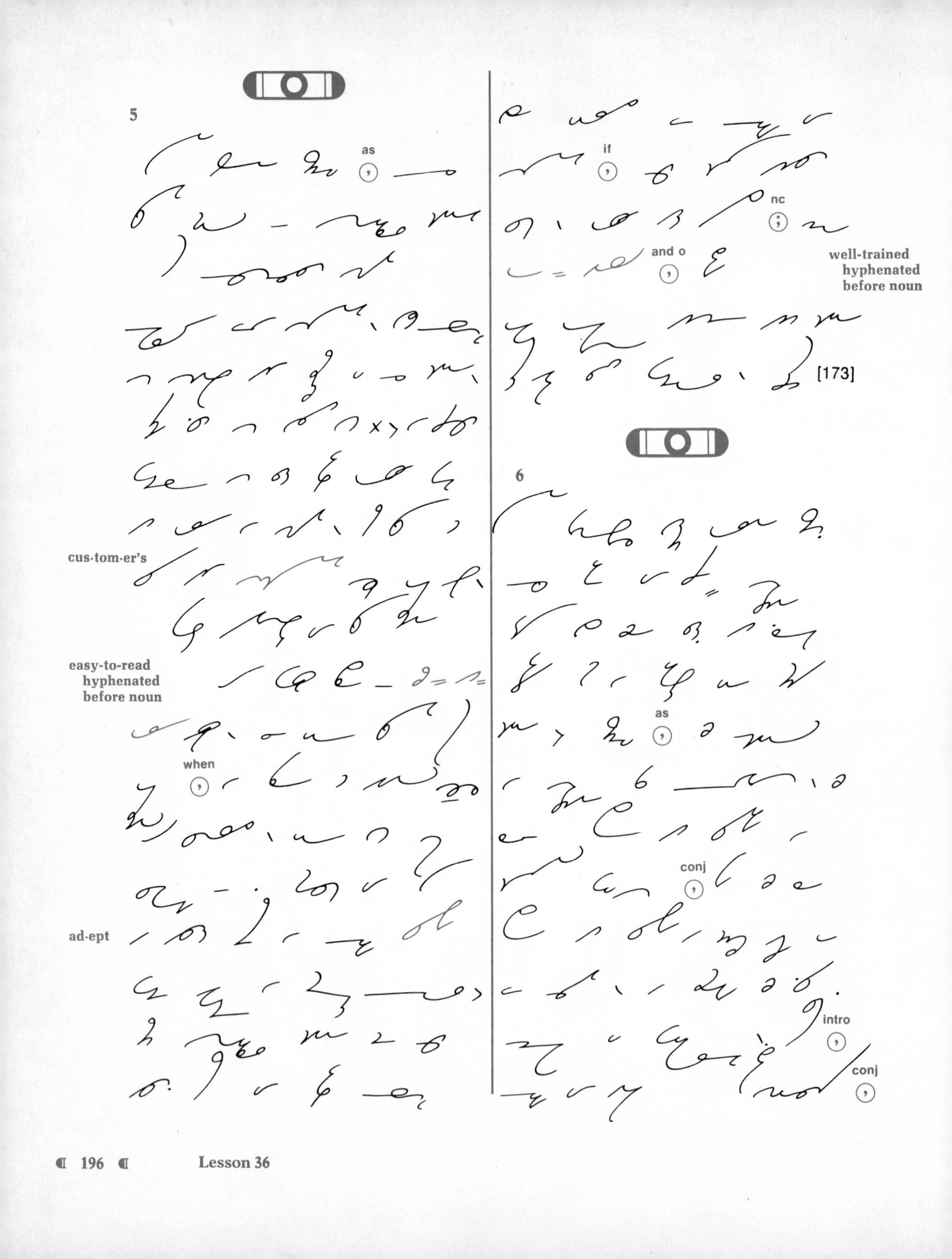

5

as

customers

easy-to-read
hyphenated
before noun

when

ad·ept

if

nc

and o

well-trained
hyphenated
before noun

[173]

6

as

conj

intro

conj

enu

min·utes' 5

few·er

intro

conj

if

[208]

7

an·nounce
self-ser·vice

402

nonr

as

geo

intro

ser

intro

[164]

Building Transcription Skills

1 **SPELLING FAMILIES ● -cede, -ceed, -sede**

The sound *seed* in words may be spelled *cede, ceed,* or *sede.*

Words Ending in -cede

cede	**con-cede**	**pre-cede**
ac-cede	**in-ter-cede**	**re-cede**

Words Ending in -ceed

ex-ceed	**pro-ceed**	**suc-ceed**

Word Ending in -sede

su-per-sede

2 **Business Vocabulary Builder**

bleak Not hopeful or encouraging.

contend To argue; to maintain.

substantiated Proven; verified.

Reading and Writing Practice

3

ad·e·quate·ly trained no hyphen after ly

check·ers

conj

ex·ceeds

bleak

intro

qual·i·fy·ing

if

re·fer

suc·ceed

par

Transcribe: 50 well-trained hyphenated before noun

if

[156]

4

ac·cept·ed

Transcribe: $5,000

ad·mis·sions

pro·ceed

fi·nal·ized

as

de·signed

ser

sales·peo·ple

on-off-cam·pus hyphenated before noun

cal·en·dar

ac·quaint·ed

ap

Transcribe: September 15 8 a.m.

Transcribe: 402 East Elm Drive

[149]

5

fall·en

Transcribe: 16 percent

ex·ceed

conj

intro

con·clud·ed

re·sis·tance

lacks

conj

con·ten·tion

re·vis·ing

conj

role

cr

[157]

6

and o

lose

low-cal·o·rie hyphenated before noun

schemes

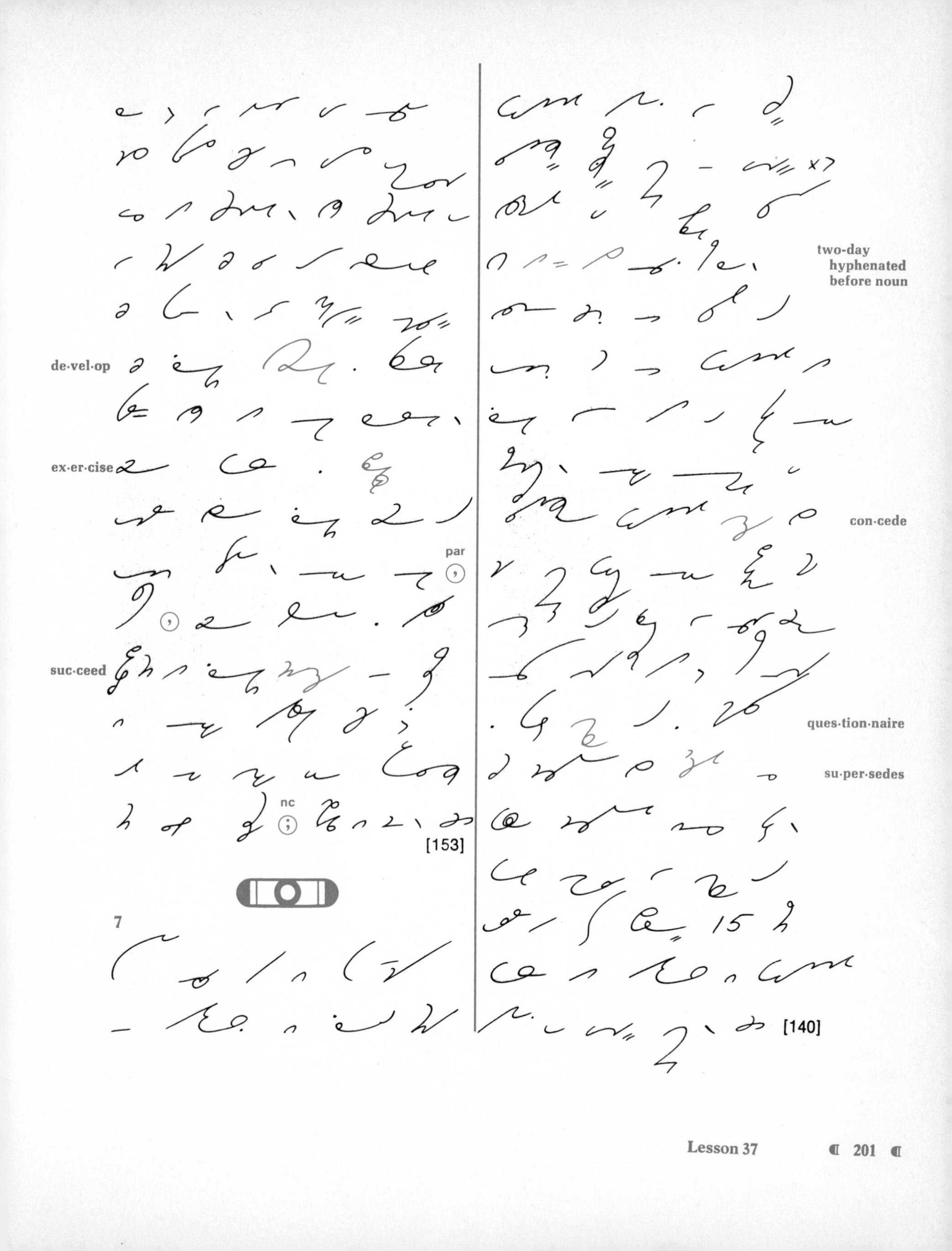

de·vel·op

ex·er·cise

par

suc·ceed

nc

[153]

7

two-day hyphenated before noun

con·cede

ques·tion·naire

su·per·sedes

[140]

Building Transcription Skills

1 GRAMMAR CHECKUP ● one word or two? (concluded)

Here are some additional expressions that may be written as one word or two words.

everyday, every day

everyday *(adjective)* Ordinary; daily.

These are my everyday (ordinary) *clothes.*

every day Each day.

Please post all transactions every day (each day) *next week.*

anyway, any way

anyway In any case.

I planned to do the work myself anyway (in any case).

any way By any method.

Get the job done in any way (by any method) *that you can.*

maybe, may be

maybe Perhaps.

Maybe (perhaps) *we can complete the job ahead of schedule.*

may be This expression is a verb.

It may be *too late.*

---

2 Business Vocabulary Builder

durable Lasting.

wholesome Beneficial to one's health; nourishing.

foremost *(adjective)* First in rank; preeminent.

resource A source of information or expertise.

Reading and Writing Practice

3

news·cast
to·day's
when
nc
week's
when
up-to-date hyphenated before noun
when
styl·ish
par
dairy
par
whole·some

Each time
if
may be
else·where
[153]

4

ac·quaint
ap
ap
coun·try's
fore·most

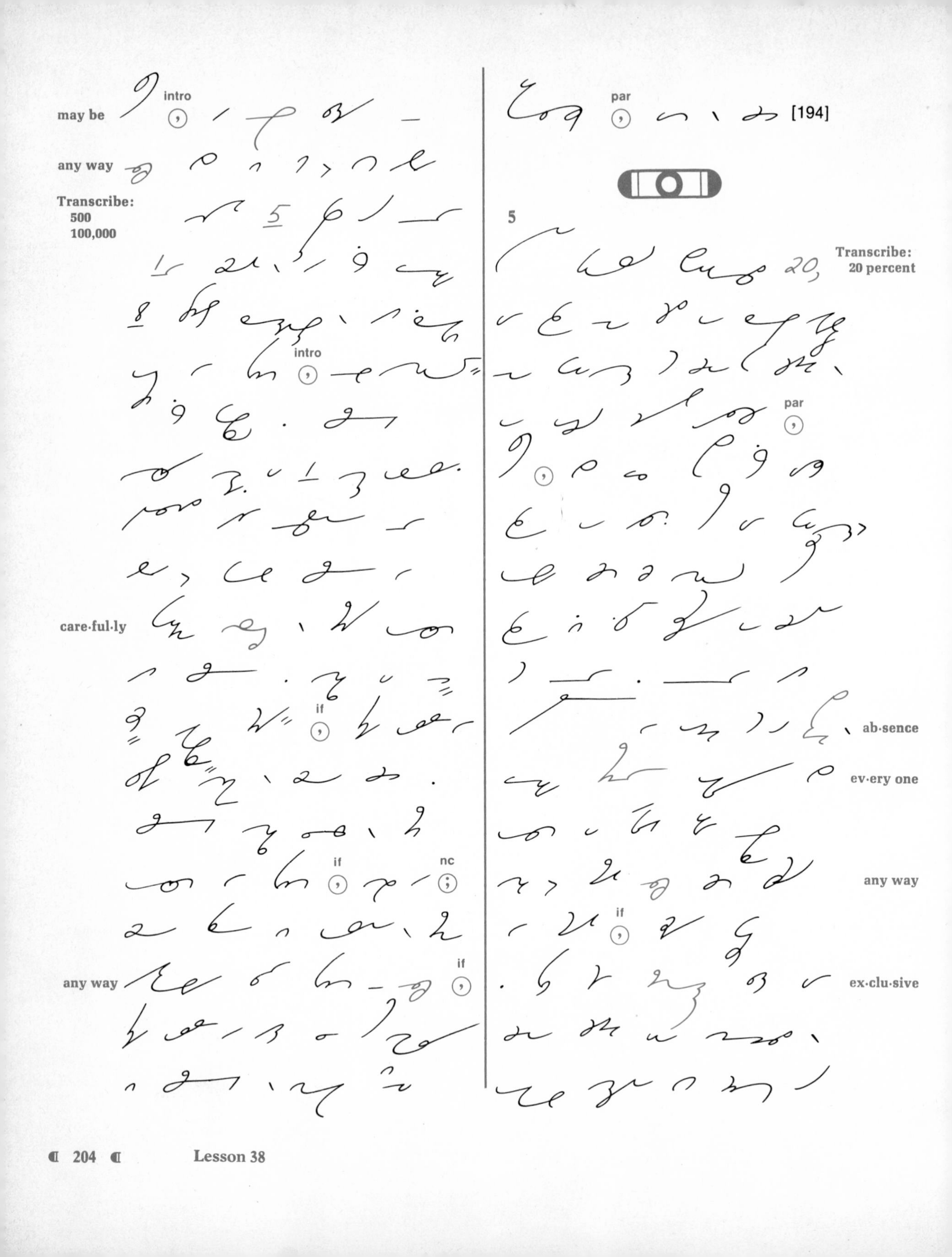

may be

intro

any way

Transcribe:
500
100,000

intro

care·ful·ly

if

if

nc

any way

if

par

[194]

5

Transcribe:
20 percent

par

ab·sence

ev·ery one

any way

if

ex·clu·sive

rec·om·men·da·tion

some·tme

cr [141]

6

50,

ev·ery·day

ser

conj

Transcribe:
8 a.m.
3 p.m.

ser

conj

ev·ery day
May·be

intro

Any·way

3

[141]

Building Transcription Skills

1 **OFFICE-STYLE DICTATION ● short transpositions**

A dictator will occasionally decide to transpose words or phrases for emphasis or for some other reason. The dictator may say:

Mr. Chan works skillfully and efficiently—make that **efficiently and skillfully.**

In your notes you would indicate the transposition in this way:

You would then transcribe the word *and* after the word *efficiently.*

long transpositions

There will be times when the dictator will decide to transpose a sentence or even an entire paragraph. When this happens, circle the material to be transposed and indicate the new position with an arrow.

2 Business Vocabulary Builder

dilemma A problem seemingly incapable of satisfactory solution.

channel *(verb)* To focus or concentrate on a particular activity.

solely At the exclusion of everything else; singly.

Illustration of Office-Style Dictation

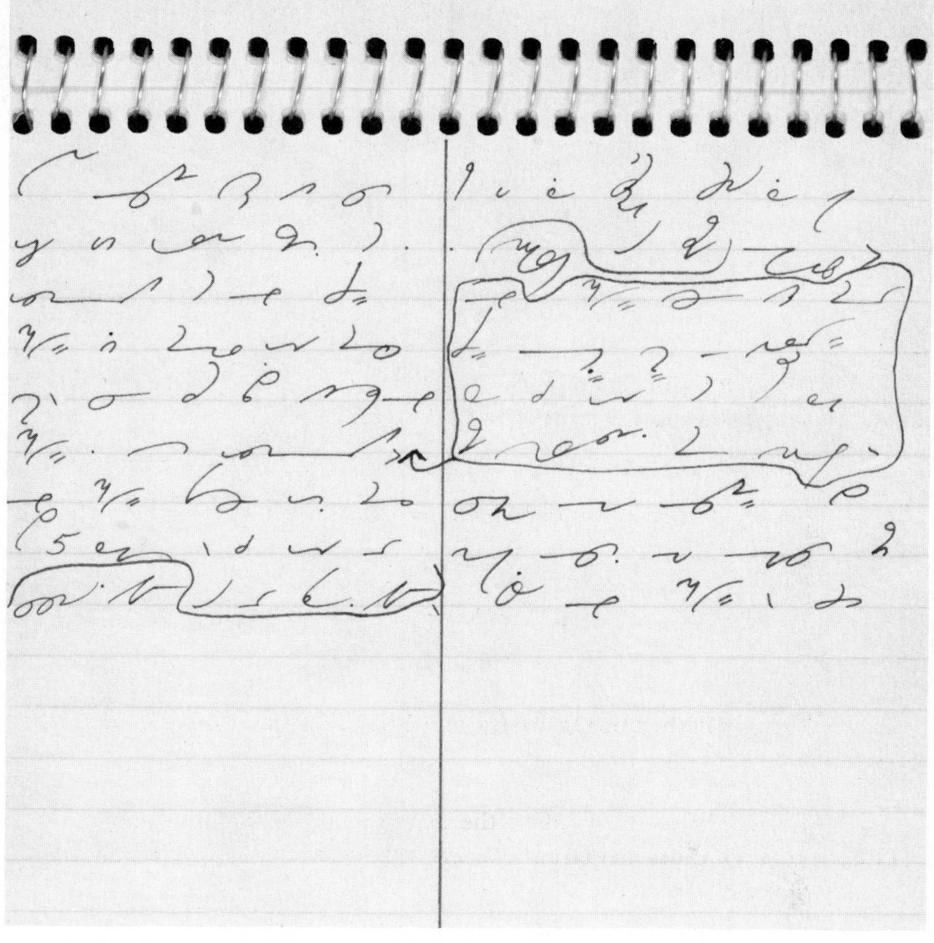

Reading and Writing Practice

3

di·lem·ma

chil·dren's

per·suade

ser

har·vest

intro

loaves

intro

acres

150

pruned

ser

conj

chan·nel

full-time
part-time
hyphenated
before noun

intro

[161]

4

intro

isq

Farm·ers'

intro

Co·op·er·a·tive

ex·ists

intro

sole·ly

intro

intro

high·est

intro

non·prof·it intro

intro

its

[152]

5

judge

Live·stock ser

conj

ac·cept

nc

Transcribe:
15th
16th
17th

par

[118]

6

coun·try's

years'
def·i·cits

intro

abun·dant·ly

conj

intro

com·mod·i·ties

conj

en·deav·ors

[181]

7

if

fast·est-grow·ing hyphenated before noun

intro

enu

ben·e·fits

al·most

and o

up-to-date hyphenated before noun

[157]

Transcribe: $85

Building Transcription Skills

1 COMMON PREFIXES • ir-

ir- In many English words, the prefix *ir-* means *not*.

irreplaceable Not capable of being replaced.

irregular Not regular; not steady.

irrelevant Not relevant; not applicable.

irreparable Not capable of being repaired.

irresponsible Not responsible; lacking a sense of responsibility.

irrespective Regardless of; without consideration of.

irreducible Not capable of being reduced.

2 Business Vocabulary Builder

prompted Urged; caused to take action; incited.

counteract To make ineffective; to neutralize.

appreciably Noticeably.

unwarranted Having no justification; groundless.

Reading and Writing Practice

3

can·ning

as

can·nery

Transcribe: January 1, 1960,

ex·pand·ed

intro

salm·on

par

shrimp

ser

ex·cel·lent

conj

ir·reg·u·lar

intro

con·tact

if

[186]

4

pub·lic·i·ty

nc

ir·re·spec·tive

Transcribe:
15 percent

15,

conj

ap·pre·cia·bly

farm·ers'

intro

un·war·rant·ed

[154]

5

de·sign

if

build

plow

fa·tigue

ac·ces·si·ble

ir·rep·a·ra·ble

if

some·time

[136]

6

fourth

geo

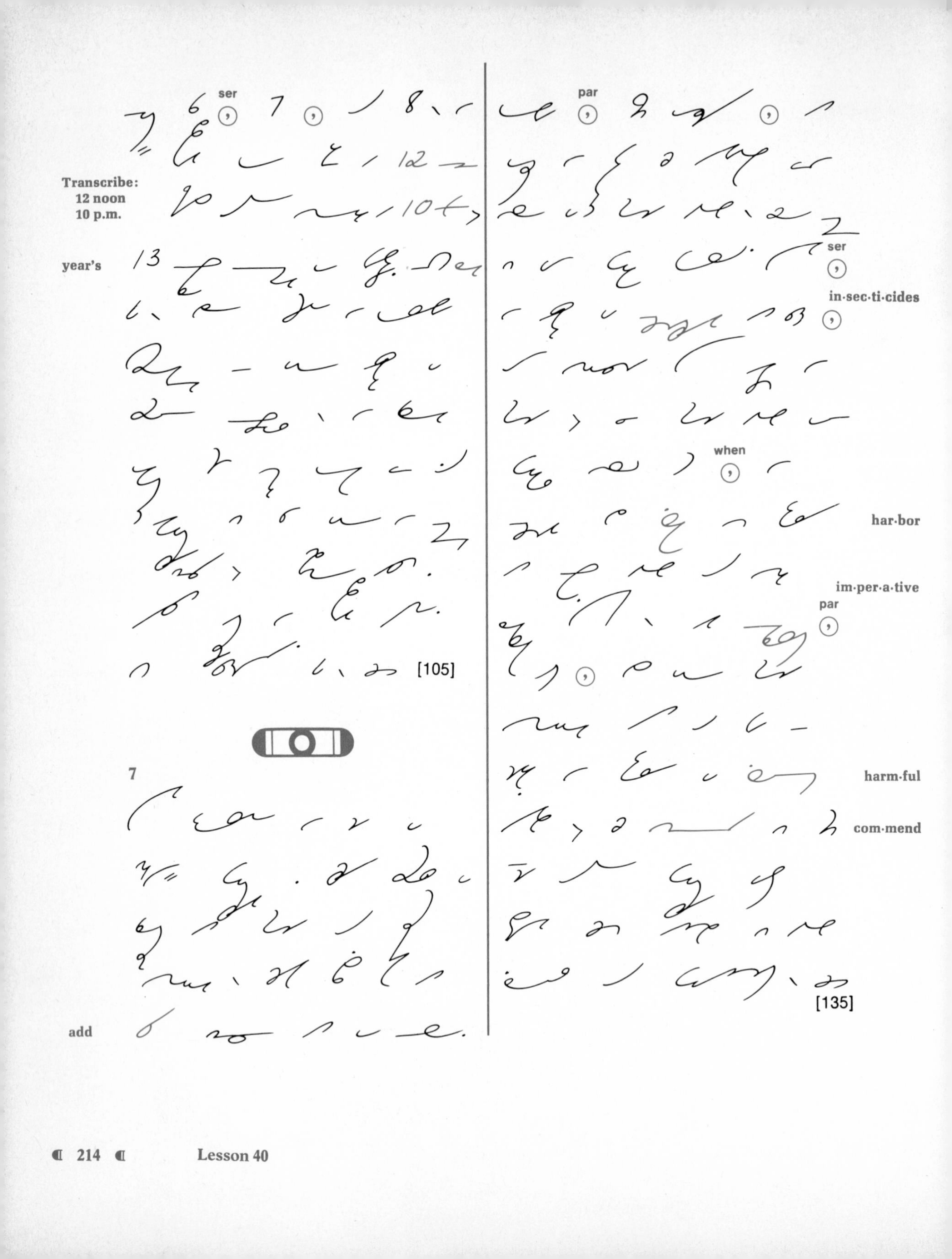

ser

Transcribe:
12 noon
10 p.m.

year's

[105]

7

add

par

ser

in·sec·ti·cides

when

har·bor

im·per·a·tive

par

harm·ful

com·mend

[135]

PART

ARRANGING MEETINGS AND TRIPS

During one dictation session, Mr. Franklin asked Marie to make travel arrangements for Ms. Valdez and him. They were going to visit one of the branch offices to meet with some of the sales representatives and would need airline reservations and hotel accommodations for the following week. Before Marie took care of those arrangements, however, Mr. Franklin asked that she set up a meeting of the marketing staff for the next day. The meeting would probably last all morning, and its purpose was to discuss the previous month's sales performance. Marie jotted down all the necessary information in her shorthand notebook.

When she returned to her desk, Marie first reserved the conference room for the meeting. She then telephoned each of the eight staff members who were to attend to let them know of the meeting because it was being scheduled on such short notice. Marie confirmed the meeting by memo, stating the date, time, place, and agenda, and delivered each memo personally. She also noted the meeting on Mr. Franklin's calendar and on her own calendar.

The first thing Marie intended to do the next morning was to see that the conference room was in order—making sure that there were enough chairs; placing folders, pads, and pencils at each place; and supplying sufficient copies of any reports that would be needed during the meeting. Afterwards, it would be Marie's responsibility to see that the conference room was left in the same neat condition in which she had found it.

Marie consulted the airline guide and wrote down (in order of preference) several departure and return flights that would best fit into the scheduled plans. By using this source now, she would save time when she called the airline to make the reservations. The hotel guide was also a handy reference because she was able to choose the hotel nearest the branch office so that the two travelers would not have to go a great distance to and from the office each day. When she made the hotel reservations, she asked the reservation clerk to send written confirmation.

While she was on the phone with both the airline and the hotel clerks, Marie kept Mr. Franklin's calendar open in front of her to be sure of the scheduled dates. When the arrangements were completed, she wrote the details on Mr. Franklin's calendar and on her own calendar and prepared four copies of an itinerary—one each for Mr. Franklin, Ms. Valdez, Ms. Valdez' secretary, and herself. Marie was always especially careful to keep both calendars up to date and consulted them each time she scheduled appointments for Mr. Franklin. It would be embarrassing to both her boss and her if she had to cancel an appointment because of a conflict.

On days like this one, Marie truly realized and appreciated the importance of good organization.

Building Transcription Skills

1 **TYPING STYLE STUDY ● capitalization**

General Classifications Names Personal Titles

☐ **1** Do not capitalize common nouns like *company* that represent general classifications.

Our company *will open a new office.*

☐ **2** Use the following forms for titles in the address, salutation, and body of business letters.

Mr. *Smith*	Miss *Lopez*	Dr. *Samuels*
Mrs. *Jackson*	Ms. *Pulaski*	

☐ **3** Other titles, such as *professor, manager,* or *senator,* are spelled in full. They are capitalized only when they are used with names.

I will give the report to the professor.

Did you meet Professor Barnes?

---

2 Business Vocabulary Builder

traveler's checks Guaranteed checks that may be used like cash.

letter of credit A letter from a bank guaranteeing a person's check at another bank.

surplus Excess; more than enough.

Reading and Writing Practice

3

geo

Eu·rope

conj

trav·el·er's

help·ful

prompt

par

[117]

4

prob·a·bly

geo

per·mit·ted

cer·tif·i·cates

Transcribe: $5,000

intro

if

sur·plus

par

re·ceive

one-year hyphenated before noun

fur·ther as·sis·tance

if

555-6491

if

29 EAST CANYON AVENUE, SANTA FE, NEW MEXICO 87501

Cable: SPLAGAR

SPLANE & GARDNER, INC.

TEL. 445-7890

February 14, 19--

Miss Pamela S. White
White Real Estate Consultants, Inc.
345 West Third Avenue
Chicago, IL 60607

Dear Miss White

For the past several months my company has been considering purchasing a new building in the Springfield, Illinois, area. We hope to use the new building as a regional sales office and as a warehouse.

Last week we located a building that we think will be suitable. It is in the eastern part of Springfield, and it contains about 50,000 square feet of floor space. The building is owned by Madison and Company and is currently leased to the Midwest Motor Company. However, their lease will expire in two months, and they do not plan to renew it.

Madison and Company would like $200,000 for the building, and our real estate people feel that this is a fair price. However, they have recommended that we contact you to find out if you feel that this price is in line with other real estate in the general area.

Will you do us a favor, Miss White? Can you go to Springfield sometime during the next week or so to look at this building? If you recommend that we purchase it, we will probably go ahead with the financial arrangements in the next few weeks.

We will be looking forward to hearing from you, Miss White. You can call us at the above telephone number to let us know when you will be able to go to Springfield.

Very sincerely yours

Jeffrey Stone

Jeffrey Stone
Vice President

cl

Long letter, full-blocked style, open punctuation

[159]

5

col·lege

ap

En·glish

Transcribe:
$100
$200

with·held

if

intro

intro

[250]

6

wel·come

7

enu

if

ap

Transcribe: eight

intro

and o

ac·cept

short-long-term hyphenated before noun

cap·i·tal

ser

ad·ept

if

[141]

[157]

Building Transcription Skills

1 SPELLING FAMILIES ● -ly added to words ending in e

Most words ending in *e* retain the *e* when the ending *-ly* is added.

bare-ly	**ac-tive-ly**	**nice-ly**
com-plete-ly	**name-ly**	**sure-ly**
mere-ly	**for-tu-nate-ly**	**unique-ly**
like-ly	**sin-cere-ly**	**late-ly**

In the following words, however, the *e* is dropped when *-ly* is added.

tru-ly	**du-ly**	**whol-ly**

2 Business Vocabulary Builder

impeccable Without defects or errors.
unmarred Unblemished; not damaged.
financial advisor One who gives advice about investments.
expedites Speeds up.

Reading and Writing Practice

3

and o

im·pec·ca·ble
un·marred

Transcribe:
ten

ex·pand·ed

nc

suc·cess·ful

ser

ob·tain·ing

when

low-in·ter·est hyphenated before noun

[154]

4

ad·vi·sor

conj

re·mod·el res·i·dence

home-im·prove·ment hyphenated before noun

par

aware

add·ing

conj

ap

low-cost hyphenated before noun

par

[145]

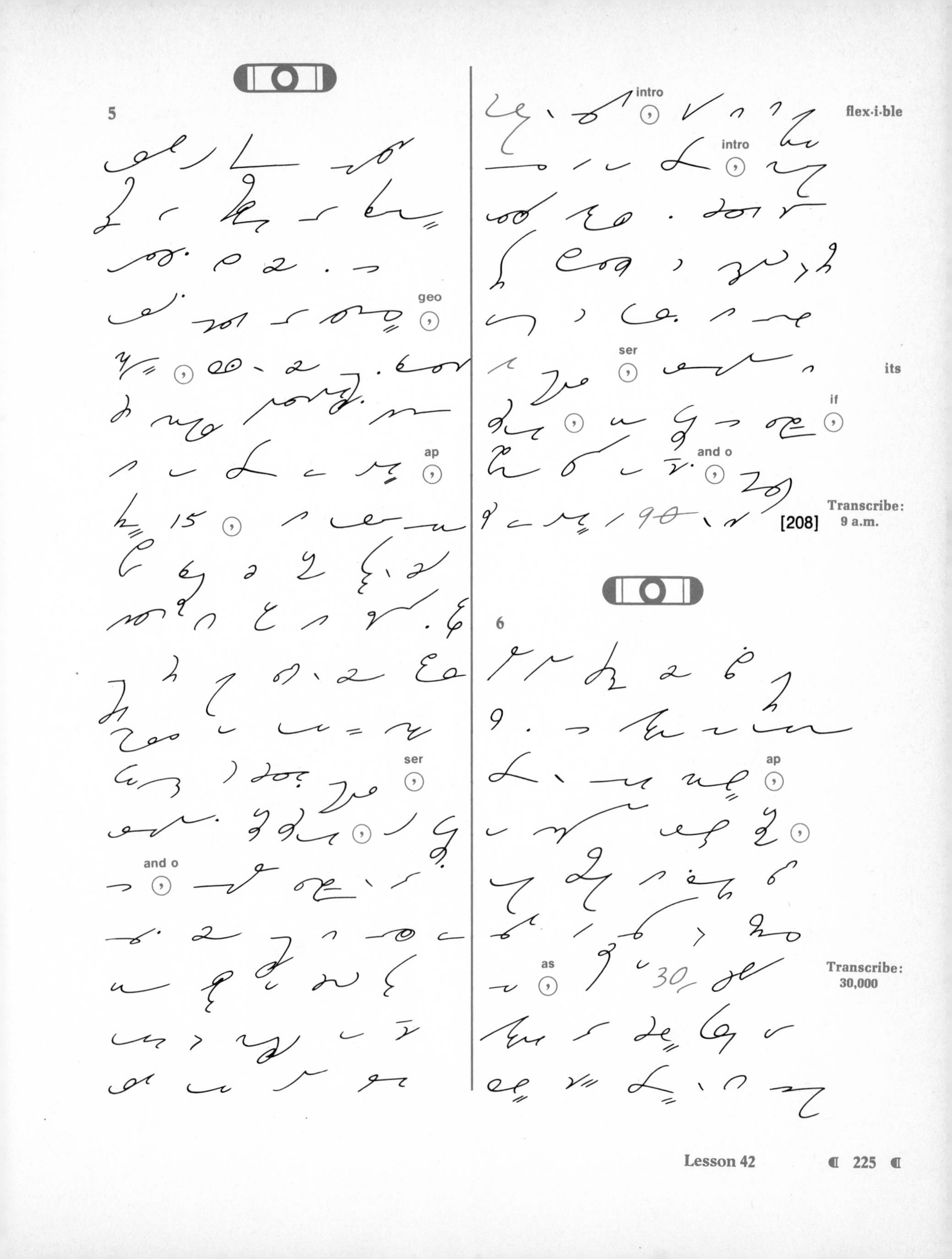

5

geo

ap

ser

and o

intro

flex·i·ble

intro

ser

its

if

and o

Transcribe: 9 a.m.

[208]

6

ap

as

Transcribe: 30,000

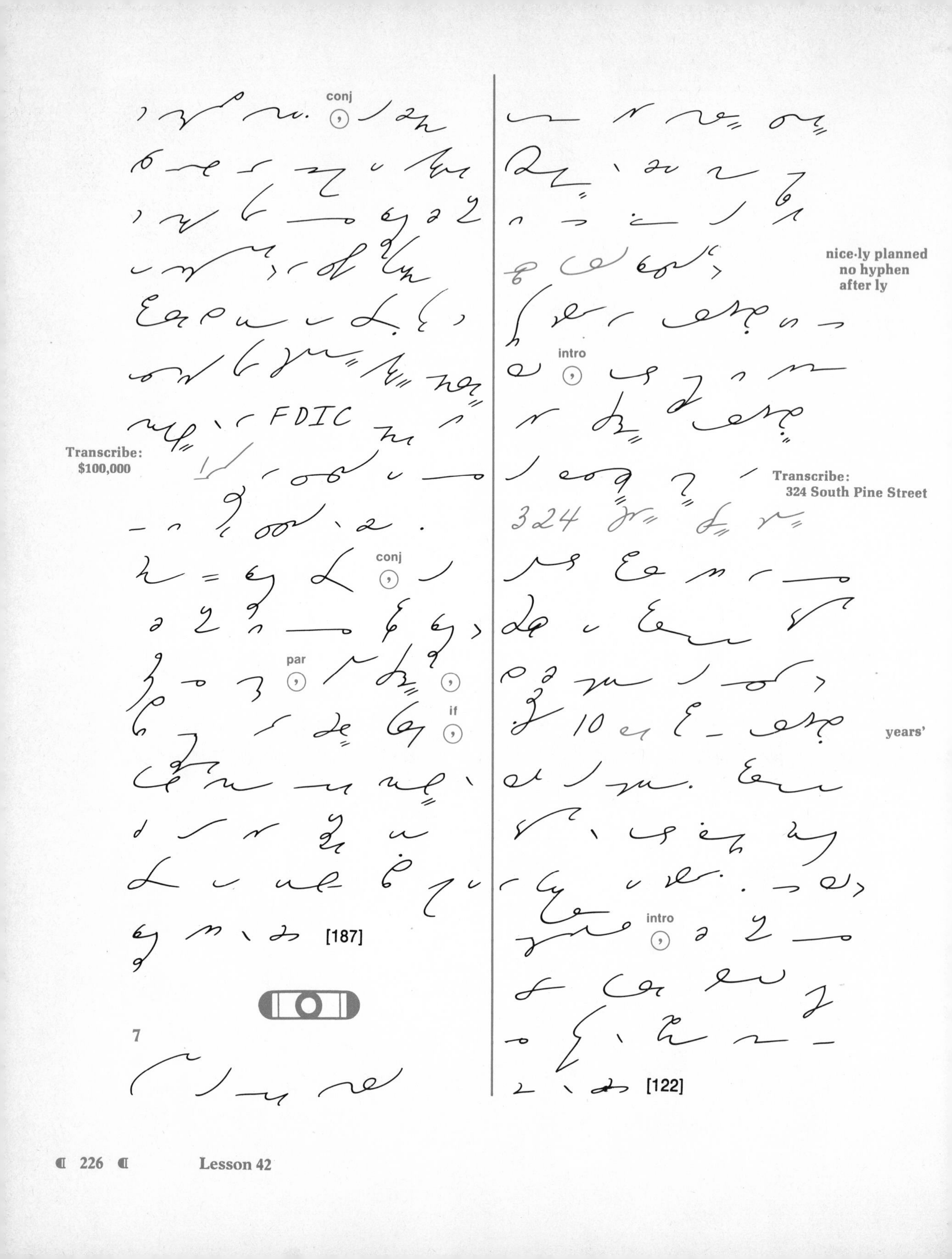

conj

FDIC

Transcribe: $100,000

conj

par

if

[187]

7

nice·ly planned
no hyphen
after ly

intro

Transcribe: 324 South Pine Street

324

10

years'

intro

[122]

Building Transcription Skills

1 ACCURACY PRACTICE

Follow the procedures suggested on page 178 as you work on this Accuracy Practice.

Group 1	Group 2	Group 3
written	get	theirs
regular	gather	ours

practice drill

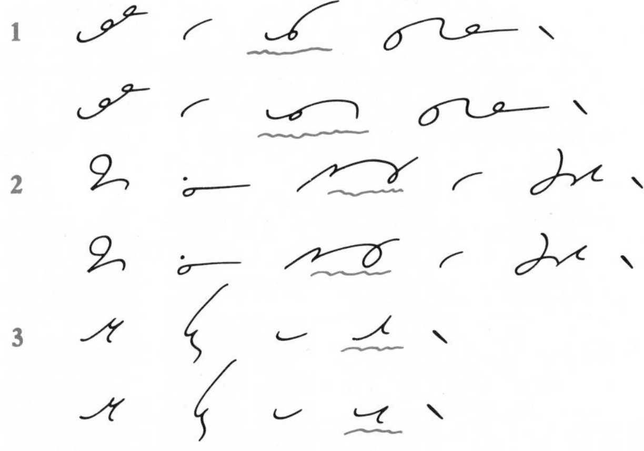

1 *Return the* written *agreement.*
Return the regular *agreement.*
2 *Ask him to* get *the facts.*
Ask him to gather *the facts.*
3 *Those boxes are* theirs.
Those boxes are ours.

2 Business Vocabulary Builder

stock split Extra shares of stock issued by a company to its investors.

common stock Stock in a company that does not pay a specific dividend.

annuity contract A contract entitling an investor to a fixed income for a specified number of years.

Reading and Writing Practice

3

an·nu·al

cr

wel·come

char·ac·ter·izes nc

[80]

4

an·nu·ity nc

intro with·in

gath·er da·ta

dis·cuss

par

choose

great·est

geo

ap

Feb·ru·ary

Transcribe: No. 12145

[145]

5

as

ap

13

board

intro

de·creased

conj

Transcribe:
$50
1,000

50

conj

intro

un·til

ap

17

nc

50

40

when

suf·fered

nc

fault

par

ours
theirs

conj

[187]

6

conj

com·pa·ny's

You have already learned how to place short and average-length letters by judgment. In this lesson you will take up the placement of long letters (those containing more than 200 words) by judgment.

On page 231 you will find Letter 5 of Lesson 41 of *Transcription* as it was written in shorthand by an experienced stenographer. You will also find the transcript of that letter made on a typewriter with elite type. The shorthand notes for the letter required a column and a half.

Make a shorthand copy of Letter 5 to determine how much space this long letter requires in your shorthand notebook. Try to fix in your mind the space your shorthand requires in your notebook for a long letter.

Whenever your notes for a dictated letter require approximately the same amount of space in your notebook, here is what you should do:

☐ **1** Set your margin stops for 1-inch margins at the left and at the right.

☐ **2** Insert your paper and type the date on the third line below the last line of the letterhead.

☐ **3** Start the inside address about six lines below the date (about four lines below the date if your machine has pica type).

☐ **4** Then transcribe the body of the letter.

Whenever a letter requires more than a column and a half of shorthand, consider carefully whether you should make it a one-page letter or a two-page letter. If you decide to type it as a one-page letter, you may find that you do not have enough space for the closing, with the result that you may have to retype it.

If you have the slightest doubt whether a letter will fit on a single page, play it safe; widen your margins and type it as a two-page letter.

STATE COLLEGE
1250 Main Street Portland, OR 97520

October 2, 19--

Oregon Funding Association
1100 River Road
Portland, OR 97208

Gentlemen:

Several professors at the college in Portland have expressed an interest in starting a combination savings and retirement plan with the Oregon Funding Association. Professor Dennis O'Brien, head of the English department, has been elected president of this group.

These professors are interested in a plan whereby they can each deposit from \$100 to \$200 a month and have you invest it in stocks or mutual funds for them. They are also interested in having their deposits automatically withheld from their paychecks and deposited directly to their accounts with your association.

If you have such savings plans, may they be used as retirement programs? What is the rate of interest the association pays? When may a professor start retirement payments?

The group of professors would like to have this program go into effect by
the first of the year. Since this is the month of October, they would ap
ciate receiving answers to the above questions within the next week or sc
They would also appreciate receiving any other information or advice you
be able to give them. In addition, please send me copies of any informat
you send to Professor O'Brien.

Professor O'Brien and his committee are anxiously awaiting your reply.

Yours very truly,

Albert H. Landau
Dean of Faculty

fps

and o

few·er

Transcribe: 50

50

intro

and o

Transcribe: $1,000

if

5

if

if

5

3

nc

ap

[183]

7

conj

if

up to date no noun, no hyphen

[83]

Building Transcription Skills

1 OFFICE-STYLE DICTATION ● short insertions

Dictators frequently make changes in their dictation. They may insert a word or phrase in a sentence that has already been dictated. They might say:

Please return the form as soon as possible—make that **enclosed form.**

You must be alert so you can find quickly the point at which the insertion is to be made. When you find it, insert the added word or phrase with a caret, just as you would in longhand thus:

Illustration of Office-Style Dictation

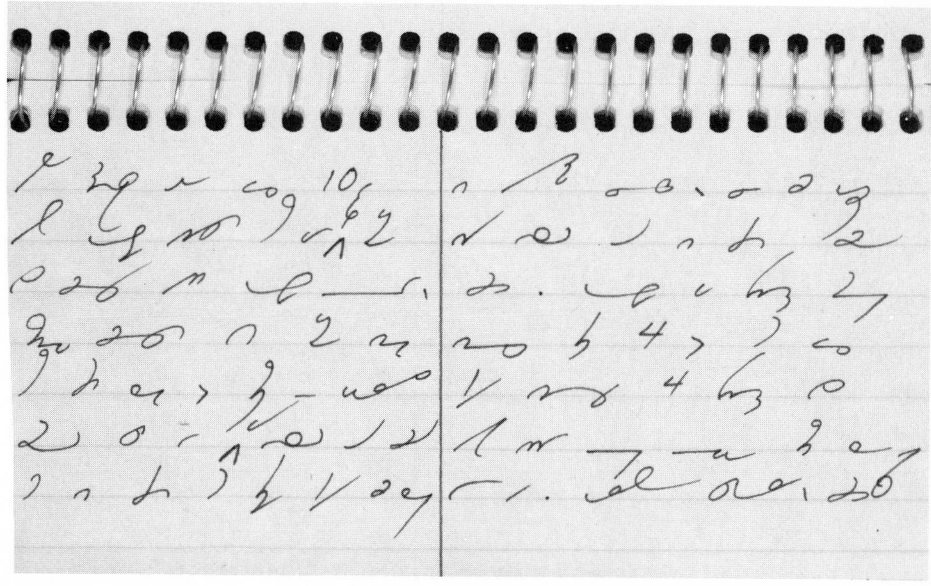

2 **Business Vocabulary Builder**

exempt *(adjective)* Free from; excused from.

liquidate To convert into cash.

clarification Explanation.

Reading and Writing Practice

3

ex·empt

ser

de·pen·dents

an·swer

cr

or·ga·ni·za·tion

if

Transcribe: $2,000

conj

tax-ex·empt

cr

[153]

4

ex·treme·ly

Transcribe: $5,000

nec·es·sary

sign

as·sis·tance

cr

par

[95]

5

an·nu·ity

re·ceive

intro

state·ment

May·be

conj

coun·sel·or

thought

Transcribe: 7 percent

[141]

6

sel·dom

conj

grate·ful

if

ren·der

[105]

7

al·ways

conj

days'

Transcribe:
30 cents
$100

intro

nc

if

ser

[155]

8

if

when if [89]

pass·book

up to date no noun, no hyphen

9 TRANSCRIPTION QUIZ

You are already familiar with the Transcription Quiz from your work with the other books in Series 90. In *Gregg Shorthand for Colleges, Transcription,* these quizzes will become more challenging. There will be one quiz in each chapter.

As you read each Transcription Quiz, decide what punctuation should be used and what words have been omitted from the shorthand. If any one of a number of words makes sense, select the one that fits most logically and makes the sentence read most smoothly.

Then make a shorthand copy of the letter, inserting in your notes the punctuation marks and the missing words.

[128]

Building Transcription Skills

1 **COMMON PREFIXES ● inter-**

inter- The prefix *inter-* means *between; among; in the midst of.*

interstate Between or among states.

interfere To come between; to break into.

interrupt To break into or between.

intervene To come in between.

interval A period between.

international Between or among nations.

2 **Business Vocabulary Builder**

consented Agreed to; permitted.

reflects Illustrates; makes apparent.

sound *(adjective)* Steady; firm; stable.

Reading and Writing Practice

3

ser

wel·comed

Transcribe: 100,000

when

fi·nan·cial·ly

agree·ment

par

when

[121]

4

intro

ser

rep·u·ta·ble

intro

nc

per·son·al

as

ref·er·ences

intro

ac·knowl·edged

re·ceipt

con·sent·ed

if

fur·ther

hes·i·tate

con·tact

[164]

5

conj

fourth

com·pa·ny's

Transcribe:
$2
$4

year's

[138]

6

pro·ce·dures

par

al·most

ap

stock·bro·ker

conj

stock·hold·er's

if

nc

if

[197]

7

geo

Transcribe: six

nc

intro

intro

and o

high·ly ef·fi·cient no hyphen after ly

ap

Transcribe: five

intro

and o

ex·cel·lent

if

nonr

[153]

SHARPENING SKILLS

Marie realized that she must always be alert to opportunities to increase those skills that would make her an increasingly effective office employee.

Shorthand is the written language of the secretarial profession because it speeds the time between input and output of information in the office; its complete mastery is essential for success as a secretary. Marie, therefore, decided to make a special effort to sharpen her shorthand skills.

Marie had kept her shorthand theory book from school, and one evening she reviewed all the theory. She was surprised that it required only about two hours to complete this task and decided to make this extra effort periodically.

Also, Marie had been keeping a list of the difficult and unusual words that occurred in dictation on the job as well as a list of the phrases Mr. Franklin used repeatedly. She practiced writing these words and phrases so that she could write them without hesitation. She knew that this practice would help her to enlarge her writing vocabulary and thus make her increasingly useful to her employer.

Usually Marie had little difficulty reading her notes, but when the dictation was unusually fast, some of her outlines became distorted. By taking notes from shorthand tape recordings and from the radio, Marie practiced writing outlines in correct proportion so that she could better handle rapid dictation.

Last, but not least, Marie used her shorthand to take telephone messages, to make notations as she processed incoming mail, to organize and maintain her calendar, and to do all the research she was assigned. She realized that shorthand is the quickest and most efficient way of taking any kind of notes and messages.

Good transcription skills—including a knowledge of good grammar and punctuation—go hand in hand with good shorthand skills. Mr. Franklin relied on Marie to correct automatically any errors he may have made during dictation.

Since Marie had also kept her reference manual from school, she was able to brush up on any points of grammar and punctuation about which she was unsure. Sometimes, during the workday, she came across a specific problem in transcription and took the time at home to review it so that she would not have trouble in the future.

Of course, there were certain transcription practices that did not require study but did require skill in checking facts such as days and dates. Marie was always alert to catch such errors and correct them because she knew that this was her responsibility and that Mr. Franklin appreciated her thoroughness.

One additional thing that Marie took time for was to keep up with any courses she might take that would help her improve her performance on the job. She planned to take one or two short courses each year if time permitted.

Building Transcription Skills

1 **SIMILAR-WORDS DRILL ● principal, principle**

principal First; highest in rank; main; money.

I spoke with the *principal* of the school.
This is the *principal* problem.
I will repay the *principal* and the interest.

principle Rule; standard; general truth.

Follow the correct *principle,* and you will solve the problem.

2 **Business Vocabulary Builder**

aspect Phase; part.

milestone An important event; a turning point.

astonished Amazed; surprised.

Reading and Writing Practice

3

As·so·ci·a·tion

res·i·dents

geo

ap

coun·sel·ing

Transcribe:
482 West 26 Street

ap·point·ment

well-trained
hyphenated
before noun

and o

ad·vis·able

per·son's

one's

when

prin·ci·ples

de·ci·sions

if

[207]

4

conj

pro·fes·sion·al

quite
proud

as·sis·tance

Transcribe: four

conj

Transcribe: $1,000

if

Transcribe: 8 percent

conj

prin·ci·pal

if

par

par

and o

[188]

5

as·ton·ished

Transcribe: $187.65

intro

as

prin·ci·pal

ap

prin·ci·pal

nc

Transcribe: $100

Transcribe:
No. 106

book·keep·er

cr

[177]

6

conj

ad·ept

prin·ci·ples

when

and o

com·plete

ex·pen·di·tures

self-in·ter·est

treat

if

intro

con·ve·nient·ly lo·cat·ed
no hyphen
after ly

[164]

Building Transcription Skills

1 **SPELLING FAMILIES ● forming -ed and -ing derivatives of words ending in l**

When the last syllable of a word ending in *l*, preceded by a single vowel, is accented, the *l* is doubled in forming derivatives ending in *-ed* and *-ing*.

com-pel	**com-pelled**	**com-pel-ling**
con-trol	**con-trolled**	**con-trol-ling**
dis-pel	**dis-pelled**	**dis-pel-ling**
ex-cel	**ex-celled**	**ex-cel-ling**

When the last syllable is not accented, the *l* is not doubled.

can-cel	**can-celed**	**can-cel-ing**
mod-el	**mod-eled**	**mod-el-ing**
to-tal	**to-taled**	**to-tal-ing**
trav-el	**trav-eled**	**trav-el-ing**
equal	**equaled**	**equal-ing**

2 Business Vocabulary Builder

astute Clever; having good judgment.
dispelled Cleared away.
projected Estimated; planned for.

Reading and Writing Practice

3

com-pelled

Transcribe: March 3

to·taled

re·paid

conj

par

re·ceived

re·fused

con·ten·tion

conj

as

par

[161]

4

al·ways
mod·eled

as·tute

when

dis·pelled

intro

en·roll·ing

conj

def·i·nite·ly

conj

Transcribe:
four

Transcribe: $10,000

son's

tu·ition

ser

ten-year hyphenated before noun

if

[164]

5

over·due

owed

conj

intro

great

ob·li·ga·tion

if

com·pelled

re·voke

par

op·por·tu·ni·ty

cr

conj

can·celed

lose

[142]

6

ap

mort·gage

nonr

Transcribe: six

prin·ci·pal

to·taled

month's

par

debts

ac·cor·dance

if

par

im·poses

bear·ing

[96]

7

due

[149]

Building Transcription Skills

1 **GRAMMAR CHECKUP ● common errors**

Many people often confuse various pairs of words such as *bring* and *take.* In this lesson you will study three pairs of expressions that could cause grammar errors. Be sure to use the correct words when you are writing business letters.

bring, take

bring To carry toward. (*Bring* indicates motion *toward* the speaker.)
Please bring *the papers to me.*

take To carry away from. (*Take* indicates motion *away from* the speaker.)
Take *this report to the manager.*

let, leave

let To permit; to allow.
Let *me help you.*

leave To depart; to move or go away from.
I will leave *in a few minutes.*
Hint: If you are in doubt as to whether *let* or *leave* is correct, substitute *permit* and *depart.* If *permit* makes sense, use *let;* if *depart* makes sense, use *leave.*

either, or; neither, nor

either, or One or the other.
You may have either *the booklet* or *the bound copy.*

neither, nor Not one or the other; not either.
He accepted neither *the book* nor *the report.*

---

2 **Business Vocabulary Builder**

honor *(verb)* To accept.
enjoy To have for one's use or benefit.
survey *(noun)* A study; an examination of the facts.

Reading and Writing Practice

3

stayed geo

Feb·ru·ary when

nc

hon·or intro

ei·ther

nei·ther

nc intro

Un·for·tu·nate·ly intro

re·fused

par

nc

[124]

4

conj

con·cerned

fi·nances

trav·el·er's

opin·ion

cr [65]

5

as

ar·range·ments

re·duced

per·son·al

Transcribe: five

nei·ther

[93]

6

intro

conj

choose

ser

yachts

well con·struct·ed no noun, no hyphen

its

conj

abun·dant

conj

[110]

7

Transcribe: six

ap·pre·ci·ate

as·signed

[101]

8

enu

Transcribe: December 31

ini·ti·ate

if

[93]

Building Transcription Skills

1 **OFFICE-STYLE DICTATION ● long insertions**

You are aware that office-style dictation often presents problems that must be corrected quickly and clearly. You know that you are to mark the dictator's changes in your notes so that you can transcribe the material accurately if the dictator changes the order of words, sentences, or paragraphs. There are times, however, when the dictator will make such a lengthy insertion that you cannot use the caret as you would in longhand.

Here are the steps to follow if a long insertion is to be made:

☐ 1 Write a large *A* in a circle at the point where the new material is to appear.

☐ 2 Draw two heavy lines after the last sentence that was dictated. These lines will separate the insert from the rest of the dictation.

☐ 3 Write "Insert *A*" under the two heavy lines and circle it; then write the dictated insertion.

☐ 4 Draw two heavy lines to indicate the end of the insert.

☐ 5 Subsequent insertions in the same letter can be spotted and identified quickly with *B*, *C*, and so on.

2 **Business Vocabulary Builder**

reassure To assure again; to restore to confidence.
means *(noun)* The resources or methods used to achieve an end result.
rudimentary Elementary; basic.

Illustration of Office-Style Dictation

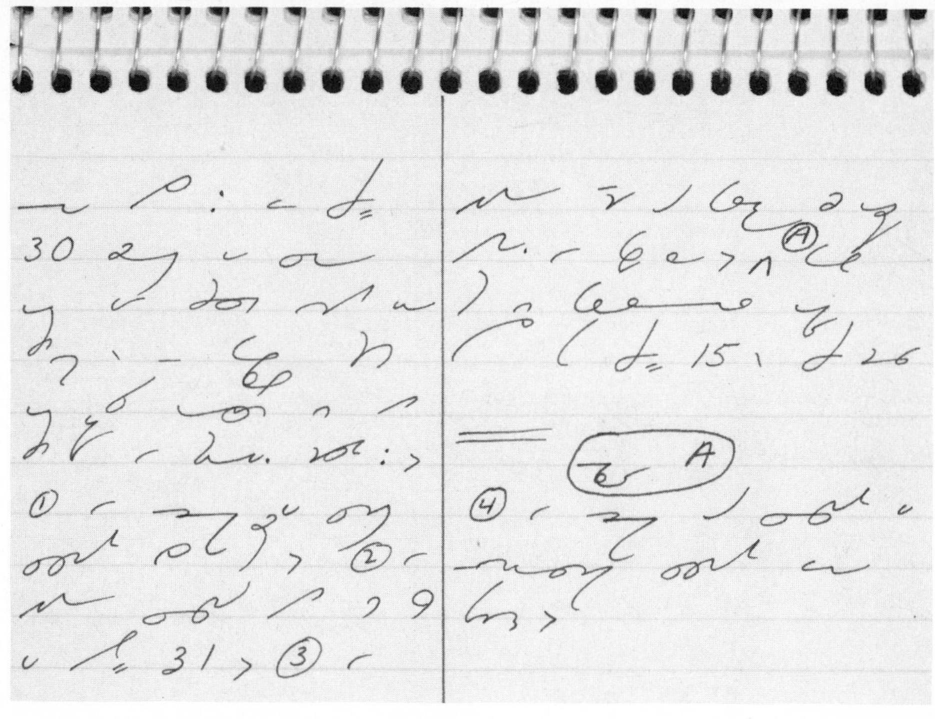

Reading and Writing Practice

3

re·as·sure

nei·ther

nc

com·pli·cat·ed

quite

enu ser

conj

strict con·fi·dence

par

ser

[161]

4

Wednes·day ap

Transcribe: 703 26th Street

703 26

par nc

suc·cess·ful

ex·cit·ing and o

re·mod·el

if

ob·tain

if

if

intro as·sist

nc

and o well-trained hyphenated before noun

[168]

5

sub·mit·ted

bur·den

and o

ru·di·men·ta·ry

if

ser

con·tact

[148]

6 Transcription Quiz Supply the necessary punctuation and the words that have been omitted from the shorthand.

[107]

Building Transcription Skills

1 COMMON PREFIXES ● multi-

multi—The prefix *multi-* means *many; much; many times over; more than one or two.*
multiple Consisting of more than one; many.
multiply To increase in number many times over.
multitude A great number; many.
multinational Involving more than two nations.
multimedia Involving several media.
multiplex Having many parts; transmitting several messages simultaneously.

---

2 Business Vocabulary Builder

compound interest Interest that is earned on both the original principal and previously earned interest.
accumulating Increasing; building up.
proportionately In a corresponding manner; in a related manner.

Reading and Writing Practice

3

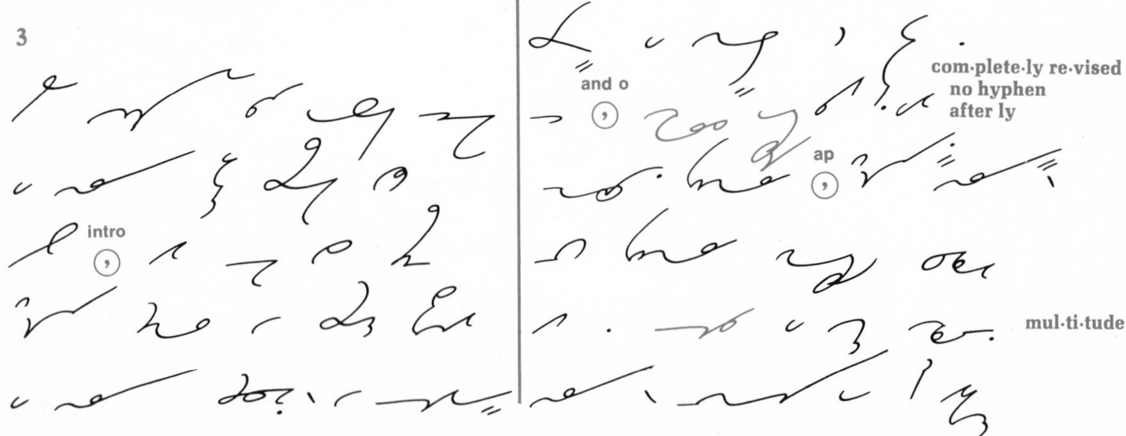

ad·vis·able

enu

es·ti·mate

if

sign

self-ad·dressed

when

[149]

4

when

watch

every day

intro

com·pound·ed

conj

day-to-day

ever-in·creas·ing
hyphenated
before noun

intro

sense

idle

if

nc

[126]

5

as

re·ceiv·able

pace

par

Transcribe: $100,000

Transcribe: $250,000

pro·por·tion·ate·ly

if

intro

worse

intro

al·most

past due no noun, no hyphen

conj

if

year's

[158]

6

ap

Transcribe: 21st of April 25

Transcribe: 1407 32d Street

geo

conj

Transcribe: $2,000

conj

du·pli·cate

conj

par

ours

nc

un·pleas·ant

lose

conj

conj

[251]

7

quite

lose

re·ceives

nc

if

cr

if

par

days'

[101]

COMPOSING LETTERS

One of the major responsibilities that Marie had been given by Mr. Franklin was the handling of routine correspondence. Marie was to compose letters that fell into the following categories: acknowledgment, request, thank-you, follow-up, and transmittal letters. Also, there were instances when Mr. Franklin simply told Marie in general terms what he wanted to say and let Marie compose the actual letter.

In writing these letters, Marie followed the basic principles of effective communications: "the seven Cs."

Consideration A sincere, considerate tone can be achieved by thinking of the reader and asking, "How would I react to this letter?" Marie realized the importance of stating her thoughts tactfully.

Completeness Knowing everything that must be included is essential when writing a letter. Marie found it helpful to also ask herself, "Is this all the information that is needed?"

Clearness A letter must also be clear and easy to understand. Marie made sure that she understood the purpose of the letter and organized the information in a clear, logical way so that the reader would have no trouble understanding the meaning of the letter.

Conciseness Wordiness can cloud the meaning of a letter as well as waste the reader's time. Marie made an effort to eliminate any unnecessary words that did not clarify the meaning.

Concreteness Good letter writing requires specific, to-the-point vocabulary that best conveys the meaning to the reader. Marie was careful to avoid vague, meaningless words.

Courtesy The mere use of *thank you* and *please* does not make a letter courteous. The courteous writer's attitude is characterized by promptness in responding, consideration of the reader's feelings, and cooperation in dealing with the matter at hand. Marie always kept these points in mind.

Correctness Naturally, every letter must be perfect—no errors in grammar, typing, or spelling. In addition, facts and figures must be accurate; Marie did not want to cause embarrassment to the company, her boss, or herself.

Much of the routine correspondence was sent out under Marie's name rather than Mr. Franklin's. And it was up to Marie to keep track of follow-up correspondence, which she did by using a tickler file—a file that she was sure to check every day.

Taking on this responsibility relieved Mr. Franklin of time-consuming correspondence and helped to make the office operation more efficient.

Building Transcription Skills

1 SIMILAR-WORDS DRILL ● cents, sense, scents

cents Amounts of money less than a dollar; pennies.

The subscription will cost only a few *cents* per day.

sense Meaning; judgment; feeling.

The letter does not make any *sense*.
Common *sense* is a favorable attribute.
He has a *sense* of obligation.

scents Odors; smells.

These perfumes have strong *scents*.

2
Business Vocabulary Builder

patented All rights to an invention protected by the government for a specified period of time.
intermittently Periodically.
ludicrous Laughable; amusing; absurd.
schemes *(noun)* Crafty plans.

Reading and Writing Practice

3

chim·ney

Un·for·tu·nate·ly intro

intro

es·cap·ing

ap

Transcribe: 30 percent

fac·to·ry-trained hyphenated before noun

and o

hours'

valve

cents

sense

555-8090

[198]

4

loss

nc

sat·is·fac·to·ri·ly

in·ter·mit·tent·ly

par

occasion·al·ly

intro

scent

when

intro

ilq

afraid

worth·less

conj

dis·con·nect

iq

par

Transcribe: $1,000

[227]

5

life's

par

lu·di·crous

conj

sim·i·lar

nc

intro

Transcribe: 90 cents

year's

un·sound schemes

yields

intro

nc

conj

tax-ex·empt

intro

self-ad·dressed

[242]

Building Transcription Skills

1 SPELLING FAMILIES ● forming -ed and -ing derivatives of words ending in t

When the last syllable of a word ending in *t*, preceded by a single vowel, is accented, the *t* is doubled before *-ed* and *-ing*.

al-lot	**al-lot-ted**	**al-lot-ting**
com-mit	**com-mit-ted**	**com-mit-ting**
omit	**omit-ted**	**omit-ting**
per-mit	**per-mit-ted**	**per-mit-ting**

When the last syllable is not accented, the *t* is not doubled.

ben-e-fit	**ben-e-fit-ed**	**ben-e-fit-ing**
cred-it	**cred-it-ed**	**cred-it-ing**
lim-it	**lim-it-ed**	**lim-it-ing**
so-lic-it	**so-lic-it-ed**	**so-lic-it-ing**

When the *t* is preceded by more than one vowel or by a consonant, the *t* is not doubled.

coat	**coat-ed**	**coat-ing**
seat	**seat-ed**	**seat-ing**
greet	**greet-ed**	**greet-ing**
alert	**alert-ed**	**alert-ing**
at-tract	**at-tract-ed**	**at-tract-ing**
grant	**grant-ed**	**grant-ing**

2 Business Vocabulary Builder

allotted Assigned to.
renowned Famous; celebrated.
detach To separate; to take away from.

Reading and Writing Practice

3

Transcribe: One thousand

high·ly pub·li·cized no hyphen after ly

ap

al·lot·ted

Transcribe: November 15

ben·e·fit·ed

nonr

re·nowned

ap

ben·e·fit·ing

well-planned hyphenated before noun

if

de·tach cou·pon

ser

[161]

4

conj

trans·ferred

its re·al·ty

rec·om·mend·ed

geo

intro

so·lic·it·ing

ser

two-car hyphenated before noun

Transcribe: $90,000

intro

lim·it·ed

suit·able

cr

[170]

5

dis·ap·point·ed

intro

cat·a·log

ex·pect·ed

intro

nc

cred·it·ing

[118]

6

intro

cr

geo

per·mit·ted

nov·ice

if

too

conj

lim·it·ed

[138]

7

ap

Transcribe: March 21

nonr

Transcribe: 402 Main Drive

greet·ing

intro

sta·tio·nery

[103]

Building Transcription Skills

1 ACCURACY PRACTICE

Follow the practice procedures suggested in Lesson 33.

Group 1	Group 2	Group 3
ought	right	pass
should	light	base

practice drill

1 *They ought to see a doctor.*
They should see a doctor.

2 *I will choose the right color.*
I will choose the light color.

3 *I will not pass a judgment on these facts.*
I will not base a judgment on these facts.

2 Business Vocabulary Builder	**chagrined**	Distressed; disappointed.
	philatelic	Relating to the collection and study of stamps.
	face value	The value printed or written on an item.

Reading and Writing Practice

3

right

intro

ap

Transcribe:
6 p.m.
9 p.m.
816 Tenth Avenue

al·lowed

par

[147]

4

whole·sale

tow·els

geo

re·tail

conj

as·sured

prompt·ly

week's

fi·nal·ly

intro

nc

Transcribe:
100
200

nc

intro

cha·grined

conj

first-class

par

intro

else·where

[176]

5

intro

Phil·a·tel·ic

its

intro

Transcribe:
$25

ap

na·tion·al·ly rec·og·nized
no hyphen
after ly

and o

ar·ti·cles

phases

when

new·ly is·sued
no hyphen
after ly

intro

long-time hyphenated before noun

as

conj

intro

intro

ser

[239]

6

intro

ser

au·tumn

shad·ed

al·ready

bloom

intro

2107 21

Transcribe: 2107 West 21 Street

[134]

Building Transcription Skills

1 OFFICE-STYLE DICTATION ● instructions during dictation

Occasionally a dictator may wish to emphasize a word or expression and ask you to underscore it or type it in all capital letters. The dictator may say:

Every one of you should attend this meeting—type **every one of you** *in all caps. Notice that the meeting date is August 25—underscore* **August 25**—*instead of August 26.*

Draw two lines under the expression to be typed in all capital letters; draw one line under the expression to be underscored. These sentences would appear in your shorthand notes as follows:

Your typewritten transcript would look like this:

EVERY ONE OF YOU should attend this meeting. Notice that the meeting date is August 25 instead of August 26.

2 Business Vocabulary Builder

legislation Law.
accustomed Used to; in the habit of.
contingency A possible event; something that may occur.
spouse Marriage partner; a husband or wife.

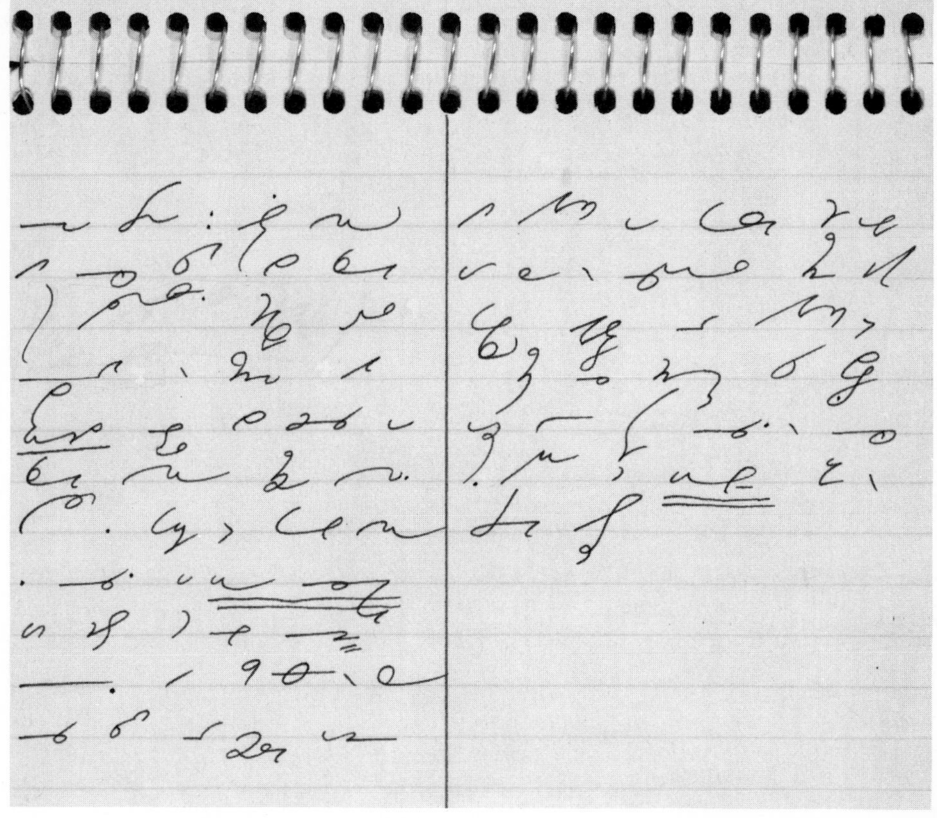

Reading and Writing Practice

3

Transcribe:
24
lug·gage

intro

ac·knowl·edg·ment

conj

an·swer

intro

dis·mayed

intro

per·son·al·ly

par

hap·pened

cr

Transcribe: 25th of August

if

can·cel

[139]

4

Phoe·nix

ap

up to date no noun, no hyphen

leg·is·la·tion

easy-to-read hyphenated before noun

Transcribe: $8.95

nc

self-ad·dressed

sat·is·fied

if

nc

owe de·cide

if

[150]

5

ac·cus·tomed

suf·fi·cient

intro

con·tin·gen·cy

if

spouse

se·vere

if

conj

ser

intro

nc

well-trained hyphenated before noun

and o

[177]

6

ex·cel·lent

re·viewed

Transcribe: six

conj

Transcribe: 20 percent

re·main·der

if

[78]

7 Transcription Quiz Supply the necessary punctuation and the missing words.

[167]

Building Transcription Skills

1 **SIMILAR-WORDS DRILL ● weight, wait**

weight The amount that something weighs.

The *weight* of the truck is seven metric tons.

wait To remain; to await.

I cannot *wait* any longer for the work to be finished.

2 **Business Vocabulary Builder**

bulky Extremely large; clumsy.

buyers Persons who purchase the stock for retail stores.

regional Relating to a specific area; localized.

Reading and Writing Practice

3

ear·ly

intro

nc

intro

bro·chures

Transcribe: three

conj

weight

and o

bulky

par

wait

par

pro·ceed

[172]

4

plan·ning

geo

Tuc·son

wom·en's

chil·dren's

some·time

conj

at·trib·ute

light·weight

en·tice

[108]

5

mow·er

geo

guides

ef·fi·cient

and o

un·in·ter·rupt·ed

conj

wait

if

conj

intro

anx·ious·ly

[164]

6

geo

as

rep·u·ta·ble

house·hold

intro

as·sist

par

ap·prais·als

min·i·mum

ac·cept

intro

if

fur·ther

[150]

7

if

ca·reer

el·o·quent

ser

lis·ten·er

ap·pear·ance

suc·cess·ful

intro

Transcribe:
7624 Main Street

7624

nc

wait

555-8206

[143]

8

ap

com·pre·hen·sive

in·curred

intro

intro

urge

its

yours

ap

nc

wait

[173]

9

intro

toured

one-fam·i·ly hyphenated before noun

nc

de·scrip·tion

wait

[77]

ACCEPTING MORE RESPONSIBILITY

After about six months, Marie realized that she was able to handle the job with ease and efficiency. She knew there were very few situations or procedures she was unable to handle on her own. She found herself taking responsibility for more and more things, with and without Mr. Franklin's specific instructions.

As she opened each day's mail, Marie now had certain procedures she followed. She read each piece of correspondence to see if there was additional information she could supply for Mr. Franklin or if he would need a particular file in order to respond. She made brief notes on the letters, when appropriate, so that Mr. Franklin would have the necessary information at his fingertips. This not only saved time for her boss but it saved time for her as well because she did not have to interrupt dictation to go back and forth to the files.

At Mr. Franklin's request, Marie now attended most of the meetings he scheduled. There were two specific benefits in Marie's going to such meetings.

First, she was able to take notes of certain points that were brought up or decisions that were made. In fact, there were several instances when she was asked to take minutes of meetings, transcribe her notes, and distribute them to the attendees so that everyone concerned had a record of what had occurred.

Second, Marie's knowledge of the company's business was greatly enhanced by the discussions. She was able to gain a better understanding of why certain procedures were followed and why certain decisions were made in relation to the performance of the company as a whole. Marie, of course, never discussed this information with anyone who was not directly involved with the meetings.

A day arrived when Marie became aware of just how much she had advanced and how much Mr. Franklin relied on her abilities as a secretary. He asked her to take a one-day trip out of town with Ms. Valdez and him to help coordinate the activities for the annual week-long national sales meeting.

Building Transcription Skills

1 **SIMILAR-WORDS DRILL ● formerly, formally**

formerly Before; in the past.

I *formerly* worked in Providence.

formally According to established form, custom, or procedure.

Let me *formally* welcome you to our organization.

2 **Business Vocabulary Builder**

alumni Persons who have graduated from a particular school, college, or university.

exotic Strikingly different or unusual.

ancestry Line of descent; lineage; family tree.

registrar An officer of an educational institution responsible for registering students and keeping their records.

Reading and Writing Practice

3

alum·ni

for·mal·ly

via geo 28 for·mer·ly 15 as cruise route intro itin·er·ary sel·dom intro lei·sure ship's and o ex·ot·ic el·e·gance [172]

4

and o ex·cit·ing conj his·tor·ic par tru·ly intro ser cul·ture an·ces·try for·mal·ly

ser

if

weeks'

for·mer·ly

intro

reg·is·trar

[239]

5

for·mer·ly

lux·u·ry

nc

ne·ces·si·ty

one's

around-the-world hyphenated before noun

Transcribe: eight

sea·shore

vig·or·ous

iq

intro

ap

yours

[165]

6

for·mal·ly

Transcribe: 10103 State Street

10103

geo

for·mer·ly

nonr

605

and o

par

ser

dra·mas

min·utes'

intro

ef·fi·cien·cy

nc

[169]

7

for·mal

conj

its

add

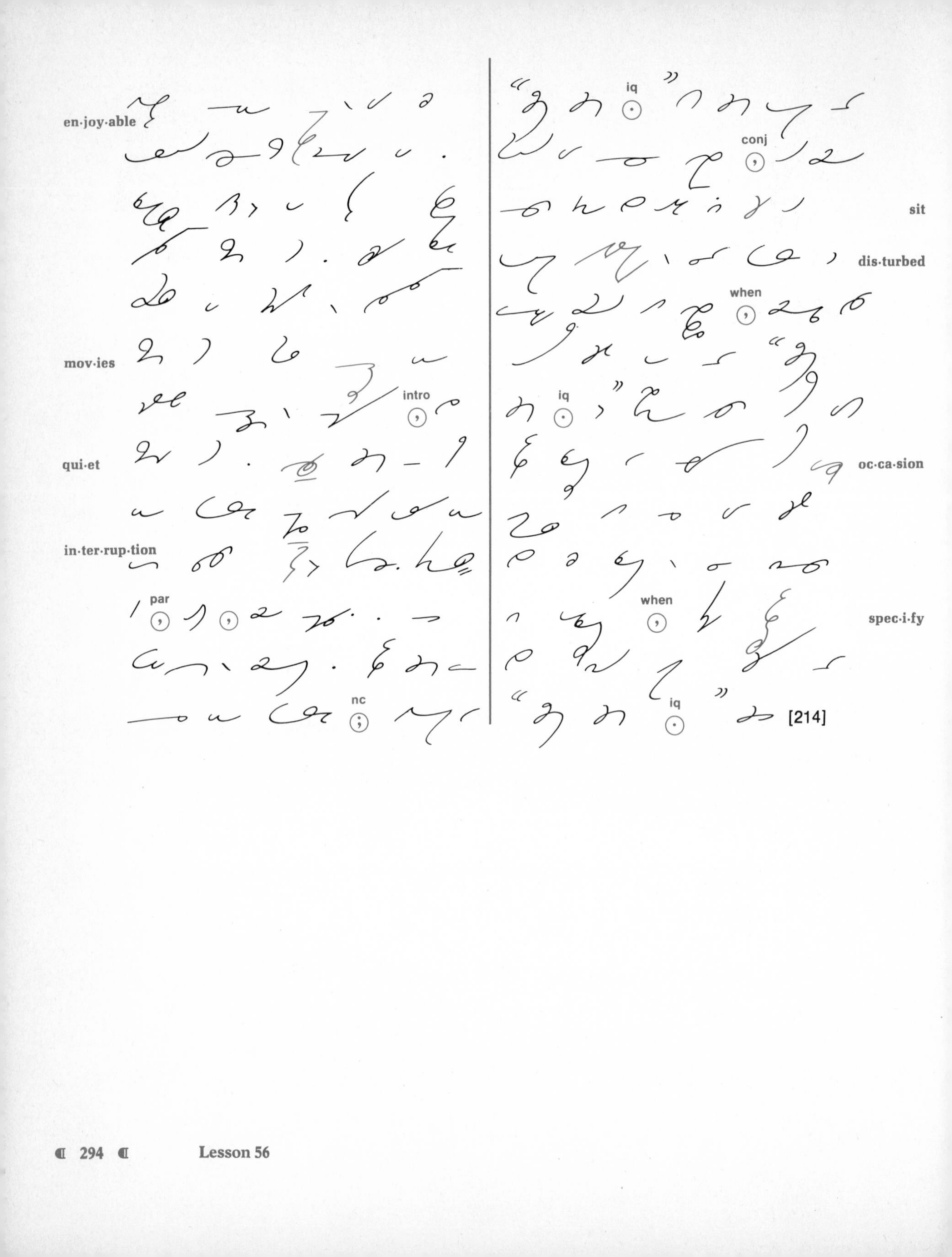

en·joy·able

mov·ies

intro

qui·et

in·ter·rup·tion

par

nc

iq

conj

sit

dis·turbed

when

iq

oc·ca·sion

when

spec·i·fy

iq

[214]

Building Transcription Skills

1 **SPELLING FAMILIES ● forming -ed and -ing derivatives of words ending in r**

When the last syllable of a word ending in *r*, preceded by a single vowel, is accented, the *r* is doubled in forming derivatives ending in *-ed* and *-ing*.

de-fer	**de-ferred**	**de-fer-ring**
oc-cur	**oc-curred**	**oc-cur-ring**
pre-fer	**pre-ferred**	**pre-fer-ring**
re-fer	**re-ferred**	**re-fer-ring**
trans-fer	**trans-ferred**	**trans-fer-ring**

When the last syllable is not accented, the *r* is not doubled.

an-swer	**an-swered**	**an-swer-ing**
cov-er	**cov-ered**	**cov-er-ing**
of-fer	**of-fered**	**of-fer-ing**
or-der	**or-dered**	**or-der-ing**

2 **Business Vocabulary Builder**

myriad *(noun)* An immense number.
trinkets Small pieces of jewelry; things of little value.
acclaim *(noun)* Praise.
bygone Past; gone by.

Reading and Writing Practice

3

sum·mer

intro

al·most

par

myr·i·ad

ser

Transcribe:
5,000
25

for·eign

intro

await·ing

when

trin·kets

if

de·ferred

par

sense

[183]

4

crit·i·cal
ac·claim

and o

Transcribe:
1,000

intro

hab·i·tat

when

sim·u·lat·ed

conj

and o

intro

of·fer·ing

if

Transcribe: $30

if

nc

week's

[226]

5

fron·tier

by·gone

in·ter·na·tion·al·ly known no hyphen after ly

ser

ser

all-day hyphenated before noun

ca·noe

sce·nic intro

mu·se·ums ser

the·aters

intro

fam·i·ly's

when

pre·ferred

sim·i·lar

[167]

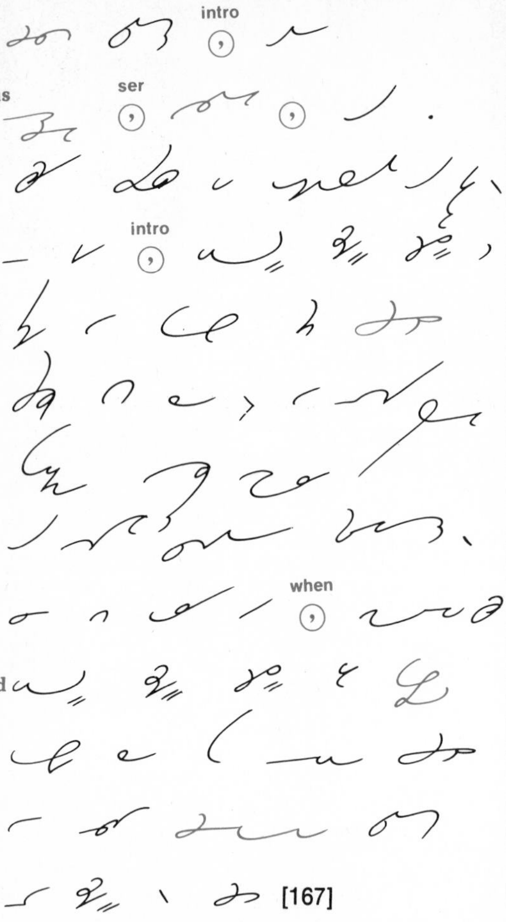

6

plan·ning

au·tumn

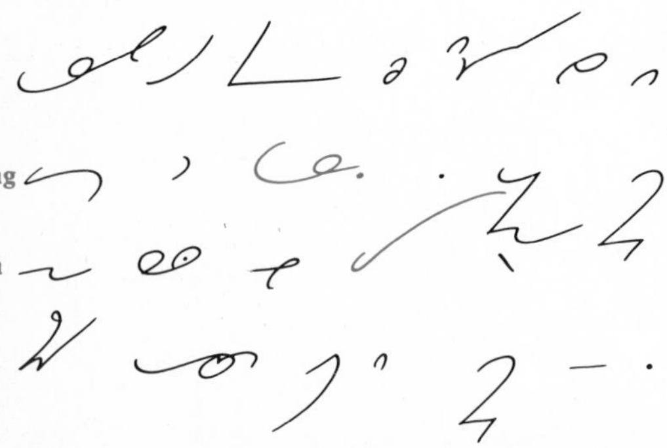

first-class

if

when

Transcribe: 3,000

conj

ac·com·mo·date

if

ap

of·fer·ing

[168]

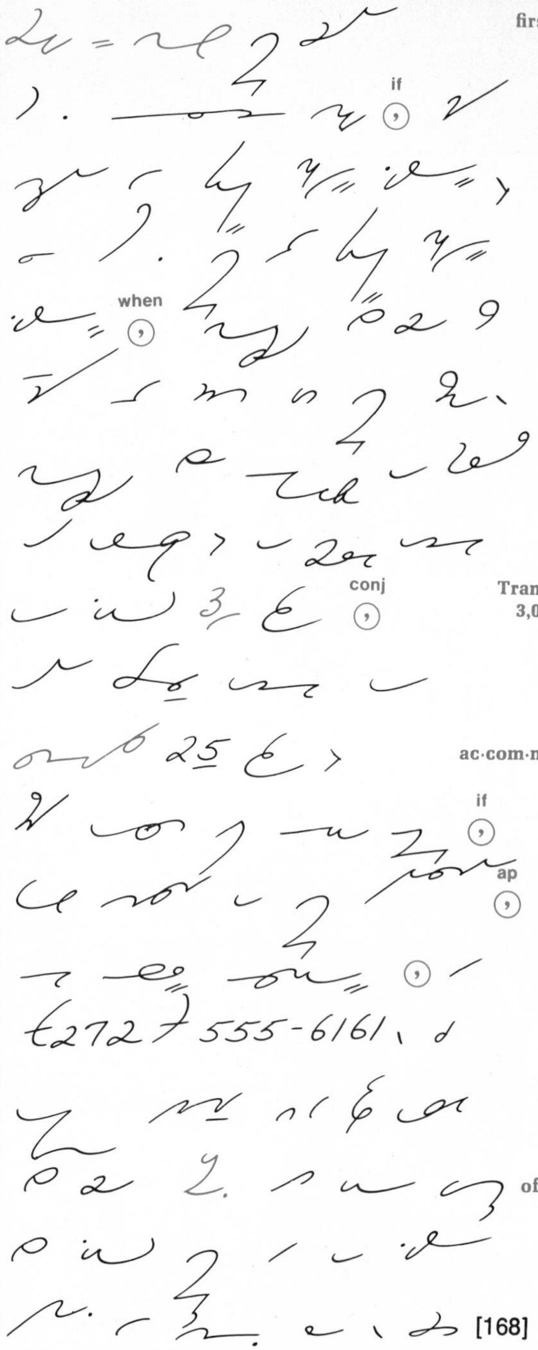

Building Transcription Skills

1 GRAMMAR CHECKUP ● less, fewer; already, all ready

Occasionally your employer, being human, will make a grammatical error. It is your job as a secretary to see that that error is corrected before the letter is submitted for signature.

less, fewer
Be careful to use the words *less* and *fewer* correctly.

less Refers to degree or amount.

She completed the work with less *effort than usual.*
We needed less *time to do the work than we ordinarily do.*

fewer Refers to a number.

He made fewer *errors today than he made yesterday.*

already, all ready
Sometimes these expressions are written as one word; sometimes they are written as two words.

already Now or previously.

It is already *time to go.*
The work is already *finished.*

all ready Everyone is prepared.

We are all ready *for the trip.*

2 **Business Vocabulary Builder**

densely Heavily; closely.

justification Reason; evidence supporting an act, idea, or belief.

destination The place which is set for the end of a journey.

Reading and Writing Practice

3

routes

Transcribe: 7 p.m.

1201 7 17 10 9

ap

res·i·dents

4 6

dense·ly

few·er

al·ready

if

pre·pared

nc

[188]

4

un·pleas·ant

ser

al·ready filled

Transcribe: 15,000

first-qual·i·ty hyphenated before noun

15,

intro

(8) 555-5016

ef·fi·cient

and o

con·ve·nient·ly lo·cat·ed no hyphen after ly

when

all ready

and o

if

des·ti·na·tion

can·cel

and o

nc

[213]

5

en·joy·able

all ready

and o

gracious

par

week-end

mountains

[103]

6

intro

de-cid-ed

prof-it

fis-cal

care-ful-ly

out-of-town hyphenated before noun

can-celed

[122]

7

ap

el-i-gi-ble

ap

nc

par

if

ser

de·duct

ser

Transcribe:
7 percent

prin·ci·pal

intro

intro

if

nc

when

[195]

8

to·day's

ap

busi·ness

its

ev·ery·day

Smith's

cr

[101]

Building Transcription Skills

1 OFFICE-STYLE DICTATION ● instructions during dictation (continued)

An effective way to stress or emphasize a few lines of typewritten copy is to indent them. If, for example, the letter is typed on a 50-space line, the indented material might be typed on a 40-space line so that it will stand out from the rest of the letter.

If prior to dictating the dictator mentions that a certain portion of a letter or report is to be emphasized, indent your shorthand notes slightly and place brackets around the material to be indented. If after dictating the dictator mentions that the material should be emphasized, merely place a single large bracket on one side of the section to be indented. The use of brackets will remind you to make the necessary indention when you are transcribing.

Illustration of Office-Style Dictation

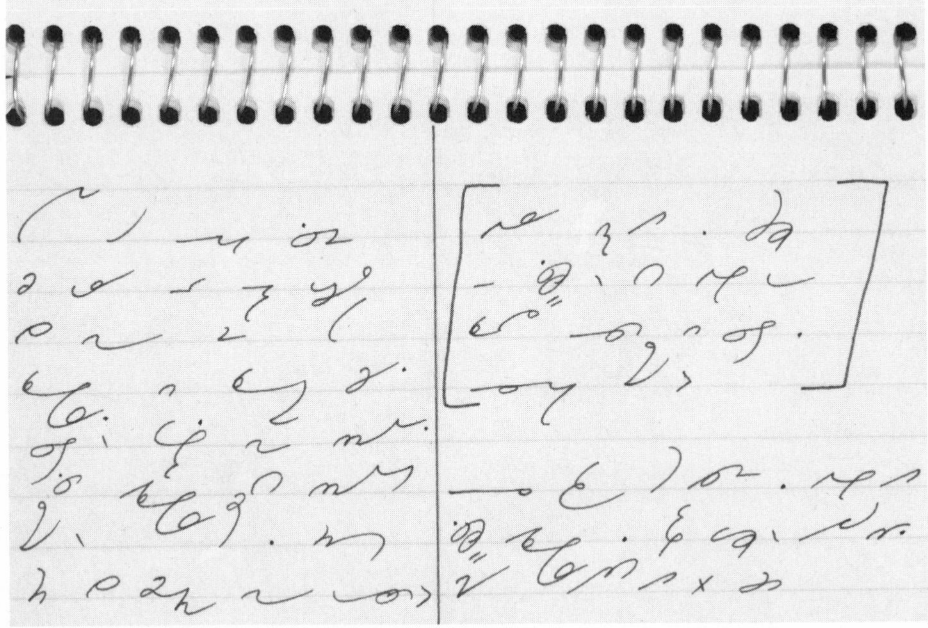

2 **Business Vocabulary Builder**

guaranteed reservation A hotel room reservation that is held past the check-in time (usually 6 p.m.) and must be paid for whether or not the person occupies the room.

accommodating *(adjective)* Helpful; obliging.

continental United States All of the states except Alaska and Hawaii.

pest infestation The inhabiting of a place by a large number of insects so as to be harmful or unpleasant.

Reading and Writing Practice

3

geo ser cr

can·di·dates

conj

so·fa

ser

intro

guar·an·tee

[89]

4

guest

intro

Transcribe: $138.50

de·fer

conj

passed

conj

po·lite

intro

ac·com·mo·dat·ing

re·cip·ro·cate

cr

co·op·er·a·tion

par

[130]

5

for·mal·ly

ap

as·so·ci·a·tions

Transcribe:
$20

Transcribe:
$25,000

ser

en·ti·tled
nu·mer·ous

when

if

de·sire

ser

intro

iden·ti·fi·ca·tion

Transcribe:
$100
1,000

par

sense

[187]

6

intro

abroad

per·mit·ted

de·struc·tion
do·mes·tic

in·fes·ta·tion

trav·el·er

en·vi·ron·men·tal

[159]

7

Transcribe:
April 5, 1960,

geo

light·weight

year's

to·tal·ly
self-con·tained

its

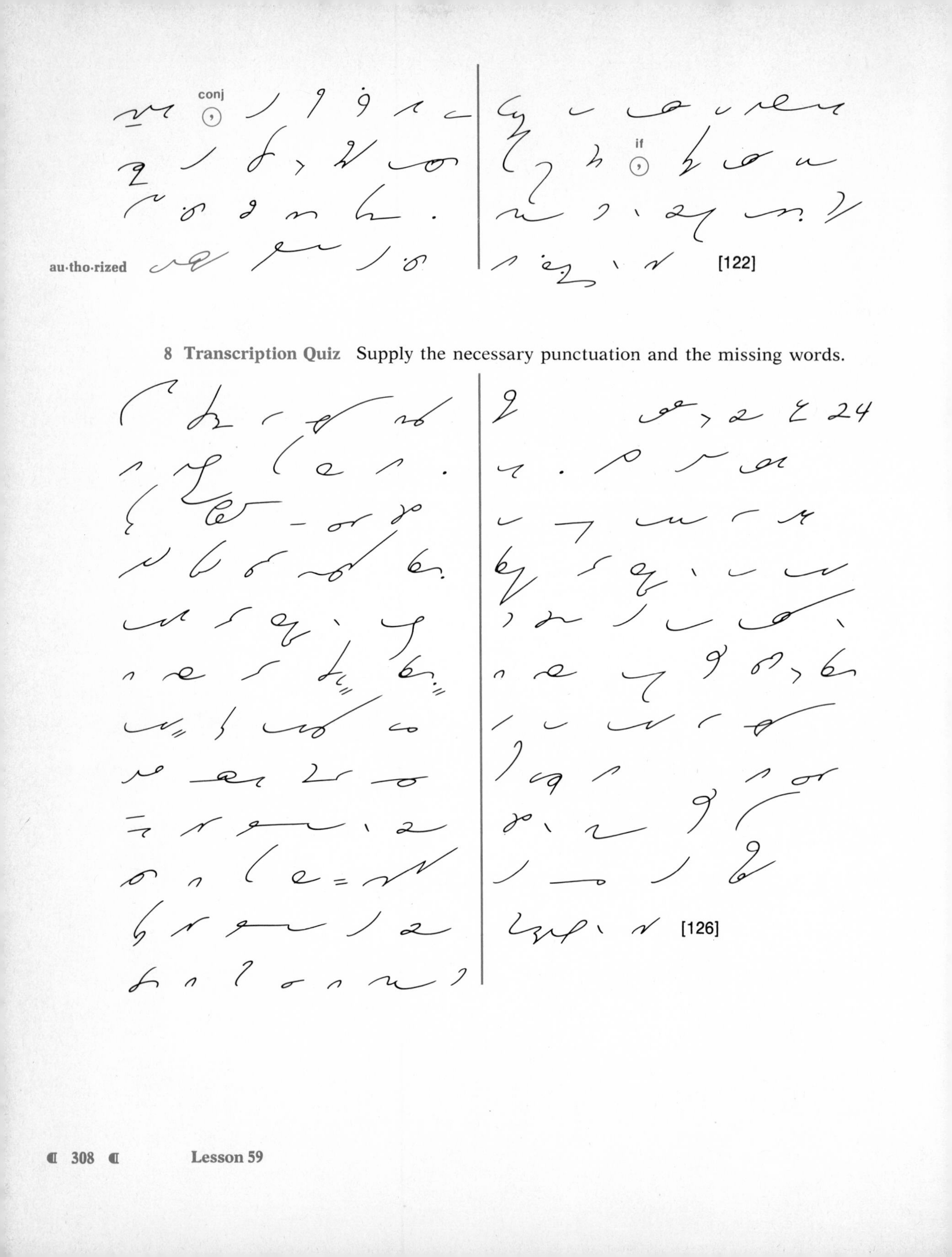

conj

if

au·tho·rized

[122]

8 Transcription Quiz Supply the necessary punctuation and the missing words.

[126]

Building Transcription Skills

1 GRAMMAR CHECKUP ● preposition at the end of a sentence

Careful writers, as a general rule, try to avoid ending a sentence with a preposition.

no

Is this the store you bought your new furniture in?

yes

Is this the store in which *you bought your new furniture?*

However, if the application of this general rule would result in an unnatural or stilted construction, the sentence may end with a preposition.

He is easy to work with.

Short questions often end with a preposition.

How many votes can you count on?

---

2 Business Vocabulary Builder

passports Formal documents issued to citizens of a country to allow them to leave and reenter that country.

visa An endorsement made on a passport granting permission for a citizen of one country to enter and leave another country.

fringe benefits Privileges (such as pension, paid holidays, and health insurance) granted by an employer to employees.

Reading and Writing Practice

3

Transcribe: 50 percent

af·ford

ef·fect

when

40

el·i·gi·ble

ac·com·mo·da·tions

enu

1

filled

ad·vice

ser

2

re·com·mend

ser

routes

coun·sel·ors

3

pass·ports
vi·sas

if

Transcribe:
$10

10/

[207]

4

as

re·call

ap

re·tire·ment

geo

conj

build

ap

21

dis·cuss

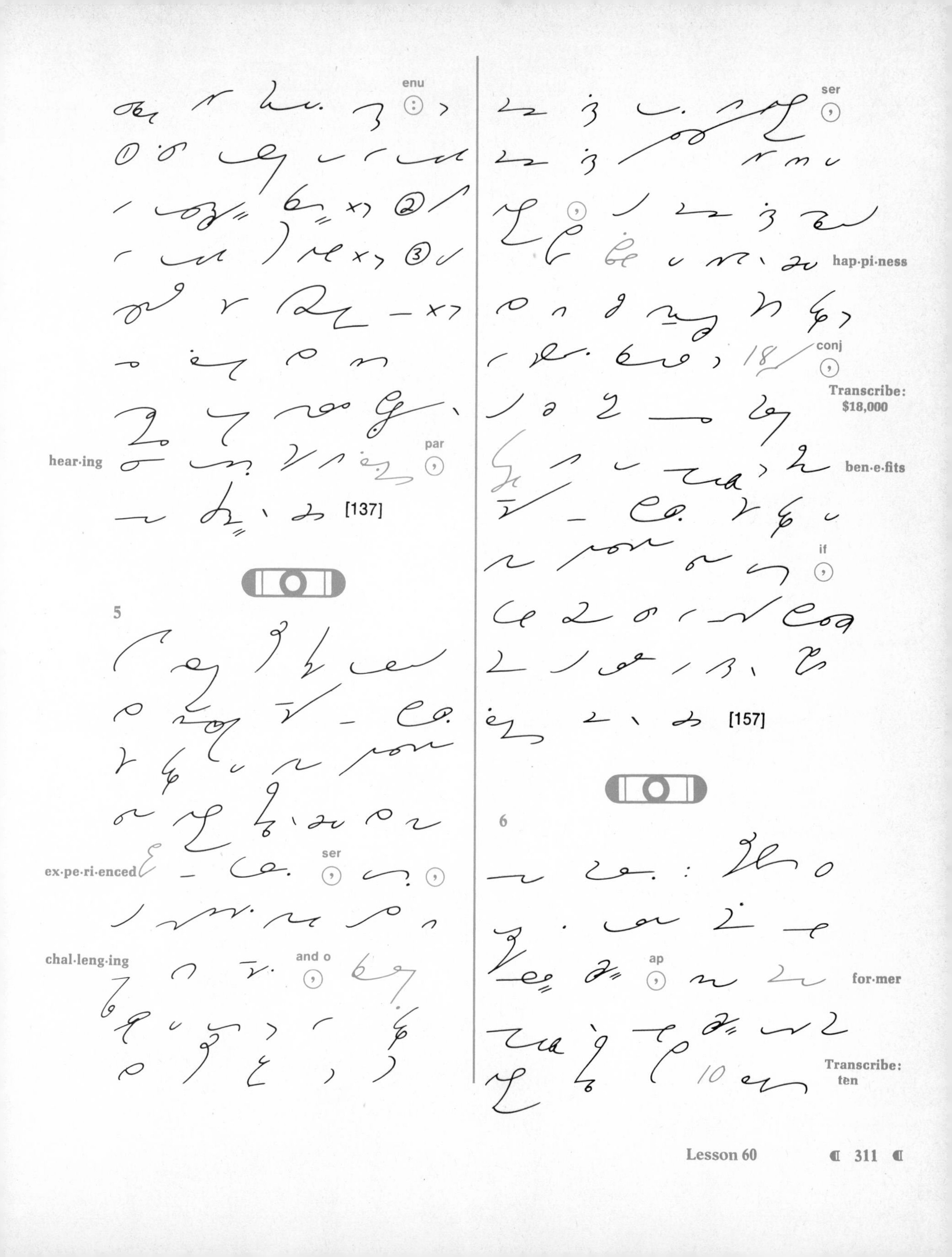

enu

hear·ing

par

[137]

5

ser

ex·pe·ri·enced

chal·leng·ing

and o

ser

hap·pi·ness

conj

Transcribe: $18,000

ben·e·fits

if

[157]

6

ap

for·mer

Transcribe: ten

re·gard·ed

grad·u·ate

conj

part-time hyphenated before noun

de·vote

par

cr

def·i·nite

ser

knowl·edge·able

self-in·ter·est

[147]

7

al·ways

ap

choose

de·luxe

ser

and o

care·free

Transcribe: $1,500

ap

[122]

PART

MOVING UP

Marie Washington had been Mr. Franklin's secretary for almost a year and a half, and Mr. Franklin was extremely pleased with her performance on the job. Marie had proved herself to be a professional secretary in every sense of the word—not only with her shorthand and typing skills but also with her organizational abilities and her willingness to take on additional responsibilities.

For example, Marie had spent considerable time reorganizing the filing system to make it more efficient. In addition, she learned quickly, knew when to ask questions, and was very helpful to anyone who needed information or assistance. Many times Marie had been called upon to handle situations that came up while Mr. Franklin was out of town. She was very adept at working with others.

Several times Marie had been asked to fill in when Ms. Carmen Valdez' secretary was out of the office. Ms. Valdez was vice president of marketing and was Mr. Franklin's boss. Marie had enjoyed working for her on these occasions.

One day Ms. Valdez' secretary announced that she would be moving to another city and would be leaving the company in two weeks. After consulting with Mr. Franklin, Ms. Valdez asked Marie if she would be interested in the job. This would be a promotion for Marie. In addition to performing regular secretarial duties, she would be responsible for supervising the work of two general office employees. Ms. Valdez was confident that Marie could easily step into the new position because she was familiar with the department and its operations.

Marie was flattered and delighted with Ms. Valdez' offer. But she was also a bit frightened as she had never supervised other employees before. She knew, though, that she couldn't turn down such a good opportunity. After thinking about it for a few days, Marie told Ms. Valdez that she would be happy to accept the new position. She felt she was ready to take on more responsibility.

Building Transcription Skills

1 **SIMILAR-WORDS DRILL ● quite, quiet, quit**

quite Totally; completely; wholly.

You are *quite* right.

quiet Tranquil; free from noise; still; calm.

The student is a *quiet* person.

quit To stop; to cease; to give up.

We will *quit* working on the project.

---

2 **Business Vocabulary Builder**

monotonous Tedious; boring.
sauna Steam bath.
critical Important; crucial.

Reading and Writing Practice

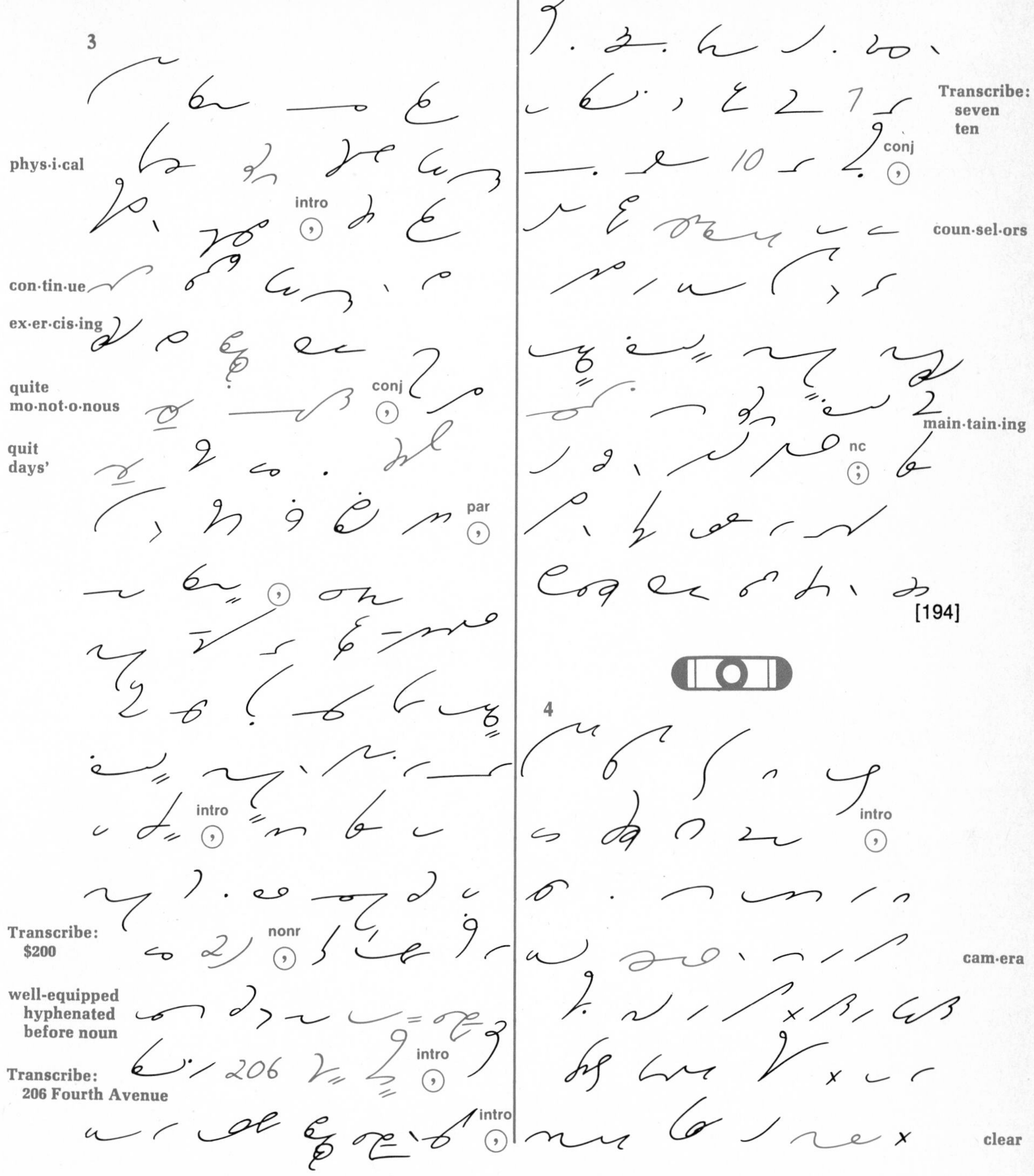

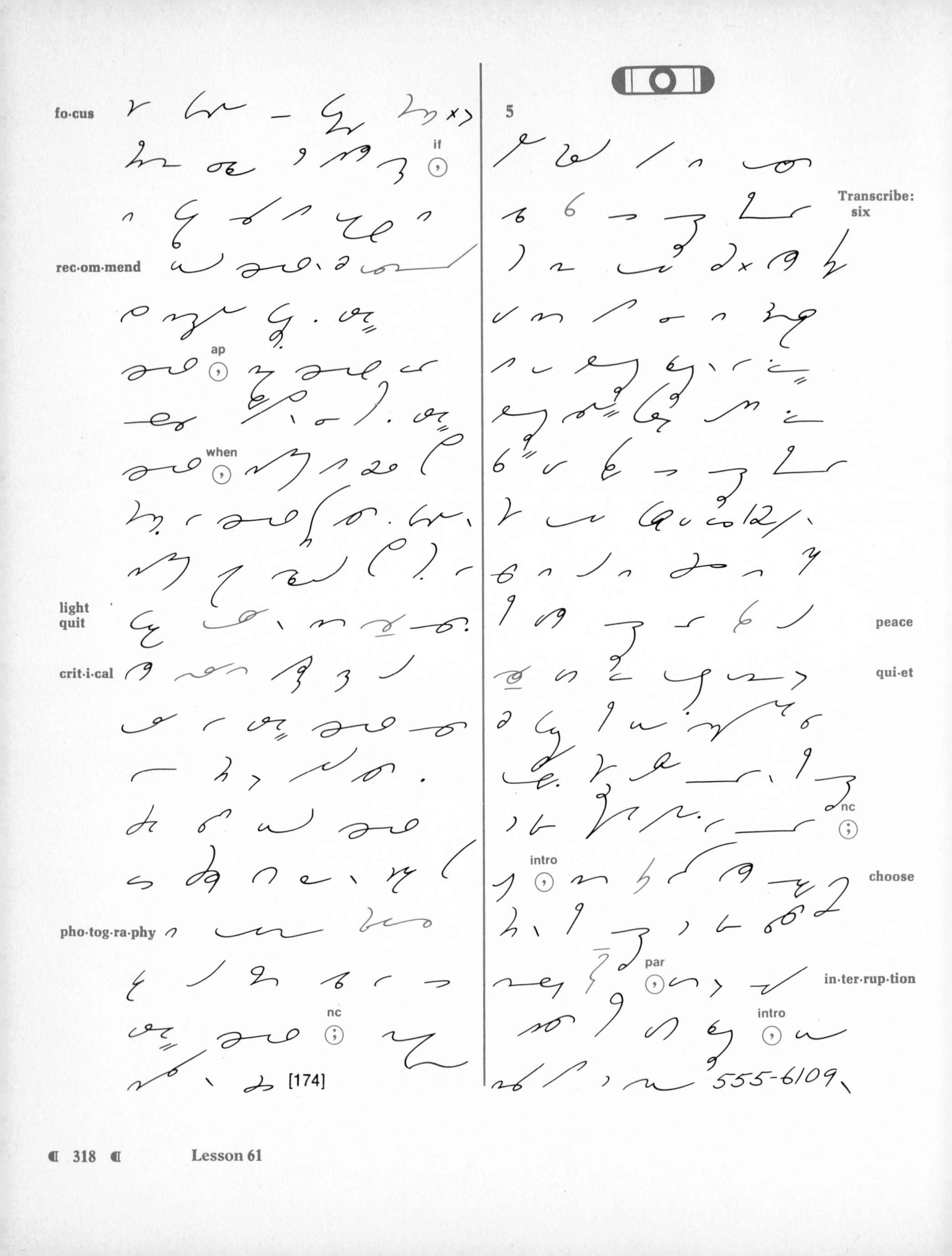

fo·cus

if

rec·om·mend

ap

when

light
quit

crit·i·cal

nc

pho·tog·ra·phy

[174]

5

Transcribe: six

peace

qui·et

nc

intro

choose

par

in·ter·rup·tion

intro

555-6109

de·vice

intro

nc

[184]

6

ar·chi·tec·ture

if

in·tri·gu·ing

ap

ser

de·cor

nc

if

Transcribe:
891 Tenth Avenue

quite

intro

[161]

7

and o

qui·et

ac·com·mo·da·tions

if

tru·ly

conj

first-class

intro

quite

[120]

8

ac·knowl·edge

ex·tend·ed

intro

intro

oc·ca·sions

and o

qui·et

quite

con·sci·en·tious·ly

intro

quit

geo

asth·ma

if

mis·take

[165]

Building Transcription Skills

1 **SPELLING FAMILIES ● double letters**

Be alert for double consonants in words; they are frequent causes of misspelling. The following list contains words that are sometimes misspelled.

Double L

al-lo-cate	**dis-al-low**	**hol-low**
al-lot-ment	**al-le-vi-ate**	**fal-la-cy**
ex-cel-lent	**chal-lenge**	**gal-lery**

Double M

com-merce	**com-mu-ni-cate**	**sum-ma-ry**
rec-om-mend	**im-me-di-ate**	**ac-com-mo-date**

Double S

as-sis-tance	**suc-cess**	**ac-cess**
nec-es-sary	**ad-mis-sion**	**pos-ses-sion**
as-sign-ment	**per-mis-sion**	**busi-ness**

2 **Business Vocabulary Builder**

Gulf Coast The coastal area along the Gulf of Mexico.

avid Enthusiastic; eager.

vicinity Area; locality; neighborhood.

Reading and Writing Practice

3

through ser

av·id

intro

dai·ly intro

amuse·ment

rec·om·mend

route

cr

as·sis·tance

and o

[131]

4

conj

plan·ning

ex·cel·lent

gal·ler·ies

Al·though

intro ba·si·cal·ly

nonr

enu

ad·mis·sion

[118]

5

as

ac·com·mo·da·tions

out-of-town hyphenated before noun

busi·ness

al·le·vi·ate

intro

10

Transcribe: ten 19206 Valley Road

nonr

19206

out of town no noun, no hyphen

if

nc

65/

[145]

6

intro

rolling

18=

chal·lenge

intro

and o

spa·cious

mag·nif·i·cent

ap

(8) 555-8016

[97]

7

re·ceived

au·di·to·ri·um
gym·na·si·um

intro

un·wise

nec·es·sary

par

nonr

80 24

Transcribe:
80 24th Street

if

[208]

Building Transcription Skills

1 ACCURACY PRACTICE

Follow the procedures described in Lesson 33.

Group 1		Group 2		Group 3	
see		as		your	
say		if		this	

practice drill

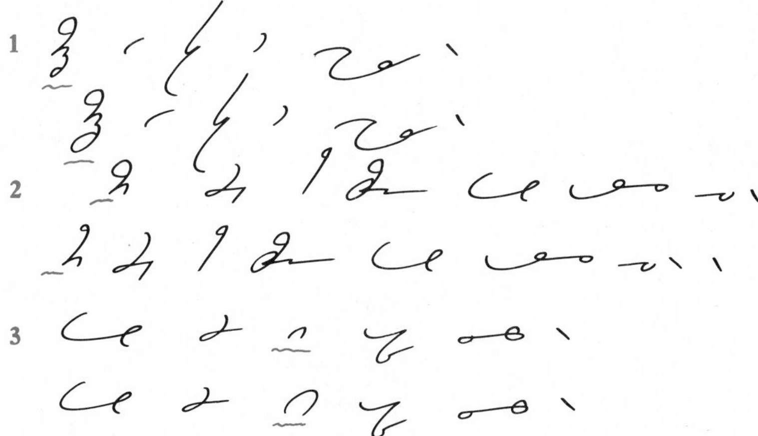

1 *As you* see, *the job is complete.*
As you say, *the job is complete.*
2 As *you finish each assignment, please let me know.*
If *you finish each assignment, please let me know.*
3 *Please send* your *report immediately.*
Please send this *report immediately.*

2 Business Vocabulary Builder

metropolis A large, important city.
intriguing Fascinating.
supersonic Faster than the speed of sound.
marinas Docks; boat basins.

Reading and Writing Practice

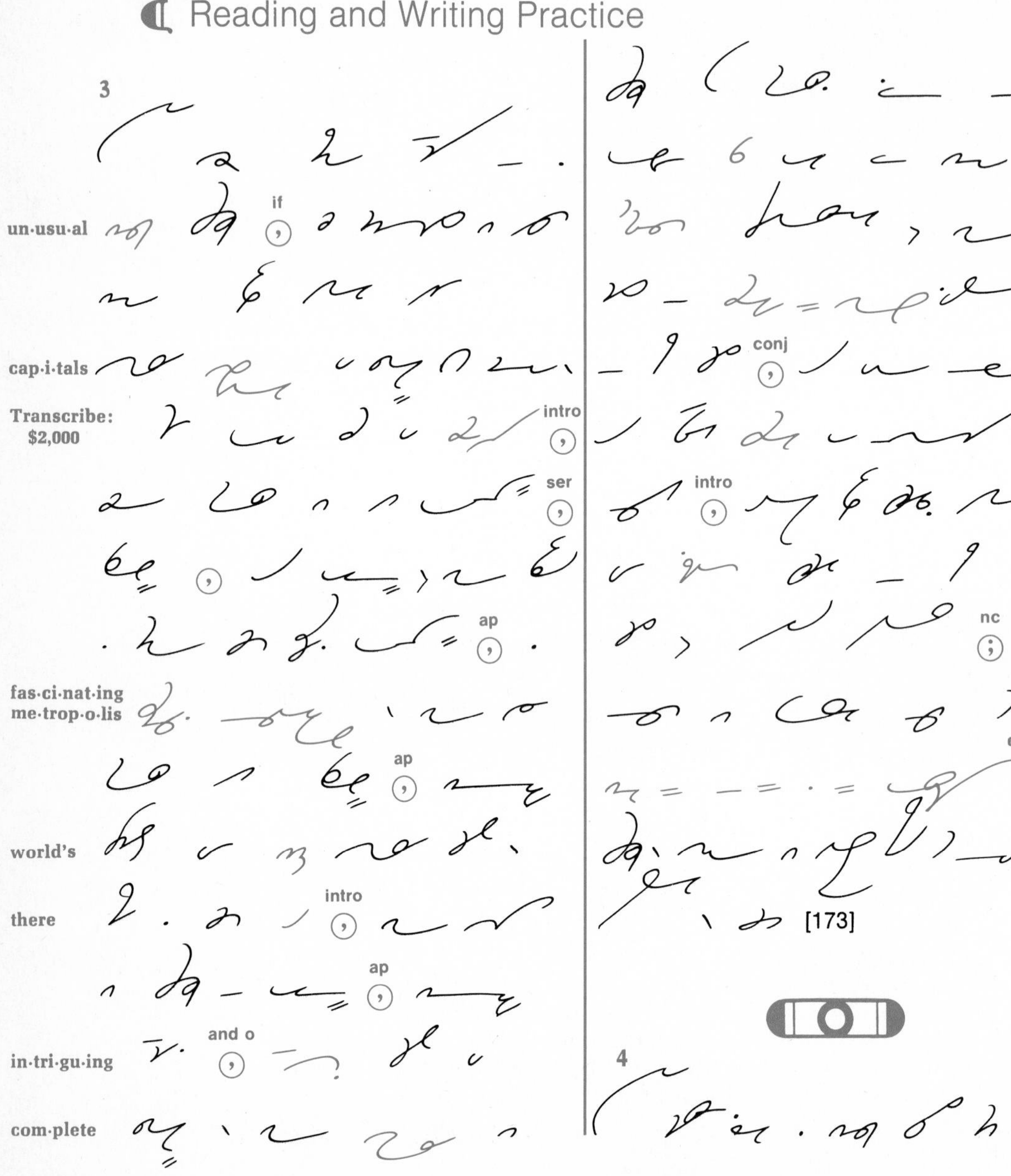

house·boat
de·scrib·ing

and o

lux·u·ri·ous

quite

Transcribe:
1,000

as

ser

ma·ri·nas

if

ser

if

nc

yours

if

[174]

5

lei·sure

ser

ex·cel·lent

choose

an·cient

Transcribe:
$1

6

if

can·celed

conj

intro

re·ceive

conj

conj

Don't

nc

conj

[229]

and o

mem·o·ra·ble

trav·el·ing

if

as

and o

par

na·tion·al·ly known
no hyphen
after ly

ser

un·sur·passed

intro

ser

and o

if

[158]

7

ap

plan·ning

dis·turbs

al·ready

qui·et

con·ges·tion

Transcribe:
7 to 9 a.m.
4 to 6 p.m.

par

in·flu·ence

cr

[173]

Letter Placement Hints

By applying the suggestions for the placement of short, average, and long letters that were presented to you in earlier lessons, you will be able to place most of your letters attractively on the page—and all of them acceptably.

Sometimes, though, you may find after typing the complimentary closing that the letter is slightly high on the page. When this happens, you can "pull the letter down" by allowing more space between the complimentary closing and the typed name; that is, instead of allowing the customary four lines below the complimentary closing, allow five or six lines. In addition, you can type the reference initials three or four lines below the typed name instead of the usual two lines.

At other times, after typing the complimentary closing, you may find that the letter appears to be low on the page. You can "lift it" by decreasing the space for the signature between the closing and the typed name to three or even two lines if necessary. Also, you can type the reference initials on the same line as the typed title.

CUSTOMARY

```
If we can be of assistance to you in the future, please do not hesitate to
contact us.
                                                                          1
                                              Sincerely yours,            2
                                                                          3
                                                                          4
                                                                          5
                                              Stephanie Michaels          6
                                              Personnel Director          7
                                                                          8
fjt                                                                       9
```

LOW

```
If we can be of assistance to you in the future, please do not hesitate to
contact us.
                                                                          1
                                              Sincerely yours,            2
                                                                          3
                                                                          4
                                              Stephanie Michaels          5
fjt                                           Personnel Director          6
```

HIGH

If we can be of assistance to you in the future, please do not hesitate to contact us.

Sincerely yours,

Stephanie Michaels
Personnel Director

fjt

As you gain experience, you will be able to place letters more attractively by deviating slightly from the placement suggestions you have learned for short, average, and long letters. For example, when a letter contains only 70 or 80 words, your experience will tell you that you will get a better-looking letter by starting the inside address twelve lines below the date rather than ten lines, as suggested for short letters.

When a letter contains 130 words, you will get a better-looking letter by starting the inside address ten lines below the date rather than the suggested eight lines for average letters.

Building Transcription Skills

1 OFFICE-STYLE DICTATION ● instructions during dictation (continued)

Some dictators never give their secretaries instructions about spelling, punctuation, and other details of transcription. Some, however, frequently do. When your employer gives instructions, it is important that you record them in your notes, no matter how simple they may seem to be.

If your employer spells a proper name, record the spelling immediately above your shorthand outline. If your employer dictates punctuation, place the marks in your notes, encircling them so that you won't try to read them as shorthand outlines.

Illustration of Office-Style Dictation

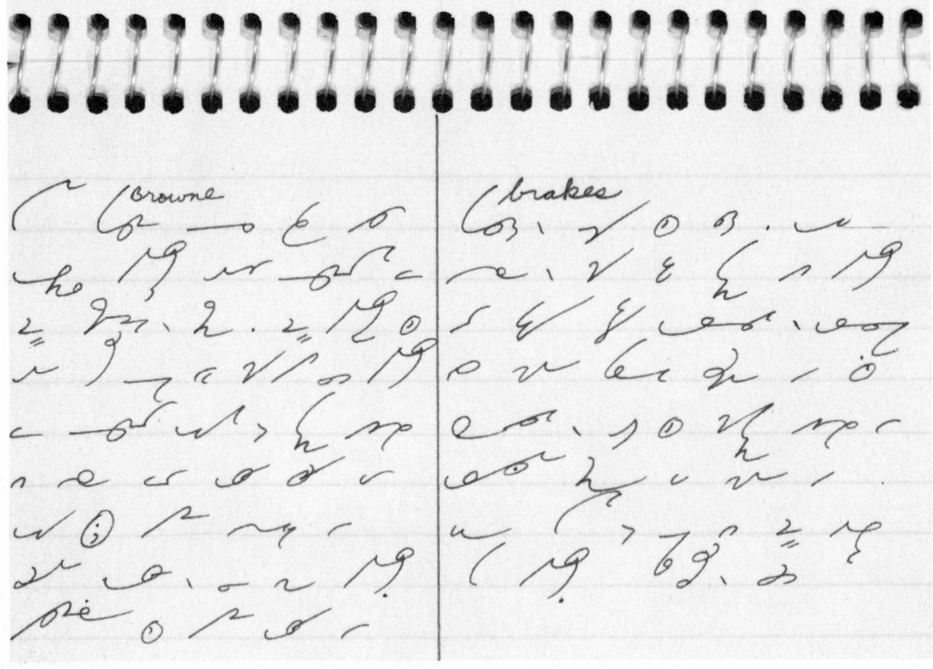

2 Business Vocabulary Builder

reinstate To restore to a previous condition or position.

coordination The ability to move parts of the body in a smooth, efficient manner.

charter member An original member or founder of an organization.

impractical Not practical.

Reading and Writing Practice

3

re·duc·ing
work·week
Transcribe:
five
four

as

its

four-day hyphenated before noun

ser

per·son·nel

Transcribe:
eight
six

un·til

ser

six-month hyphenated before noun

intro

as·sess

re·in·state

[187]

4

par·tic·i·pa·tion

ap

nc

ser

strength
co·or·di·na·tion

ser

con·cen·tra·tion
de·ter·mi·na·tion

if

intro

Transcribe:
$100

year's

conj

nc

[150]

5

Transcribe:
$3,000

conj

intro

con·crete

and o

cracked

im·prac·ti·cal

par

du·ra·ble

any·one's

ser

pool·side

conj

if

ob·li·ga·tion

par

[201]

6

if

stacked

ceil·ing

oc·ca·sion·al·ly

sel·dom

ser

sea·son·al

if

as·sis·tance

nonr

Transcribe:
9206 Fourth Avenue

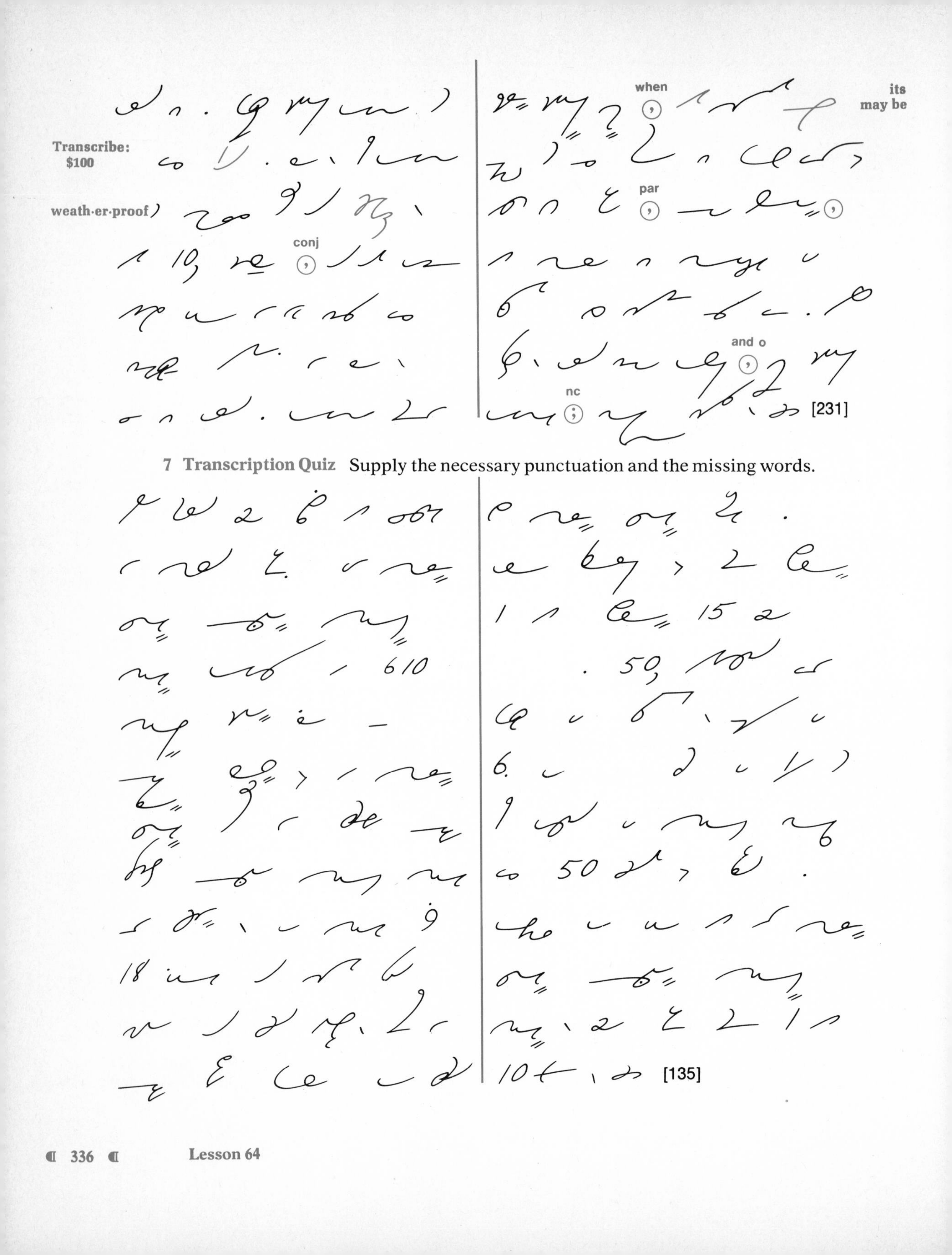

Transcribe: $100

weath·er·proof

conj

when

its may be

par

and o

nc

[231]

7 **Transcription Quiz** Supply the necessary punctuation and the missing words.

[135]

Building Transcription Skills

1 **COMMON PREFIXES ● bi-**

bi- As a prefix, *bi-* frequently means *two.*

bimonthly **1** Occurring every two months.
2 Occurring twice a month.

biannual Occurring twice a year.

biennial Occurring every two years.

bicentennial A two hundredth anniversary.

bicycle An unmotorized vehicle with two wheels.

bilingual Having the ability to use two languages fluently.

binoculars Field glasses used with both eyes simultaneously.

bifocals Eyeglasses with lenses made up of two parts.

2 **Business Vocabulary Builder**

quaint Pleasingly old-fashioned; charming.
picturesque Resembling a picture; suggesting a painted scene.
rural Relating to the country rather than the city.

Reading and Writing Practice

3

un·usu·al

if

quaint

up-to-date hyphenated before noun

and o

conj

bi·cy·cle

conj

pic·tur·esque

inns

ser

the·ater

if

ru·ral

and o

if

too

nc

for·get

[117]

4

cli·ents

ap

ser

ac·cus·tomed

han·dling

conj

par

bi·lin·gual

Transcribe: $20,000

if

[159]

5

its

bi·month·ly

intro

Transcribe:
500,000
$700,000

intro

conj

Transcribe:
1 million
$2 million

conj

phe·nom·e·nal

intro

tech·niques

if

[198]

6

1611

Transcribe:
1611 South Fourth Avenue

geo

nonr

com·plete

bin·oc·u·lars

conj

Transcribe:
10 a.m.
9 p.m.

[145]

7

as

its

rec·om·men·da·tion

def·i·nite·ly

intro

ar·ti·cles

if

nonr

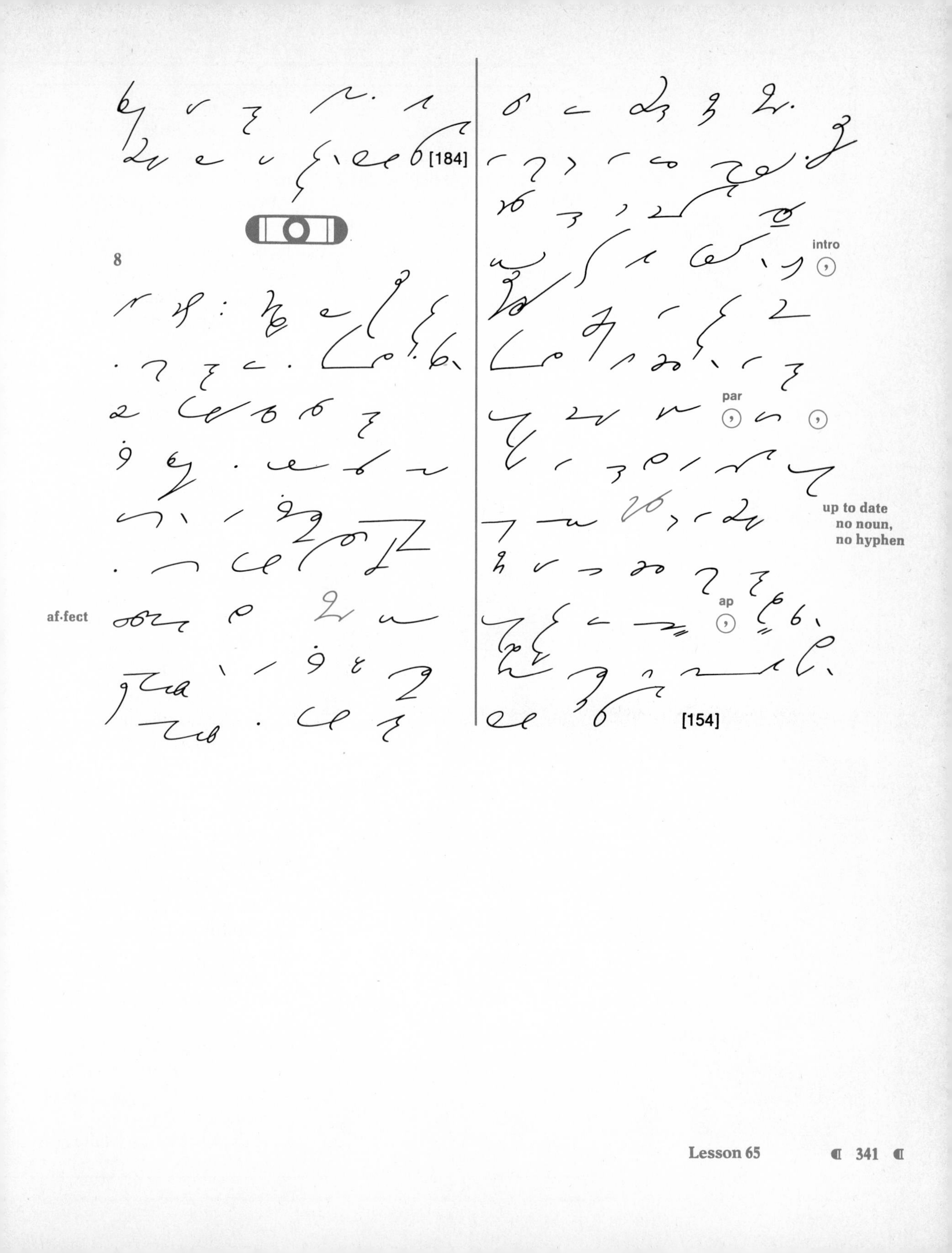

[184]

8

af·fect

intro

par

up to date no noun, no hyphen

ap

[154]

THE REPLACEMENT

Since Marie would be beginning her new job shortly, Mr. Franklin requested that Marie help him find and train a replacement before she left. They then sat down and drew up a list of requirements for the job to submit to the personnel department. The personnel department then arranged interviews with several candidates for the job.

After Mr. Franklin interviewed each candidate, he asked Marie to join them and explain in more detail the duties of the position. Marie was pleased to have so much input in the selection process; she knew that this experience would be helpful to her in the future.

After interviewing several people, Mr. Franklin narrowed the choice down to three candidates, but he was most impressed with Joshua Adams. Joshua typed accurately at 65 words a minute and took shorthand at 100 words a minute, and he had established a good rapport with both Mr. Franklin and Marie during his interview. When he was offered the position, Joshua accepted. He would work with Marie for one week before Marie began working for Ms. Valdez. This would be Marie's first experience in supervising another employee.

Marie knew that training Joshua would involve more than simply showing him where supplies were kept. She would have to spend many hours working with him so that he could carry on after she left without disrupting the office routine.

Even before Joshua arrived, Marie began to get ready. She reviewed and updated the procedures manual because she knew Joshua would depend on it to reinforce all the things she would be teaching him. She also prepared a "lesson plan" by jotting down the various tasks she did each day for a week. This list and the manual helped her put together an outline of what information she wanted to cover. This outline would also serve as a checklist so that she

could be sure she told Joshua about everything he had to know.

Marie knew that Joshua's first day on the job could be difficult for him. Marie first took Joshua on a short tour of the office and introduced him to other members of the staff. Next, she briefly reviewed the procedures manual with him, encouraging him to ask questions—no matter how trivial they might seem to be. Since Marie had a full week to work with Joshua, she would have the opportunity to show him how most things were done. Certain things she would explain as they came up and he could observe her doing them.

After going over a task thoroughly, Marie let Joshua do it. Although this was time-consuming, it would eliminate the need for Marie or Mr. Franklin to help Joshua later.

Above all, Marie was patient, cordial, and polite. She knew that procedures that seemed simple to an experienced secretary could be difficult for any new employee. She trained Joshua as thoroughly as possible. She wanted to be sure that he understood his new responsibilities and that he could handle them confidently.

Building Transcription Skills

1 TYPING-STYLE STUDY ● ages and anniversaries

Express ages in figures when they are used as significant statistics.

When you become 18 *years of age, you may vote.*

Your insurance rates increase after you are 65.

When ages are not considered significant statistics, spell them in full.

I took my three-year-old *son to the doctor.*

Spell out ordinals (*first, second,* and so on) in reference to birthdays and anniversaries.

This is our tenth *anniversary.*

Figures may be used, however, when more than two words would be needed.

We celebrated our city's 150th *anniversary.*

---

2 Business Vocabulary Builder

reprographics Duplicating and copying processes.
predicament A difficult, perplexing situation.
upshot Outcome; result.

Reading and Writing Practice

3

ser

ap·prox·i·mate·ly

Transcribe: twentieth

con·fer·ence

nonr

geo

re·pro·graph·ics

year's

du·pli·ca·tors

intro

ex·hib·it

booth

par

Transcribe: $100

three-day hyphenated before noun

if

[201]

4

well-known hyphenated before noun

dis·cov·ered

Transcribe: 11

tech·nol·o·gy

intro

and o

out-of-date hyphenated before noun

up·shot

pre·dic·a·ment

par

ser

if

may be
too

lack

months'

conj

well or·ga·nized
no noun,
no hyphen

an·a·lyze

Transcribe:
ten
eleven

10 11

re·plac·ing

out of date
no noun,
no hyphen

intro

[233]

nc

5

col·lege

Don't

par

555-

1106 [172]

6

ap

23

its

Transcribe:

125th

125

when

type·set·ting

con·vert·ed

out·skirts

geo

site

intro

if

intro

[207]

Building Transcription Skills

1 **PUNCTUATION PRACTICE ● the dash**

Use a dash instead of other punctuation when *special emphasis is required.*
Two of the students were especially helpful—Janet and Bob.

When a parenthetical expression or an expression in apposition contains internal commas, set off the complete expression with dashes.

All of the schools—Washington, Jefferson, and Lincoln—*will participate in the playoffs.*

Use a dash to set off an afterthought.

The task was assigned to Jim—or was it Joe?

2 Business Vocabulary Builder

portion Part.

instantaneously Without delay; in an instant.

apprise To inform; to tell.

Reading and Writing Practice

3

ap

conj

por·tion

ex·pen·di·tures

ser

Transcribe:
5
10
20

ser

intro

cli·ent

com·pat·i·ble

if

rep·re·sen·ta·tives

[189]

4

in·no·va·tive

intro

nonr

wait

intro

al·ready
de·pos·i·tor

intro

Transcribe:
nine
three

spe·cial·ly cod·ed
no hyphen
after ly

intro

in·sert

iden·ti·fi·ca·tion

Transcribe: $200

[186]

5

as

au·tho·rized

re·plac·ing

intro

intro

chang·ing

con·tact

ap·prise

cr

[130]

6

sec·ond

Transcribe: 25 cents

ex·ten·sions

add

intro

par

dec·o·ra·tor

intro

intro

and o

if

self-ad·dressed

[177]

7

ap

on-line

great

sec·onds'

ser

cus·tom·er's

ses·sions

in·stal·la·tion

intro

[154]

Building Transcription Skills

1 **GRAMMAR CHECKUP ● common errors**

The writer who is careful about grammar usage never uses:

different than for **different from**

no

The styles this year are different than *last year's styles.*

yes

The styles this year are different from *last year's styles.*

those kind for **those kinds**

no

I like those kind *of foods.*

yes

I like those kinds *of foods.*

between you and I for **between you and me**

no

Just between you and I, *he will not be going.*

yes

Just between you and me, *he will not be going.*

than me for **than I**

no

She types better than me.

yes

She types better than I.

2 Business Vocabulary Builder

inordinate Exceeding reasonable limits; excessive.
prevalent Generally accepted or practiced.
minimal The least possible.

Reading and Writing Practice

3

as

leased

geo

ser

fi·nan·cial

ex·per·i·ment

intro

fail·ure

months'

par

feel·ings

cr

[174]

4

cus·tom·ers'

in·or·di·nate

end-of-month hyphenated before noun

if

intro

when

for·mer·ly

ser

min·utes'

chal·leng·ing

and o

intro

con·tact

if

nc

Transcribe: 555-8806

555-8806

if

8641 27

Transcribe: 8641 East 27 Street

drudg·ery

[210]

5

mon·ey's

prev·a·lent

par

es·pe·cial·ly

intro

par·tic·u·lar

intro

min·i·mal amount

intro

let·ter·head

[161]

6

up to date no noun, no hyphen

yes·ter·day's

if

if

intro

imag·ine

intro

intro

high-speed hyphenated before noun

ser

up-to-date hyphenated before noun

and o

mo·ment's

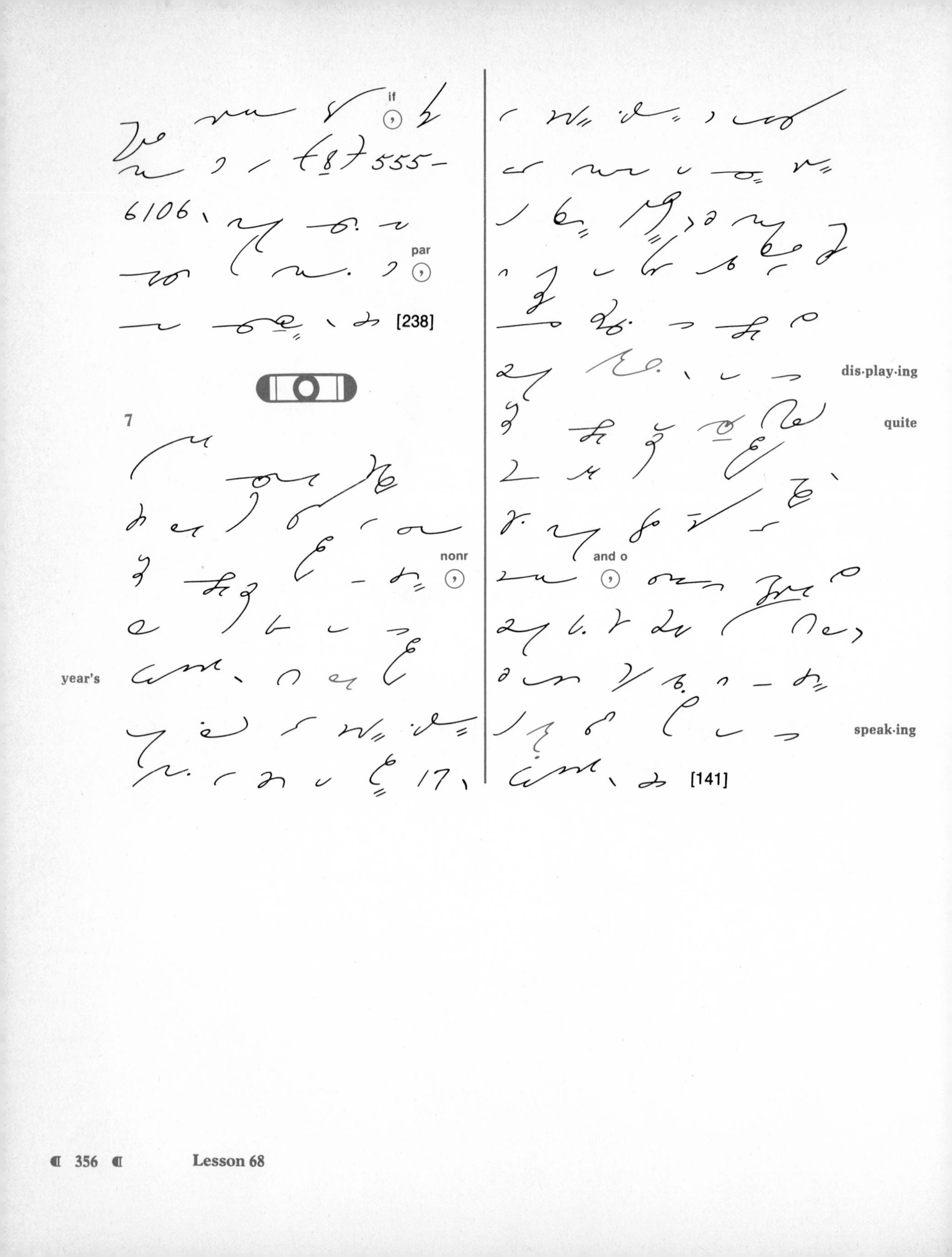

if

(8) 555-6106

par

[238]

7

nonr

year's

17

dis·play·ing

quite

and o

speak·ing

[141]

Building Transcription Skills

1 OFFICE-STYLE DICTATION ● instructions during dictation (continued)

Pay close attention to those instructions that require you to do something before you start to transcribe. In the middle of a letter, for example, the dictator may say, "Send a copy of this letter to Mr. Baker." Because you should have this type of information before you start to transcribe, you should always leave a few blank lines at the beginning of each letter to insert special instructions.

Illustration of Office-Style Dictation

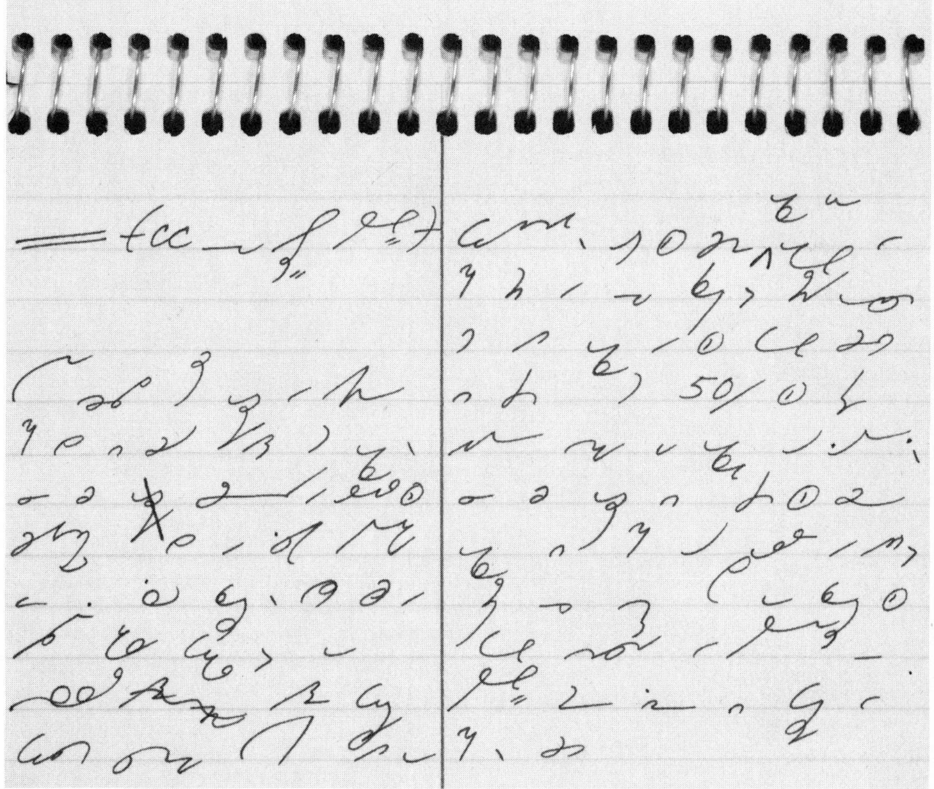

2 Business Vocabulary Builder

conducive Favorable; contributive; promoting.

sprightly Lively.

program *(verb)* To work out a sequence of operations to be performed automatically, as with a computer.

Reading and Writing Practice

3

as·so·ci·ate

if

de·scribes

choose

if

at·tached

when

re·ceive

nc

[147]

lat·er

4

intro

at·mo·sphere

con·du·cive

spright·ly

and o

and o

if

par·tic·u·lar·ly

ex·plain

ben·e·fits

if

en·joy·able

and o

[159]

5

phys·i·cal·ly

back·ache

Transcribe: 40 percent

par

rec·om·mend

pos·ture

intro

week's

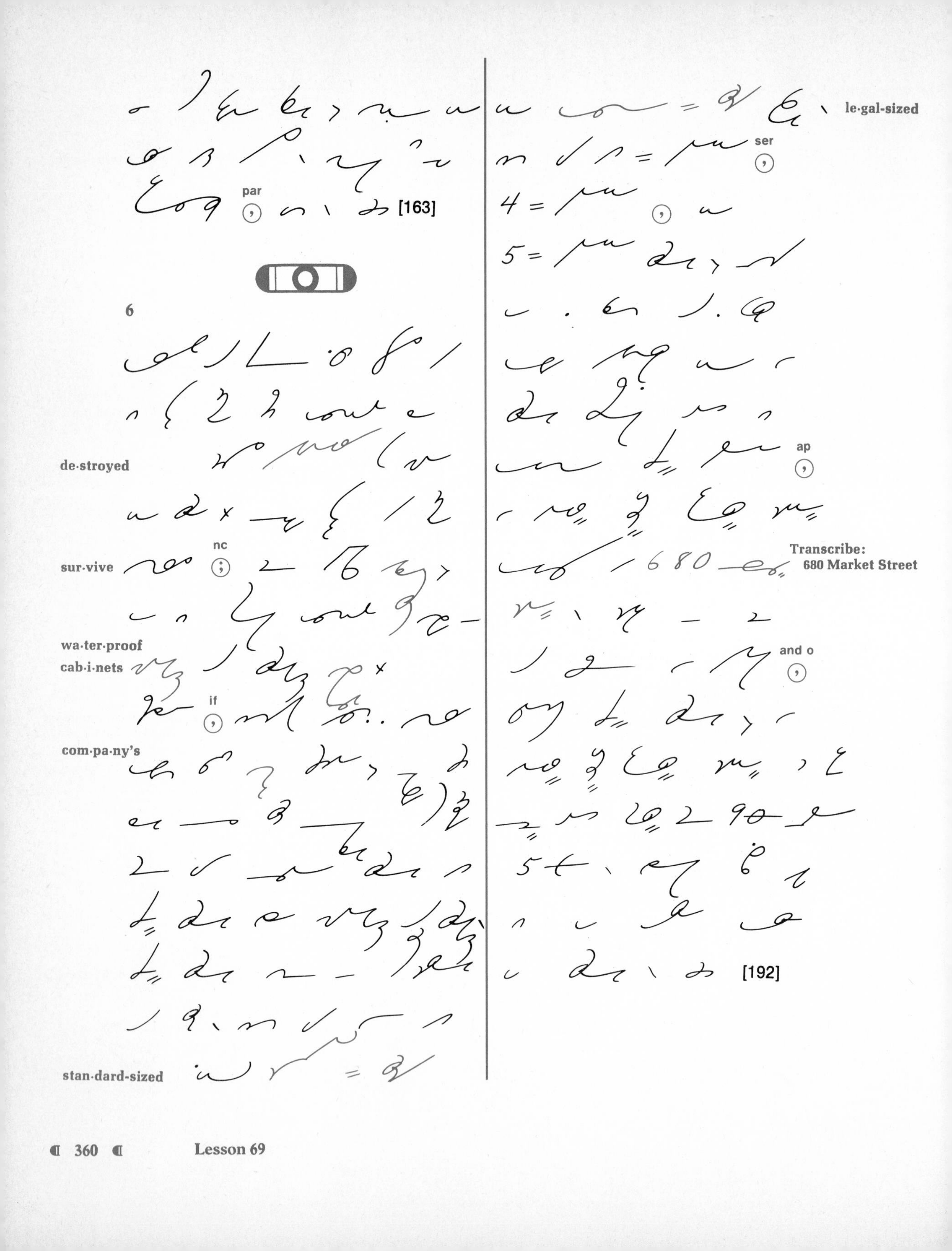

le·gal-sized

ser

par

[163]

6

de·stroyed

nc

sur·vive

wa·ter·proof

cab·i·nets

if

com·pa·ny's

stan·dard-sized

ap

Transcribe:
680 Market Street

and o

[192]

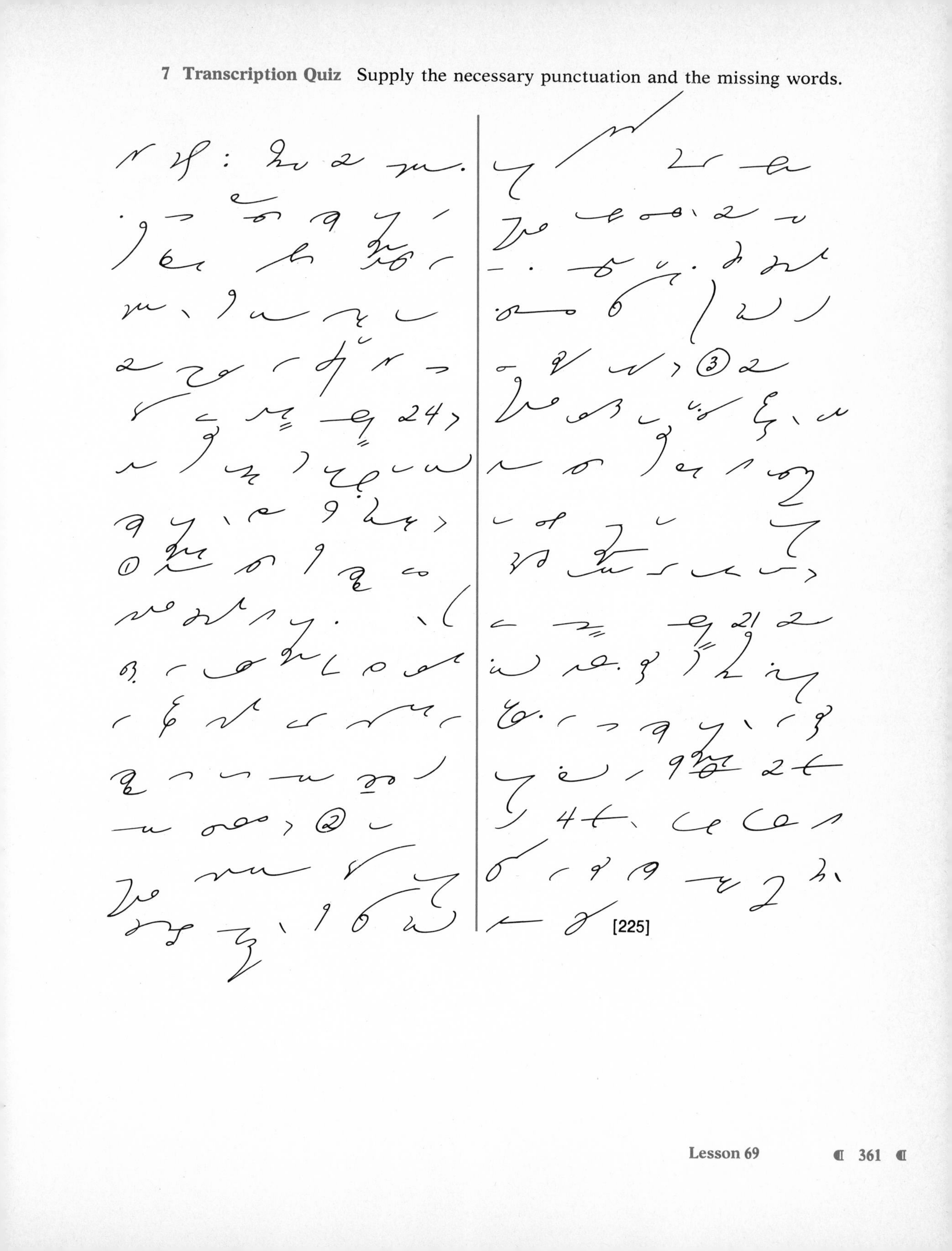

7 **Transcription Quiz** Supply the necessary punctuation and the missing words.

[225]

Building Transcription Skills

1 COMMON PREFIXES ● post-

post- 1 Having to do with the mails.
postage The charge for mailing a letter or other material.
postmark The cancellation mark of the postal service.
postal Relating to the postal service.

post- 2 Later; after.
postpone To delay or defer to a later time.
postscript A message added after a letter has been completed.
postdate To use a date that is later than the actual date.

---

2 Business Vocabulary Builder

tentatively Uncertainly; not finally.
judicious Wise; of sound judgment.
promissory note A written promise to pay a sum of money by a specified date.

Reading and Writing Practice

3

as

de·cid·ed
its

four-day
hyphenated
before noun

ap

intro

post·pone

ten·ta·tive·ly
re·sched·ul·ing

ap

Transcribe:
9 a.m.

board·room

if

if

[138]

4

as

cel·e·brat·ed
Wash·ing·ton's

men·tion

ap·par·ent·ly

cal·en·dar

clar·i·fi·ca·tion

if

ju·di·cious

rea·son

if

[145]

5

ap

con·trol·ler

post·dat·ed

conj

if

post·pone

prom·is·so·ry

par

in·ter·est

Transcribe:
14 percent

intro

[154]

6

com·pa·ny's
twen·ti·eth

and o

world's
best-known
hyphenated
before noun

intro

intro

be·lat·ed

[167]

if

ap

[127]

7

ap

8

post·age

ZIP Codes

pro·ce·dure

mail

if

de·layed

if

Transcribe:
ten
four

10

4

weigh

if

ac·cess

nc

[108]

SUPERVISING OTHERS

In her new position, Marie was responsible for supervising two general office employees. These two persons performed various duties such as taking dictation, operating special equipment, and, in general, helping out wherever there was a need. In dealing with these employees, Marie realized that the key factors were politeness, patience, and understanding.

By dictating much of the correspondence for which she was responsible, Marie was able to save herself a great deal of time—time that could be devoted to her other duties. Having been on the "other side of the desk," Marie was aware of the problems that dictators face. Even the shortest dictation session could be difficult if she was poorly organized, made numerous changes, or failed to speak distinctly.

As most of her correspondence was in response to inquiries, Marie made sure she understood what was being asked before composing a reply. She organized her thoughts and often made an outline in shorthand of the points she wanted to cover. She was conscious of observing the rules of effective communications as she dictated. By trying to anticipate the action or reaction of the reader, Marie was able to dictate accurate, effective letters.

In addition, Marie was careful to simplify the stenographer's job by giving special instructions before dictating the letter and by enunciating clearly. Although she was conscientious in her efforts to speak certain words clearly— for example, *formerly* and *formally*—she knew that it was the stenographer's responsibility to distinguish between the meanings of words that sound alike.

Finally, Marie read carefully each piece of correspondence before signing it, making sure that it conveyed her intended message and that it was correctly transcribed. She had also established a procedure of sending a copy of all her correspondence to Ms. Valdez.

Another of Marie's major responsibilities was to supervise the production of special reports and promotional pieces. Much of this material was produced on special equipment, and it was Marie's duty to see that the final product was correct and completed on schedule. By explaining in detail what had to be done to the persons doing the actual work, Marie was able to avoid costly delays. After assigning and explaining a job, Marie gave the employee an opportunity to ask questions or to ask for further information or clarification.

Marie was learning rapidly what it takes to be a top-notch supervisor.

Building Transcription Skills

1 TYPING-STYLE STUDY ● adjacent numbers

When two numbers come together in a sentence and one is a part of a compound modifier, spell out the first number and express the second in figures.

We own three 8-floor *buildings.*

However, if the second number would make a significantly shorter word, spell it out and express the first number in figures.

We received 500 four-page *booklets.*

---

2 Business Vocabulary Builder

seldom Rarely; infrequently.

token *(noun)* A symbol; a sign.

constraints Restrictions; limitations.

Reading and Writing Practice

3

Too

shop·ping

isq

iq

intro

con·fi·dence

to·ken

intro

Transcribe: two 3-day

as

nc

intro

ap

10

nonr

10

open·ing

intro

Transcribe: 5 p.m.

5

6

10

men's wom·en's

ser

chil·dren's

Transcribe: 50 percent

50

intro

9:30

and o

ad·mit·ted

for·ward

ap

10

[260]

4

ap

Transcribe: 1,000 four-page

4=

Transcribe: 10th of June

conj

re·ceived

if

can·cel

[112]

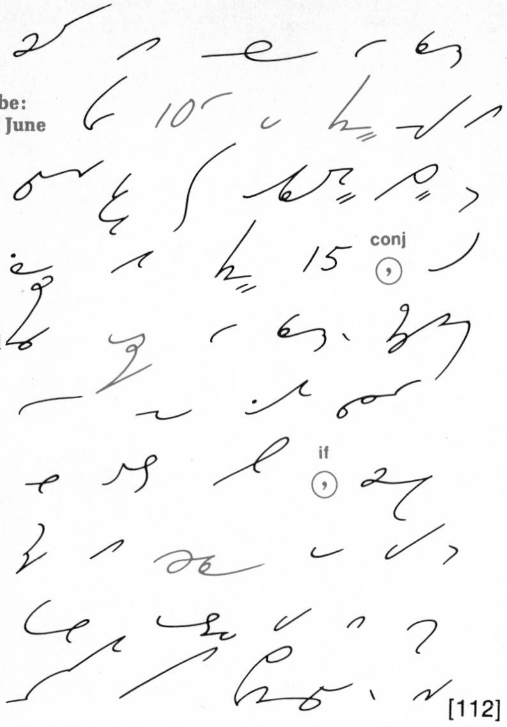

Transcribe: three 8-unit

high-qual·i·ty hyphenated before noun

intro

con·straints

com·pelled

nc

[120]

5

as

6

intro

crit·i·cal

ac·com·mo·da·tions

head·quar·ters

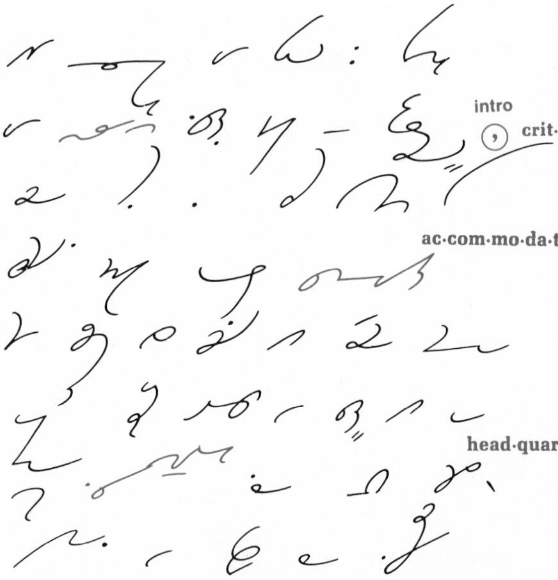

oc·ca·sions

Transcribe: three 2-bedroom

long-term hyphenated before noun

if

prom·is·ing

if

long run

[265]

7

twen·ti·eth

geo

intro

intro

Transcribe: 1,000 eight-page

Transcribe: six

pen·cil

if

cr

[139]

8

po·ten·tial

pro·ce·dures

han·dling

and o

prac·ti·cal

sen·si·ble

nonr

Transcribe: 100 two-page

cr

[175]

Building Transcription Skills

1 **PUNCTUATION PRACTICE ● parentheses**

Place parentheses around explanatory expressions to de-emphasize such expressions.

Our next meeting will be held in the conference room (not the auditorium).

Place parentheses around reference information.

Our expenses are substantially higher this year (see the attached expense report).

Use parentheses to enclose numbers or letters that accompany enumerated items within a sentence.

Please include these items in your report: (1) name, (2) address, (3) education, and (4) work experience.

2 **Business Vocabulary Builder**

commended Praised.

relevant Pertinent; relating to the matter at hand.

premiere *(noun)* The first performance or showing.

Reading and Writing Practice

3

au·to·mo·tive

com·mend·ed

tech·niques

rel·e·vant

to·day's

par

Transcribe: two

sim·i·lar

Transcribe: Fourteen

cop·ies

14

if

and o

[179]

4

ben·e·fit

Transcribe: 10 percent

10,

intro

ser

elec·tron·ic

Transcribe:
610 East 21 Street

610

21

[170]

5

pre·miere
the·at·ri·cal

ded·i·cat·ed

The·ater

intro

conj

rare·ly

intro

per·for·mances

Transcribe:
216 Elm Drive

216

ev·ery one

[144]

6

ap·point·ment

and o

par

Transcribe:
ten

10

main·tain·ing

high-qual·i·ty
hyphenated
before noun

en·roll·ment

when

im·ple·ment·ing

par

[149]

7

ar·ti·cle

ap

nonr

intro

conj

Al·though

con·tro·ver·sy

intro

ve·hi·cles

cur·tailed

par

intro

[190]

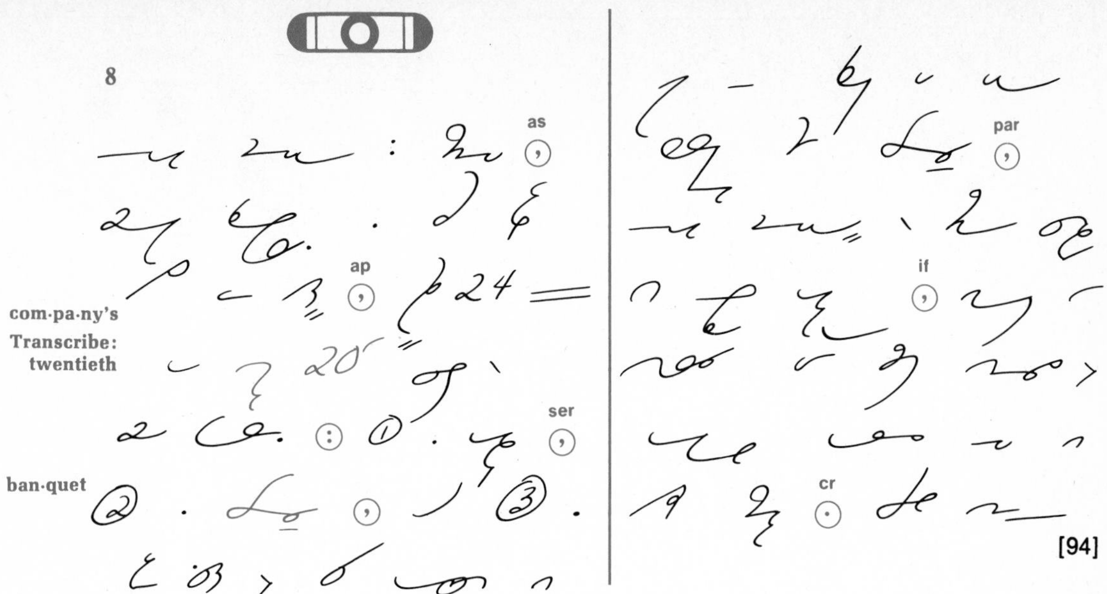

There is no substitute for advanced planning. A good secretary makes out a schedule for each day. The most important jobs are listed first, and the least important jobs are listed last. Consequently, at the end of the day, even if all the work is not complete, at least the most important jobs will have been finished.

Building Transcription Skills

1 ACCURACY PRACTICE

Follow the procedures outlined in Lesson 33.

Group 1	Group 2	Group 3
red	test	affect
lead	text	effect

practice drill

1 *Fill in the answers with a* red *pencil.*
Fill in the answers with a lead *pencil.*

2 *I will examine the* test.
I will examine the text.

3 *Your decision will* affect *the settlement of the argument.*
Your decision will effect *the settlement of the argument.*

2 Business Vocabulary Builder

formulated Developed; prepared according to a special formula.

time deposit A bank deposit payable at a specified time after deposit.

prevailing Most frequent; common.

Reading and Writing Practice

3

plan·ning

re·cep·tion

as

ap

will·ing·ness

af·fect·ed

as·set

conj

nonr

Transcribe:
2717 Route 21
6 p.m.

2717

21

ap

15

6

if

15

nc

Re·tain

ad·mis·sion

if

[197]

4

gas·o·line

ef·fect

par

and o

con·vert·er

lead
rec·om·mend

par

de·te·ri·o·rate

ser

rav·ages

and o

intro

ap

for·mu·lat·ed

when

intro

[227]

5

Transcribe: three 2-year

al·lowed

conj

prin·ci·pal

as

intro

re·deem

par

re·in·vest

pre·vail·ing

par

if

[157]

6

ful·ly equipped no hyphen after ly

geo

three-month hyphenated before noun

intro

intro

Transcribe: 555-8616

555-8616

pho·to·graph·ic

intro

nc

va·lid·i·ty

[176]

During the first week or two on your new job, you may find that your employer's dictation is somewhat more difficult than the dictation you took in class. You will not be accustomed to your employer's dictating habits and style, and you may not be familiar with the vocabulary and terminology of the business. If you have developed a good reserve of speed, you will have little trouble writing unfamiliar words and expressions in full in shorthand. As you become more accustomed to your employer's dictating habits and more familiar with the language of the business, you will find the task of taking dictation less difficult.

To make your job even easier, take notice of the words and expressions your employer uses again and again. After several weeks on the job, you may find it helpful to devise shortcuts for these expressions. For example, if your employer uses the term *audiovisual materials* repeatedly, you might write it:

instead of in full:

You can easily see how much time and effort such a shortcut will save.

When considering devising shortcuts, keep the following two points in mind:

□ **1** Your employer must use the expression *frequently.* A shortcut for a word or expression that is used infrequently will only cause you to hesitate when taking dictation and may cause difficulty when you are transcribing your notes. The shortcut must come to mind immediately if it is to be of any value to you; this will happen only if the expression it represents is used again and again.

□ **2** The shortcut must be distinctive so that you will not confuse it with any other shorthand outline.

Guard against the temptation to devise too many shortcuts, especially in the early stages of a new job. Some beginners get the false impression that if a few shortcuts will save time and effort, many shortcuts will simplify their work even more. Unfortunately, that is not the case.

Here are examples of some shortcuts you might devise if you worked in:

1 A lawyer's office

Testimony, plaintiff, defendant, Supreme Court, abstract of title.

2 An investment office

Shareholder, stockholder, stock market, stock exchange.

3 An accountant's office

Accounts receivable, accounts payable, profit and loss.

4 An insurance office

Insurance policy, endowment policy, cash value, policyholder.

5 A bank

Savings account, checking account, mortgage, interest rate.

6 A doctor's office

Physical examination, hospital, fracture.

7 A personnel office

Application blank, personal interview, employment test, in-service training.

8 A publisher's office

Manuscript, galley proof, page proof, editor in chief.

Remember: Devise shortcuts *only* for words and expressions that occur repeatedly in your dictation.

Building Transcription Skills

1 **OFFICE-STYLE DICTATION ● instructions during dictation (concluded)**

A dictator will occasionally stop dictating to tell you to verify names, amounts, or other data. The dictator may say:

Your representative, Ms. Greenfield, called on Tuesday—please check the spelling of her name and verify the day she was here.

In your notes, the instructions should appear as follows:

By indicating immediately above your shorthand outlines that you are to check the day and the spelling of the name, you will be sure that you do so before you type them.

Illustration of Office-Style Dictation

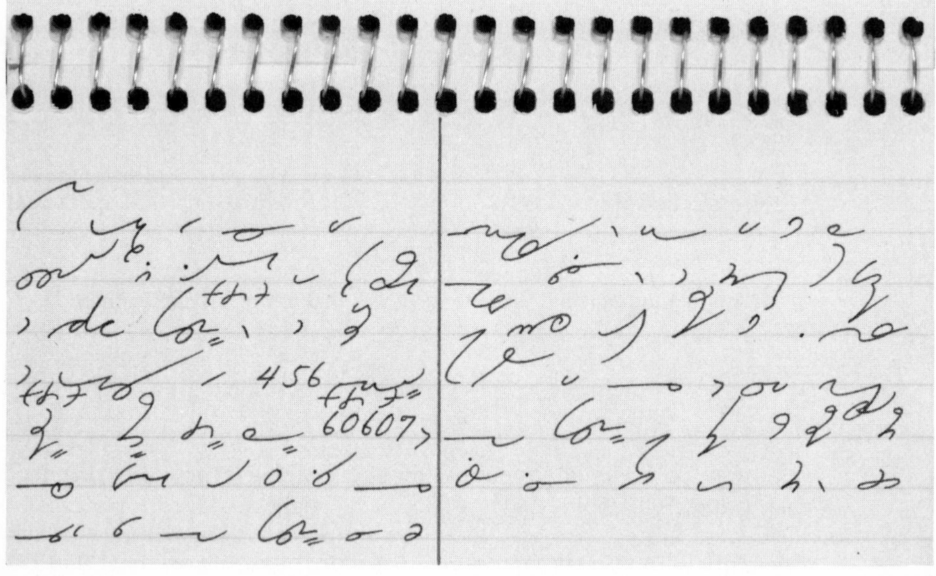

2 Business Vocabulary Builder

ambassadors Official or unofficial representatives.

rapport A good relationship, especially one of mutual trust.

deliberation Thoughtful, lengthy discussion and consideration by a group of persons.

Reading and Writing Practice

3

as

trav·el·ing

journ·ey

conj

year's

en·roll·ment

se·lect·ed

am·bas·sa·dors

ser

rap·port

pro·spec·tive

ser

com·mit·ments

Transcribe: 50 percent

[162]

4

pa·tience

re·mod·eled

conj

too

ac·com·mo·date

as

dou·bled

ap

ad·mit

spe·cial·ly priced
no hyphen
after ly

[130]

5

intro

de·lib·er·a·tion

de·ci·sion

unan·i·mous

conj

as

Transcribe:
$50

as

ser

conj

intro

de·duct·ible

[199]

6

ex·am·ined

conj

of·fend

fault

conj

if

apol·o·gize

if

ev·ery one

[137]

7

ser

com·mend·ed

siz·able

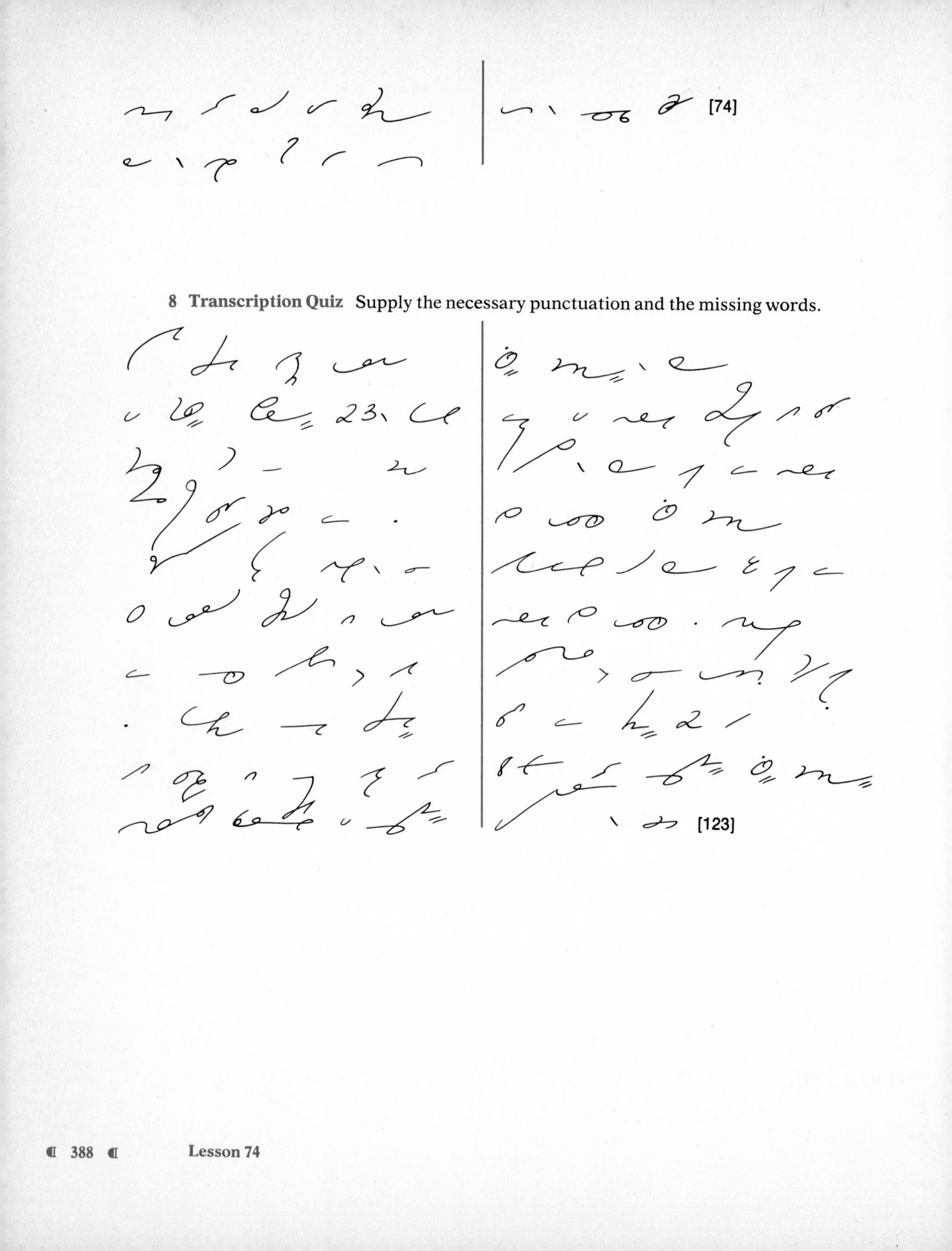

[74]

8 Transcription Quiz Supply the necessary punctuation and the missing words.

[123]

Building Transcription Skills

1 **SIMILAR-WORDS DRILL ● course, coarse**

course A series of classes; a route or direction.

I am taking a *course* in science.
We will take the proper *course* of action.

coarse Rough in texture.

That material is very *coarse*.

2 **Business Vocabulary Builder**

gesture *(noun)* An action expressing an attitude, especially as a sign of good intentions.

recourse An alternate action.

delicate Fine; dainty.

Reading and Writing Practice

3

Transcribe: three

par

re·ceived
nei·ther

intro

ges·ture

if

re·course

at·tor·neys

course

par

[138]

4

as

ser

din·ing

chose

del·i·cate

ap

dec·o·ra·tors

mea·sure·ments

stayed

thor·ough

when

brought

nc

coarse

def·i·nite·ly

conj

Transcribe: No. 608

nonr

nc

yours

intro

re·made

[212]

par

con·sent year's

course

hon·o·rar·i·um

al·lot·ting

if

nc

fi·nal·ize

par

[156]

5

ser

for·tune prin·ci·pal

conj

6

mo·ti·va·tion

when

im·ple·ment·ed

mo·rale

conj

past

tech·niques

cr

[133]

7

cal·en·dars

course

fourth

Transcribe:
nine
five

lead

as

na·tion·al·ly rec·og·nized
no hyphen
after ly

nc

[144]

8

busy

course

par

as

intro

re·ac·tions

ques·tion·naire

Transcribe: Ninety

nc

90

brief

conj

sim·i·lar

year's

[158]

If a job needs to be done, the professional secretary either does the job or sees that someone else completes it. When a truly professional secretary is at work, no job—big or small—is neglected because it is "no one's specific responsibility." The secretary sees that it becomes someone's responsibility.

FUTURE ADVANCEMENT

In both positions that she had held at All-Sports Supply Company, Marie found that she was given every opportunity to demonstrate her capability in doing whatever task she was assigned and to take on additional responsibilities. Her willingness to do a job—and do it well—was evident to both Mr. Franklin and Ms. Valdez. Encouraging Marie to take on additional responsibilities not only saved their time but also helped Marie to grow on the job and to learn more about the company's operations.

Thinking of possible future advancement, Marie took advantage of the various sources that might be helpful to her. She always read the company's "house organ" (newspaper) to keep up to date about new developments in the company that could offer new opportunities for her. As the company regularly posted job openings, Marie was informed about positions for which she might qualify. She also met with Mrs. Stanley in the personnel department to discuss career paths that might be open to her.

When the opportunity for advancement did come, Marie wanted to be ready; therefore, she thought about self-improvement. In addition to maintaining the skills needed in her present position, Marie began thinking about going back to school for training in areas that would increase her chances for promotion. She obtained several college catalogs and looked into the advanced courses sponsored by the company.

Marie's career outlook was good—and it had all started because she had strived to do the very best on every job she undertook.

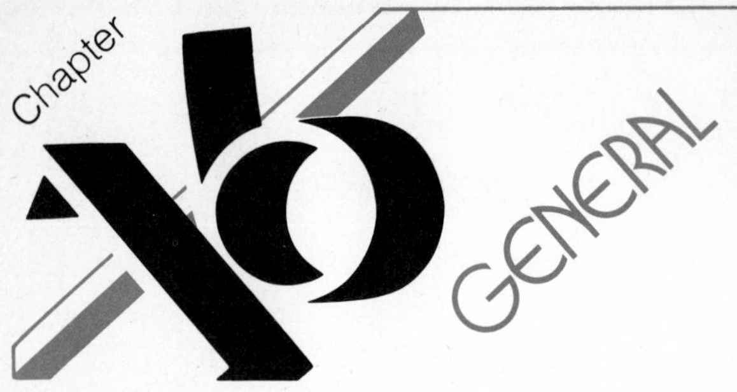

Building Transcription Skills

1 **TYPING-STYLE STUDY ● fractions and mixed numbers**

☐ **1** Spell out most fractions that stand alone. Separate the elements with a hyphen.

Only two-thirds *of the members returned their ballots.*

☐ **2** In technical writing express fractions in figures, using a diagonal to separate the elements.

2/70 3/35

☐ **3** A mixed number (a whole number and a fraction) is written in figures.

The interest rate on our loan was 8½ *percent.*

☐ **4** Spell out a mixed number that begins a sentence. Remember to hyphenate the fractional element.

Four and one-quarter *inches of rain fell yesterday.*

2 Business Vocabulary Builder

group life insurance An insurance policy covering the lives of all those in a specified group.

precipitation The amount of water resulting from rain, snow, and so on.

floodplain Level land that may be submerged by floodwaters.

Reading and Writing Practice

3

Transcribe: 100

qual·i·fy

Transcribe: one-half

when

Transcribe: $50,000

ef·fect

nc

signed

phys·i·cal

intro

ex·cel·lent

Transcribe: two-thirds

if

Transcribe: 555-6108

par

[216]

4

al·most

conj

Transcribe: 4½

and o

intro

quan·ti·ties

Transcribe: Three and one-half

intro

pre·cip·i·ta·tion

conj

dol·lars

flood·plain

intro

loss

intro

nc

ease

com·pa·ny's

sit

[194]

5

whole·sale

Transcribe: 3½

enu

1/16-inch 3/16-inch hyphenated before noun

intro

intro

par

[147]

6

Transcribe: 5½ percent

com·pute

intro

dai·ly

if

com·mer·cial

if

[134]

7

Transcribe: 14½ percent 1½ percent

as

intro

nonr

cr

[90]

Building Transcription Skills

1 PUNCTUATION PRACTICE ● exclamation point

Use an exclamation point to express strong feelings—enthusiasm, surprise, urgency, disbelief.

That's impossible! I don't believe it!

Use an exclamation point after a single word to express intense feeling.

Congratulations! We are proud of you.

2 Business Vocabulary Builder

commemorate To celebrate; to do something in honor of a special event.
variance An exception.
ordinance A law.
petition *(noun)* A formal written request.

Reading and Writing Practice

3

proud

ac·com·plish·ment

conj

past

per·son·al

com·mem·o·rate

nc

ex·cit·ing

and o

geo

if

nc

re·al

[146]

4

vari·ance

or·di·nance

Transcribe: \ Fifth Avenue

intro

sig·na·tures

20,

Transcribe: 20 percent

site

conj

pe·ti·tion

and o

shop·ping

555-8106

nc

[184]

5

plan·ning

Transcribe:
8109 62d Street

8109 62

geo

intro

first·hand

struc·ture

if

ex·ceed·ing·ly

par

[164]

6

50,

ser Transcribe:
50 percent

ev·ery day

one-stop
hyphenated
before noun

in·cred·i·ble

ser

at·tire

Transcribe: 7420 First Street

7420

10

nc

if

[115]

7

Col·lege

en·rolled

par

match

al·ways

[125]

8

to·day's

dis·sat·is·fied

ap

glow·ing

par

past

[122]

9

ap

ser

Transcribe: two

el·i·gi·ble

cast

bal·lot

nc

re·al·ly

Transcribe: one-half

nc

[142]

inter-office memorandum

To	Martha Buckingham	From	C. J. Creswell
Dept.	Inventory Control	Dept.	Personnel
Floor or Branch	33	Floor and Ext. or Branch	29
Subject	Meeting for New Employees	Date	June 2, 19--

You are invited to attend a meeting for new employees on June 15 in Room 201. The meeting will begin at 9 a.m.

You will learn about the various departments of the company and their contributions to our business. You will also meet a number of the executives of the company.

If you have any questions about our organization and its policies, you will have an opportunity to ask them at this meeting. After this meeting you will have a better picture of our organization and the products it makes.

C.J.C.

hh

Interoffice memorandum

Building Transcription Skills

1 **GRAMMAR CHECKUP ● common errors (concluded)**

Writers who are careful about their grammar never use:

try and for **try to**

no

Try and *visit us soon.*

yes

Try to *visit us soon.*

writer for **I**

no

The writer *believes this statement is true.*

yes

I *believe this statement is true.*

the reason is because for **the reason is that**

no

The reason is because *our prices are too high.*

yes

The reason is that *our prices are too high.*

2 **Business Vocabulary Builder**

defray To provide for the payment of; to pay.
commence To begin; to start.
binding *(adjective)* Imposing an obligation.
breach of contract Failure to comply with the terms of a contract.

Reading and Writing Practice

3

past

Transcribe: 2,000

na·tion·al·ly rec·og·nized no hyphen after ly

intro

mi·nor

Transcribe: 30 percent

intro

re·mained sta·ble

so·lic·it·ing

de·fray

Transcribe: $1 million

nc

intro

sum

goal

intro

first-class

pledge

[249]

4

spon·sor·ing

an·tique

ser

com·mence

nc

vil·lages

intro

Transcribe:
four 2-day

am·ple

too

nc

Don't

conj

[218]

5

intro

ad·vis·ing

yes·ter·day's

ap

signed

conj

Transcribe:
$3,000
two $100 payments

nc

par

fur·ther

breach

conj

up to date
no noun,
no hyphen

if

15

if

law·suit

as

ob·tain·ing

ex·treme·ly

par

Transcribe:
15th

[239]

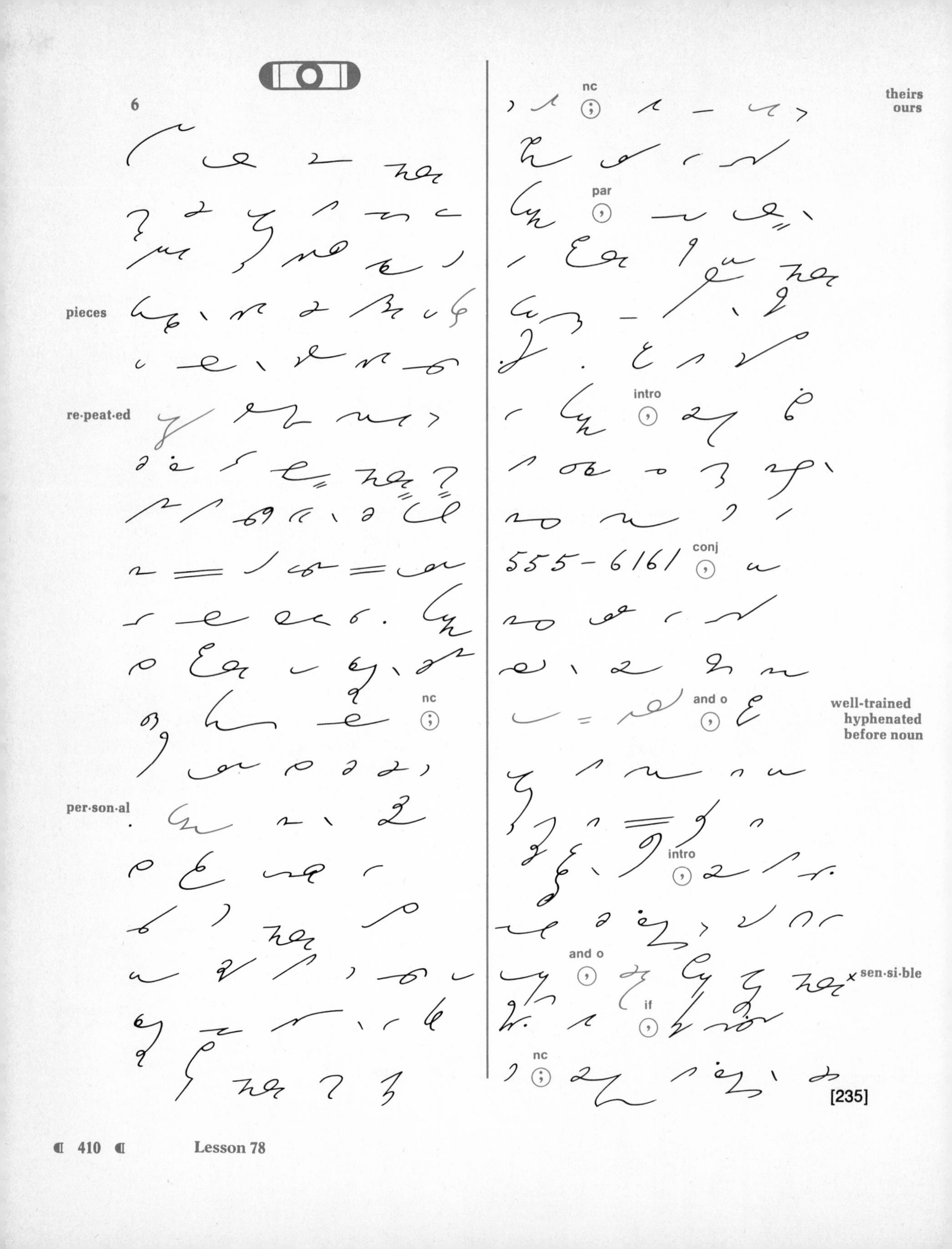

6

pieces

re·peat·ed

nc ;

per·son·al

nc ;

theirs ours

par ,

intro ,

555-6161

conj ,

and o ,

well-trained hyphenated before noun

intro ,

and o ,

sen·si·ble

if ,

nc ;

[235]

There will be times when your employer will have an important letter or report to dictate to you. Because of its importance, revisions may have to be made before a letter or report is typed in final form. You may be asked to "dash off a rough draft" for your employer to review.

Dear Mrs. Carson:

Thank you for your letter of ~~January~~ February 5 about your gas bill for the month of January. I can certainly understand you concern about the large increase in your bill as compared with the corresponding period last year.

I have checked into the matter myself, Mrs. Carsen, and I have found that the bill is actually correct. Although ~~you-have-we~~ your bill [for the month] was substantially higher than it was for January of last year, you actually used more gas. and I am sure you know that the price of gas has risen nearly 10 percent.

Thanks for your understandnig and cooperation in this mateer. If you have any further questions about your bill, I hope you will call me.

Cordially
~~Sincerely~~ yours,

When you are given such instructions, you should:

☐ **1** Type the rough draft on inexpensive manuscript paper—not letterhead paper. (Do not make a carbon copy.)

☐ **2** Double-space the material and leave wide margins so that your employer will have plenty of room for corrections and additions.

☐ **3** Strike over incorrectly typed letters and cross out wrong words if necessary (something you would never do on a final copy).

☐ **4** Submit the rough draft to your employer as soon as you take it out of the typewriter without even proofreading it (something else you would never do with a final copy).

For most dictation, your goal should be to submit for your employer's signature only letters that are mailable—with no errors of any kind. But when your employer says, "Dash off a copy," do just that!

Building Transcription Skills

1 OFFICE-STYLE DICTATION ● extensive changes

Good dictators will make only occasional changes in their dictation. Some, however, have difficulty organizing their thoughts and will make many changes. If you find that your employer makes many changes while dictating, it would be advisable to write in only one column of your notebook, using the second column for insertions or changes.

Illustration of Office-Style Dictation

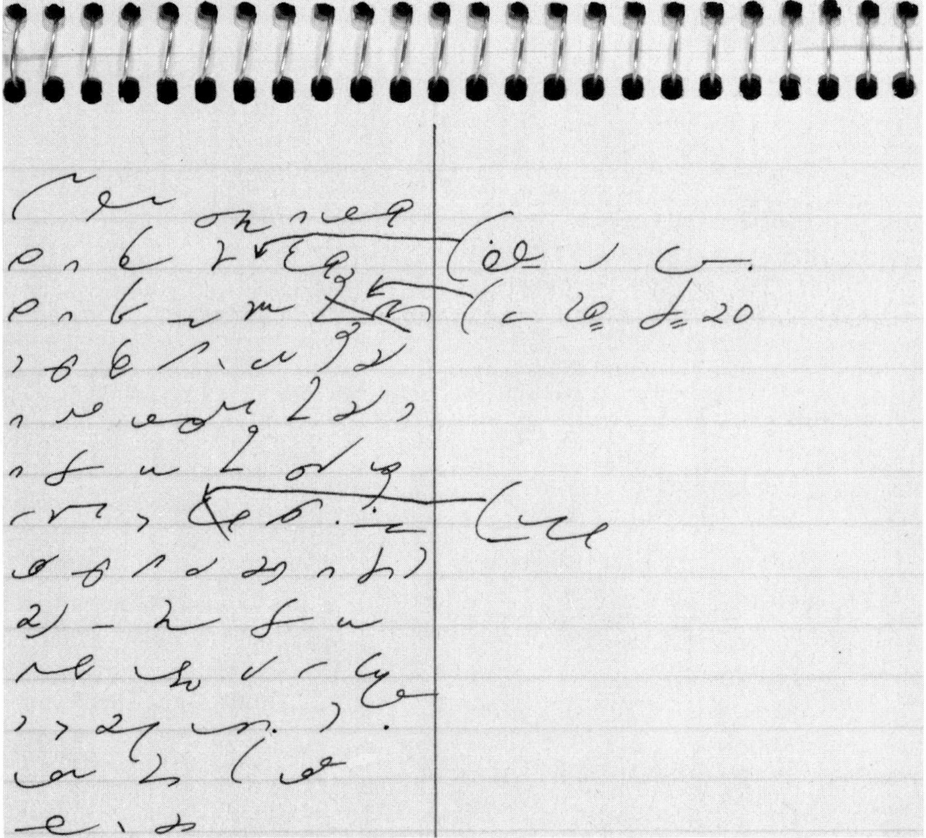

2 **minimize** To reduce or keep to a minimum.

Business Vocabulary Builder

controversy Dispute; a discussion marked by opposing views.

proposed Put forth for consideration; suggested.

Reading and Writing Practice

3

as

in·stall·ing

Transcribe: eight

and o

old-fash·ioned

intro

de·lays

nonr

pa·tient

min·i·mize

[136]

4

great con·tro·ver·sy

shop·ping

intro

busi·ness

and o

com·mer·cial

al·low·ing

Per·mit·ting

com·mis·sion·ers

[204]

5

manu·script

Transcribe: March 14

nc

ex·ceed·ing·ly

nc

wom·en

for·ward·ing

nonr

re·spon·si·ble

par

[122]

6

intro

its

896

23 nonr

geo conj

com·plete

intro

Transcribe:
nine
six

[150]

7

intro

re·ceiv·ing

intro

conj

intro

par

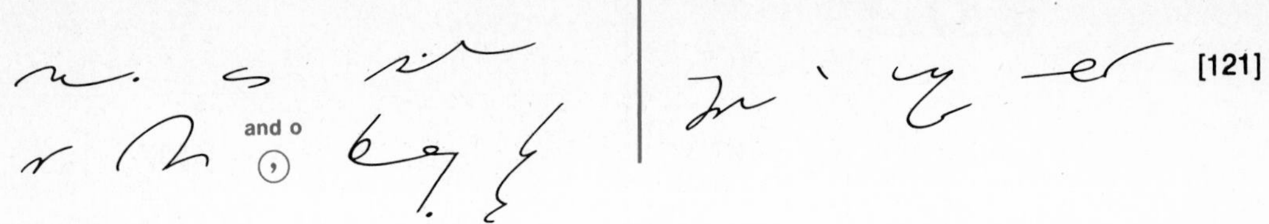

8 Transcription Quiz Supply the necessary punctuation and the missing words.

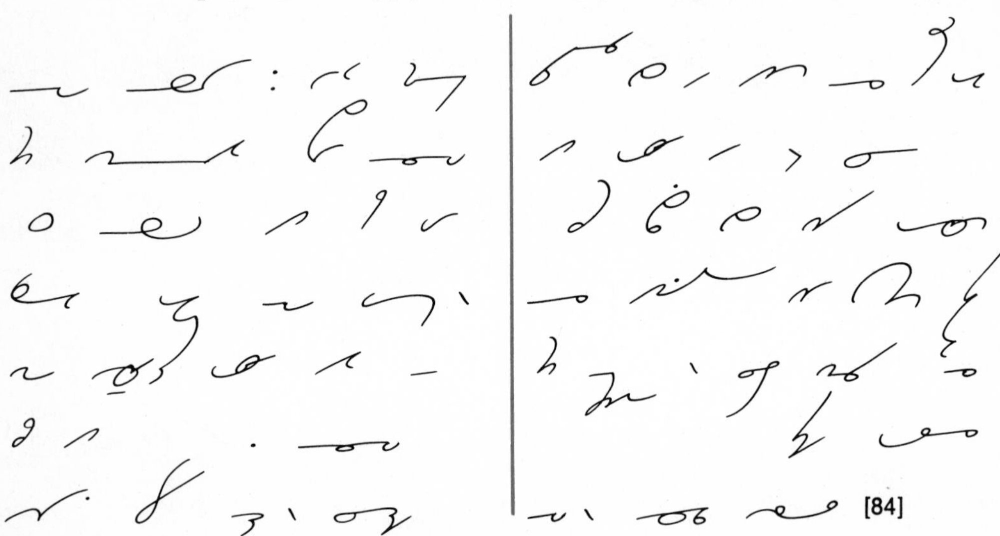

Quite often, the secretary is the only employee with whom a person outside the company deals. The company's reputation, therefore, can depend on the impression created by the secretary.

Building Transcription Skills

1 **SIMILAR-WORDS DRILL ● wear, ware**

wear To be clothed in; to have on; apparel.

I always *wear* a heavy coat in the winter.
Our store specializes in children's *wear*.

ware An article of merchandise (often used in combination with another word).

I will buy the *hardware* supplies I need.

2 **Business Vocabulary Builder**

software The entire set of programs, procedures, and related documentation associated with a computer system.

educators Teachers.

postponing Deferring; putting off to a later time.

Reading and Writing Practice

3

com·put·er

Transcribe:
5
10
20

ser

gram·mar

and o

intro

soft·ware

de·signed

par

if

ap

ar·ea

ed·u·ca·tors

[164]

4

wear·ing

cho·sen

oc·ca·sion

Transcribe:
six

if

nonr

Men's

geo

when

re·ceive

ad·vice

conj

re·com·mend

well-trained hyphenated before noun

and o

nc

[159]

5

Hard·ware

nonr

Transcribe: July 1, 1950,

1950

de·cid·ed

catch

ser

post·pon·ing

par

loy·al

intro

Transcribe: one-half

par·tic·u·lar·ly

ap·pro·pri·ate

nc

agree

[210]

6

dis·grun·tled

ilq

when

oc·ca·sion·al·ly

iq

sim·i·lar

nc

intro

enu

ours

ac·cept

week's

par

intro

ad·vise

[155]

APPENDIX

Recall Drills

JOINED WORD ENDINGS

1 -ment

2 -tion

3 -tial

4 -ly

5 -ily

6 -ful

7 -ble

8 -ther

9 -ual

10 -ure

11 -self, -selves

12 -ort

13 -tain

14 -cient, -ciency

DISJOINED WORD ENDINGS

15 -hood

16 -ward

17 -ship

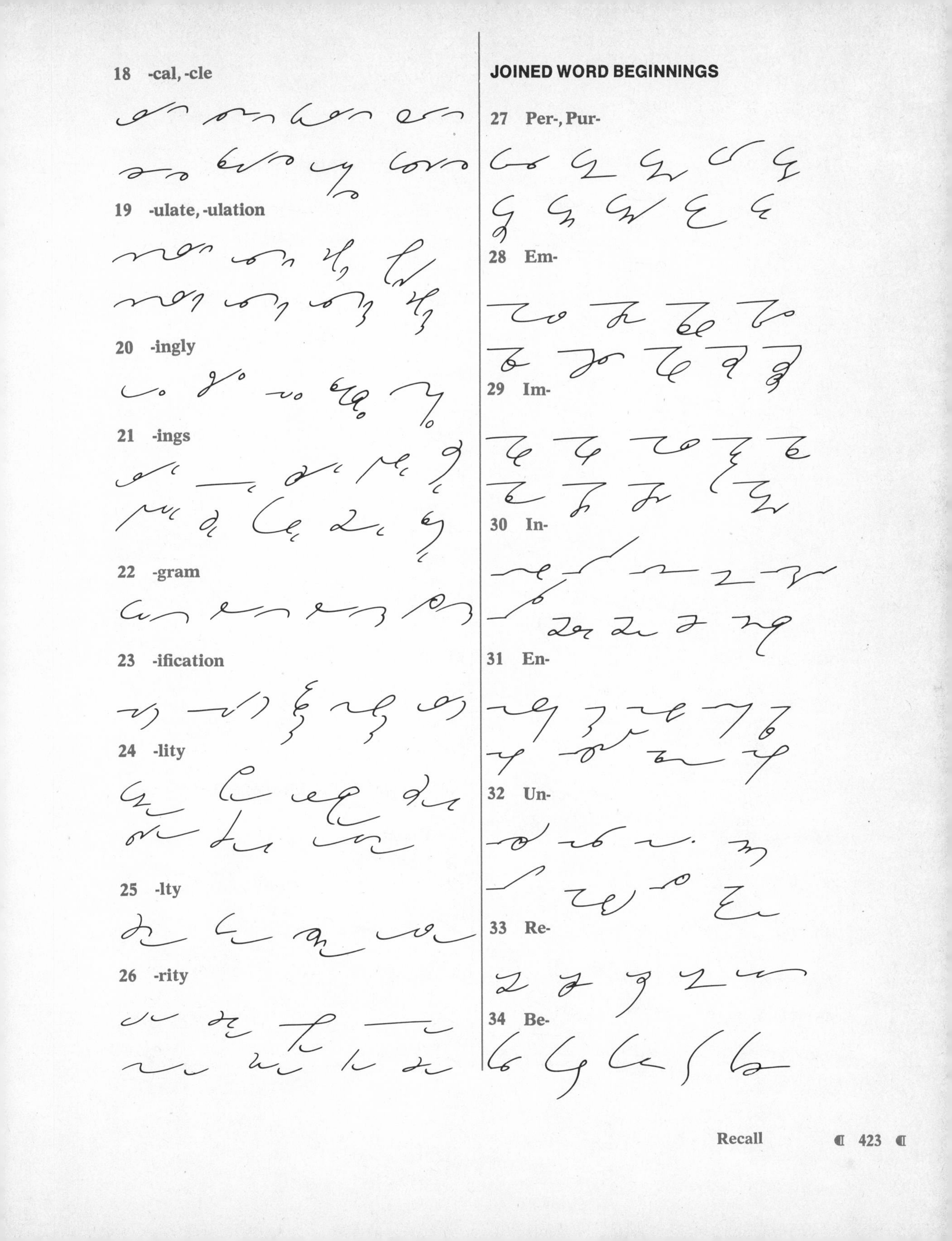

18 -cal, -cle

19 -ulate, -ulation

20 -ingly

21 -ings

22 -gram

23 -ification

24 -lity

25 -lty

26 -rity

JOINED WORD BEGINNINGS

27 Per-, Pur-

28 Em-

29 Im-

30 In-

31 En-

32 Un-

33 Re-

34 Be-

35 De-, Di-

36 Dis-, Des-

37 Mis-

38 Ex-

39 Com-

40 Con-

41 Sub-

42 Al-

43 For-, Fore-

44 Fur-

45 Tern-, Etc.

46 Ul-

DISJOINED WORD BEGINNINGS

47 Inter-, Etc.

48 Electr-, Electric

49 Super-

50 Circum-

51 Self-

52 Trans-

53 Under-

54 Over-

Addresses for Transcription

(The numbers of the following names and addresses correspond to the numbers of the supplementary letters in *College Dictation for Transcription, Series 90.*)

CHAPTER 1

Lesson 1

1 Mr. Harold Franklin, Personnel Manager, General Supply Company, 224 West Missouri Avenue, Houston, TX 77007

2 Mr. John H. Freeman, 64 Elm Street, Raleigh, NC 27602

3 Mr. Leonard James, 375 Lakewood Drive, Decatur, IL 62521

4 Mr. George Morris, 335 Commonwealth Avenue, Atlantic City, NJ 08401

5 Memorandum from John Pratt to A. J. Calvin

6 Mrs. Alice Clyde, General Manager, Baker Industries, 33 East Fourth Street, Davenport, IA 52802

Lesson 2

7 Mrs. Rhonda Oliver, Dawson Industries, 389 Commercial Avenue, Cleveland, OH 44101

8 Mrs. Teresa Smith, Twin Cities Credit Corporation, 1100 Madison Street, Minneapolis, MN 55401

9 Ms. Holly Young, Manager, Wilson and Company, 31 South Baker Road, Lexington, KY 40507

10 Memorandum from Jane Williams to Frank Brown

11 Ms. Kathy Elliot, 575 Rogers Lane, Billings, MT 59101

12 Mrs. L. R. Tate, Fifth Street Art Institute, 655 Fifth Street, Milwaukee, WI 53202

Lesson 3

13 Mr. Dean Phillips, Marketing Director, National Development Corporation, 22 East Avenue, Baltimore, MD 21233

14 Memorandum from Fred Roberts to John Foster

15 Memorandum from George Farmer to A. L. Franks

16 Memorandum from James Sherman to The Staff

17 Memorandum from Bill Rogers to Lois Layton

18 Memorandum from May Green to The Staff

Lesson 4

19 Mr. Martin Taylor, Maryland State Employment Service, 64 Crayton Avenue, Baltimore, MD 21233

20 Mr. John Samuels, Burns and Lloyd Enterprises, 538 North Riverview Drive, St. Louis, MO 63155

21 Mr. John R. Taylor, Western School District, 500 Burlington Avenue, Los Angeles, CA 90052

22 Memorandum from Allen Ames to Edward Farley

23 Mr. Raymond Foster, 2586 North State Street, Boston, MA 02109

24 Mr. T. R. Smith, Franklin Publishers, 15 Arthur Road, Easton, MD 21601

Lesson 5

25 Mr. Samuel Elton, International Airlines, 36 Federal Heights, Albuquerque, NM 87101

26 Mr. Don Strong, State College of Idaho, 37 North Shoshone Avenue, Boise, ID 96813

27 Memorandum from Betty Parsons to Allen Frost

28 Ms. Diane Mason, Bluffdale Textiles, Inc., 555 East Allen Street, Davenport, IA 52802

29 Memorandum from Ann Brown to Stan Walker

30 Memorandum from Sharon Jones to The Staff

CHAPTER 2

Lesson 6

31 Memorandum from Dorothy Marks to The Staff

32 Memorandum from Sue Phillips to William Miller

33 Memorandum from T. J. Peterson to The Staff

34 Miss Kathleen Madison, Northwest Engineering Corporation, 467 Jackson Road, Tacoma, WA 98402

35 Memorandum from Edith Davis to George Baker

36 Mr. Gary Roberts, Roberts Manufacturing Company, 762 Northeast Division Street, Portland, OR 97208

Lesson 7

37 Mr. John T. Drake, 38 East Wilshire Boulevard, Chicago, IL 60607

38 Memorandum from T. L. Stockton to Jordan Williams

39 Mr. James C. Church, The Clarkson Corporation, 628 North Walsh Avenue, Orlando, FL 32802

40 Memorandum from Ann Moore to Frank Blair

41 Memorandum from Larry Miller to John Morton

42 Memorandum from Rosa Lopez to Allen Fields

Lesson 8

43 Miss Roberta Fitzgerald, 311 Worth Street, Staten Island, NY 10310

44 Memorandum from Don Anderson to All Employees

45 Mr. Victor Sanchez, 34 East Morris Avenue, Atlanta, GA 30334

46 Memorandum from Roger Best to Brenda Miller

47 Mrs. Ann Casey, Marketing Director, Northrup Media Center, 695 Fifth Avenue, Richmond, VA 23219

48 Memorandum from Harry Gordon to The Staff

Lesson 9

49 Mr. Edward Blair, 83 North 35 Place, Birmingham, AL 35203

50 Memorandum from Mary King to All Employees

51 Memorandum from J. R. Kent to Charles Mann

52 Memorandum from Jane Patton to The Staff

53 Mr. Frederick Davis, Personnel Manager, Williams Manufacturing Company, 459 East Cullimore Street, Atlanta, GA 30304

54 Memorandum from Lee Davis to Leonard James

Lesson 10

55 Mr. Thomas R. Marks, Great Lakes Electronics, 16 Washoe Drive, Detroit, MI 48102

56 Memorandum from Doris Johnson to The Staff

57 Mr. Steven Bradley, Bradley Consultants, Inc., 350 South Clarkston Street, Cleveland, OH 44101

58 Mr. Allan Bradford, 389 North Adams Avenue, Denver, CO 80202

59 Memorandum from Joan Harrington to John Church

60 Mr. Robert Blair, United Manufacturers, 818 North Phillips Boulevard, Birmingham, AL 35203

CHAPTER 3

Lesson 11

61 Ms. Jean Garcia, State Environmental Commission, 721 West Fifth Avenue, Portland, OR 97208

62 Mr. Neal Maxwell, Savannah Oil Company, 682 East 48 Street, Savannah, GA 31401

63 Memorandum from Jill Smith to All Store Managers

64 Miss Patricia Watson, 671 Ridge Boulevard, Farmington, IL 61531

65 Miss Rachel Roberts, President, City Commission, 1200 Main Street, Lexington, KY 40507

66 Resident, 934 North Georgia Avenue, Jacksonville, FL 32201

Lesson 12

67 Mr. Frank Willis, President, Baker Enterprises, 164 East Gardenia Circle, Gary, IN 46401

68 Mr. Manuel Lopez, 1238 South Davis Street, Des Moines, IA 50318

69 Mr. Lawrence Samuels, Samuels Associates, 1224 Powell Boulevard, Madison, WI 53703

70 Mrs. Doris Pine, Wilson's Auto Parts, 350 Brookside Avenue, Manchester, NH 13101

71 Mr. Benson Ellsburg, Vice President, Energy Research Associates, 165 East Pioneer Way, Billings, MT 59101

72 Mr. Christopher Conlan, 325 Camden Road, Silver City, NM 88061

Lesson 13

73 Ms. Betty Allen, Western State College, 48 Johnston Circle, Palo Alto, CA 94304

74 Mr. Max Lane, Lane Consultants, Inc., 3285 South Fourth Avenue, Covington, KY 41011

75 Mr. D. L. Martin, Energy Research Commission, 685 La Mesa Drive, Fort Madison, IA 52627

76 Memorandum from Marie Yates to Ellen Brown

77 Mrs. Adrian Sparks, 95 Mustang Drive, Reno, NV 89501

78 Resident, 750 Bard Avenue, Wichita Falls, TX 76301

Lesson 14

79 Memorandum from George Fox to Sandra Washington

80 Mr. Ralph Ward, Webster Industries, 141 North Canyon Road, Phoenix, AZ 85026

81 Mrs. Patricia Yates, 87 Ponderosa Way, Beaver Falls, NY 13305

82 Mr. Jared Strong, State Conservation Commission, 905 Fulton Street, Greenwich, CT 03860

83 Mrs. Dolores Cunningham, 375 North Grovecrest, Lincoln, NB 68501

84 Resident, 1475 West Hawthorne Boulevard, Wilmington, DE 19899

Lesson 15

85 Miss Elaine Edwards, 750 Northeast Avenue, Evanston, IL 60203

86 Mr. Milton Fraser, Division of Wildlife Resources, 1475 Hawthorne Boulevard, Charleston, WV 25303

87 Mr. Ronald Lee, Chairman, East Valley Environmental Committee, 963 Hatch Street, Albany, GA 31702

88 Ms. Janice Parker, 475 Grove Avenue, Wilmington, DE 19899

89 Manning Institute of Technology, 728 Sixth Avenue, Decatur, IL 62521

90 Mr. Arthur L. Morgan, 3869 South Main, Kansas City, MO 64109

CHAPTER 4

Lesson 16

91 Mr. Gordon R. Jones, Lexington Agency, 400 South Main Street, Reno, NV 89046

92 Ms. Ruth C. Chester, 438 Fifth Avenue, Cleveland, OH 44119

93 Memorandum from Ellen Agronski to Dan White

94 Mr. Milton R. Harrington, 95 West Temple Street, Independence, MO 64050

95 Ms. Ruth Brown, 1383 Sycamore Place, Honolulu, HI 96813

96 Ms. Mary R. Franklin, 372 North Meridian Road, New Bedford, MA 02741

Lesson 17

97 Mr. Carl E. Lane, 87 West Oak Hills Boulevard, Reno, NV 89501

98 Ms. Phyllis Best, 1428 North Teton Drive, Boise, ID 96813

99 Mr. Harold R. Benson, 3852 Bayou Boulevard, St. Petersburg, FL 33706

100 Ms. Geraldine Elton, 502 Darby Circle, Lake Charles, LA 70601

101 Resident, 621 Orchard Drive, Spokane, WA 99210

102 Mrs. Alice Farmer, 1841 Redwood Highway, San Antonio, TX 78206

Lesson 18

103 Miss Janet Young, American Sales and Leasing, 378 Southeast Blakely Street, Lincoln, NE 68501

104 Mr. Carl Edwards, Madison Auto Center, 59 West Mill Creek Circle, Baton Rouge, LA 60821

105 Mrs. Betty Boyle, Principal, East Side High School, 21 East Main Street, Tampa, FL 33612

106 Memorandum from Donna Mason to All Employees

107 Mr. John R. Day, 51 Harbor Drive, Columbus, OH 43227

108 Ms. Ellen Sanders, 356 North Broadway, Houston, TX 77023

Lesson 19

109 Mr. Charles C. Bennett, Manager, Western Leasing Company, 416 East University Avenue, Wichita, KS 67202

110 Mr. David Taylor, 351 Cascade Boulevard, Portland, ME 04101

111 Mr. L. R. West, Eastern Paint Shop, 3725 East Baker Street, Milwaukee, WI 53202

112 Memorandum from Jane Street to The Staff

113 Memorandum from R. D. French to The Staff

114 Mr. Dean Franklin, 87 South Lincoln Road, Little Rock, AR 72114

Lesson 20

115 Miss Debra Summers, Manager, King Auto Center, 120 East Main Street, Minneapolis, MN 55401

116 Mr. Jerome Frank, 1005 Princess Avenue, Springfield, MO 65801

117 Mr. Lawrence T. Lee, 521 South Westminster Avenue, Bridgeport, CT 06602

118 Mr. A. L. Hailey, Hailey's Auto Agency, 200 Elm Street, Burlington, IA 52601

119 Mr. James Ellis, 819 North Crystal Avenue, Medford, MA 02155

120 Mr. William Evans, 2725 Northeast Glendale Drive, Bangor, ME 04401

CHAPTER 5

Lesson 21

121 Rocky Mountain Publishing Company, 274 Chase Drive, Pueblo, CO 81001

122 Ms. Betty C. Johnson, 309 Elk Drive, Jacksonville, FL 32201

123 Mr. Albert Lyon, 46 East Fourth Avenue, Newport, KY 41071

124 Mr. W. L. Baldwin, President, Chamber of Commerce, 1010 Berkeley Street, Springfield, OH 45501

125 Mr. George L. Young, 391 East Sixth Street, Rapid City, SD 57701

126 Miss Helen Lee, 875 Cove Point Drive, Seattle, WA 98199

Lesson 22

127 Ms. Bertha Morton, National Forum, 1418 First Avenue, New York, NY 10016

128 Dr. Joseph S. Garcia, 162 South Lexington Avenue, Independence, MO 64050

129 Mr. Gerald Madison, Madison Publications, Inc., 297 James Drive, Ogden, UT 84001

130 Mr. Stanley Green, East Shore Development Company, 1200 Shore Road, Atlantic City, NJ 08401

131 Ms. Theresa Michaels, 486 Sunnyside Avenue, Ashland, PA 17921

132 Mr. Donald R. Davis, Managing Editor, The Morning Register, 790 South Greenwood Drive, Flint, MI 48502

Lesson 23

133 Mrs. Roberta Sweet, Financial Publications Company, 1717 Southwest 58 Street, Brattleboro, VT 05301

134 Mr. Clifton E. Davis, Daily Tribune, 585 Fashion Place, Wilmington, DE 19899

135 Mr. Thomas R. Taylor, The Financial Digest, 135 South Manhattan Drive, Austin, TX 78710

136 Mr. Albert Collins, Editor in Chief, Pacific Press, 872 King Road, Eugene, OR 97401

137 Educators' Publishers, Inc., 921 South Allen Park Drive, Roanoke, VA 24001

138 Mrs. Ellen Green, 728 South Third Avenue, Ashland, ME 04732

Lesson 24

139 Mrs. Patricia Smith, Personnel Director, Associated Publishers, 728 South Chicago Street, Greenwich, CT 03860

140 Mr. James Williams, General Company, Inc., 725 Grant Street, Chicago, IL 60607

141 Mrs. Denise Tate, 703 East 23 Street, Des Moines, IA 50318

142 Memorandum from James Allen to Albert Cook

143 Miss Shirley Singer, 385 Ironwood Drive, Woodstock, VT 05091

144 Ms. Sharon Berger, 838 Wilson Lane, South Bend, IN 46624

Lesson 25

145 Mrs. Colleen Bell, Dana Press, 247 North Hartford Avenue, Little Rock, AR 72114

146 Mr. Edward R. Brown, Advertising Manager, Daily News, 905 East Freeman Street, Orlando, FL 32802

147 Miss Barbara Edwards, Medford Register, 482 South Adams Street, Medford, MA 02155

148 Ms. Esther Drake, 602 Southwest Quincy, Pensacola, FL 35202

149 Mr. Thomas L. Tate, 2552 Michigan Avenue, Greenville, NC 27834

150 Miss Tanya Lee, 3232 Sunset Highway, Sioux Falls, SD 57101

CHAPTER 6

Lesson 26

151 Mrs. Lisa Fielding, 901 Cherry Lane, Reading, PA 19607

152 Miss Melissa Mason, Western Advertisers, 426 Sandhill Road, Los Angeles, CA 90052

153 Mrs. Stella Oaks, 387 Woodland Drive, Bennington, NE 68007

154 Memorandum from Thomas Adamson to Juanita Sanchez

155 Memorandum from Marcia Franklin to The Staff

156 Memorandum from Martin Cunningham to The Staff

Lesson 27

157 Miss Judy Green, Readers' Press, 870 Browning Boulevard, Knoxville, TN 37901

158 Miss Eileen Bates, 629 West Olive Street, Philadelphia, PA 19104

159 Dr. Jane L. White, Johnson Institute, 415 Sixth Avenue Plaza, Kansas City, MO 64109

160 Mr. Martin Smith, Clayton Industries, 861 Highland Drive, Green Bay, WI 54305

161 Memorandum from Ray Mason to The Staff

162 Mr. Carl A. Reed, 509 State Street, Albany, NY 12225

Lesson 28

163 Mr. Roger White, Inland Industries Corporation, 914 Post Street, Reno, NV 89501

164 Mr. Allen Gates, Lexington College, 215 Riverside Drive, Lexington, VA 24450

165 Ms. Betty Jackson, Jennings Telephone Systems, Inc., 1127 Northeast 42 Street, Roanoke, VA 24001

166 Mr. John Bridge, 37 Exchange Place, Seattle, WA 98101

167 Mrs. Arlene Amos, 962 Grand Avenue, Easton, MD 21601

168 Mr. Gordon T. Strong, Strong Construction Company, 1100 Sunrise Boulevard, Birmingham, AL 35214

Lesson 29

169 Madison Paging Systems Corporation, 131 East Main Street, Memphis, TN 38101

170 Ms. Dorothy Slater, National Telephone Systems, Inc., 1114 McArthur Avenue, St. Petersburg, FL 33706

171 Mr. Phillip R. Barnes, 404 South Roberts Street, Miami, FL 33101

172 Mrs. Rose Lake, 309 Evanston Street, Lima, OH 45801

173 Mr. Richard Moore, Suburban Telephone Company, 576 East Temple Street, Providence, RI 02904

174 Mrs. Stacy Overmeyer, Research Consultants, Inc., 194 East Truman Road, Flint, MI 48502

Lesson 30

175 Ms. Edith White, Morris and Jackson Corporation, 460 Williams Avenue, Norman, OK 73069

176 Mrs. Charlene Lopez, Southern Telephone Company, 104 Industrial Road, Miami, FL 33101

177 Mr. Dan Stern, 729 East Hollow Drive, Fairfax, AL 36854

178 Mrs. Joan Smith, 1492 Aspen Hills Drive, Durham, NC 27701

179 Miss Cynthia Adams, Personnel Manager, Sunrise Publications, 289 Douglas Drive, Beaumont, TX 77704

180 Mrs. Fay Benson, 924 Victory Road, Denver, CO 80202

CHAPTER 7

Lesson 31

181 Mrs. Alice Brown, Green Acres Landscaping Service, 402 East State Street, Lorain, OH 44052

182 Mr. Ralph R. Stern, 347 West 23 Street, 186 Raleigh, NC 27602

183 Ms. Emily Roberts, Editor in Chief, J & J Publications, 81 South Regency Street, Decatur, IL 62521

184 Mr. Christopher Jackson, 81 Mill Meadow Road, Trenton, NJ 08608

185 Mrs. Elizabeth Roberts, 2387 Emerson Terrace, Staten Island, NY 10314

186 Mr. Henry L. Powers, 872 King Road, Troy, NY 12180

Lesson 32

187 Mr. Harvey Lang, Allen Brothers, 952 North Colfax Avenue, Aurora, IL 60507

188 Memorandum from Barbara P. Tate to Tom Watson

189 Mr. Allen Miller, 183 North Fullerton, Huntsville, AL 34804

190 Southland Press, 385 Thornbush Road, Las Cruces, NM 88001

191 Mr. Donald Yates, 85 West Rochester Boulevard, Wichita Falls, TX 76301

192 Resident, 503 Oak Tree Terrace, Marion, IL 62959

Lesson 33

193 Mr. James R. Smith, Denver Community College, 529 West 14 Street, Denver, CO 80202

194 Mrs. Jennifer Boyd, Manager, World of Lights, Inc., 385 Spring Creek Drive, New Bedford, MA 02741

195 Miss Anna Evans, 251 West Thompson Avenue, Houston, TX 77002

196 Miss Susan Taylor, 7154 Ridgewood Drive, Mobile, AL 36601

197 Mrs. Marlene Yates, 351 Christopher Street, New York, NY 10005

198 Mr. Lewis Bates, 351 Harvard Drive, Atlanta, GA 30310

Lesson 34

199 Mr. J. B. Harrington, 359 East Sixth Street, Falmouth, MA 02540

200 Mr. Gordon R. Stern, 593 Queens Road, Providence, RI 02904

201 Mr. Donald P. Arnold, 34 Freeport Street, Memphis, TN 38101

202 Mr. Ralph E. Tracy, Marketing Director, Troy Electric Company, 736 Douglas Avenue, Troy, NY 12180

203 Mr. Harley Stevens, 350 East Gravely Lane, Pittsburgh, PA 15222

204 Ms. Kathleen Jackson, 535 North Stockton Avenue, Kansas City, MO 64108

Lesson 35

205 Mr. Martin Fraser, Modern Yard Enterprises, 532 Southwest 82 Place, Westport, CT 06880

206 Mr. Benjamin T. Norris, 525 Valentine Avenue, Rahway, NJ 07065

207 Mrs. Linda P. Lloyd, Stereos Unlimited, 53 Grand Forks Avenue, Scranton, PA 18503

208 Mr. Michael Jefferson, 35 East Fosbury Lane, Raleigh, NC 27602

209 Resident, 251 South Herron Street, Macon, GA 31201

210 Mr. Gary Lee, Kingsport Roofing Company, 333 Blue Lake Road, Kingsport, TN 37662

CHAPTER 8

Lesson 36

211 Dr. Claudia Moore, Eastern School of Culinary Arts, 3525 South Montoya Road, Washington, DC 20027

212 Ms. Denise White, Manager, National Department Store, 515 Norfolk Drive, Camden, NJ 08101

213 Miss Aida Rodriguez, Consumer Information Agency, 515 Lenox Boulevard, Oklahoma City, OK 73100

214 Mr. Richard Olson, P.O. Box 107, Manchester, NH 03101

215 Mr. Steven S. Nelson, 853 East Brasher Street, Helena, MT 59601

216 Mr. Martin Tracy, Fairview Diner, 964 South Pawnee Avenue, Fairview, NM 87532

Lesson 37

217 Mr. Matthew Chan, Personnel Manager, Superior Food Markets, 660 East Summerville Highway, Elmira, NY 14901

218 Dr. George L. Washington, Southern State College, 402 East Elm Drive, Milwaukee, WI 53202

219 Miss Sharon Green, Package Designers, Inc., 222 Rebel Lane, Hampton, VA 23369

220 Miss Sandra Edwards, 372 Ridgecrest Drive, Grand Forks, ND 58201

221 Ms. Kathleen Mason, Mason's Cafe, 59 Paris Avenue, Corpus Christi, TX 78403

222 Mr. Donald I. Trent, 936 Mile High Road, Denver, CO 80202

Lesson 38

223 Mrs. Rose Smith, 370 Baldwin Avenue, Bethlehem, PA 18016

224 Dawson Press, 48 North Charleston Street, Pawtucket, RI 02860

225 Ms. Lorraine Cunningham, Ft. Myers Press, 770 Hidden Valley Drive, Ft. Myers, FL 33902

226 Mr. Roy Mason, 353 Masonic Way, Dover, DE 19901

227 Ms. Denise White, Manager, National Department Store, 515 Norfolk Drive, Camden, NJ 03101

228 Gerald Gold, Esq., Attorney-At-Law, 580 North Newport Road, St. Paul, MN 55101

Lesson 39

229 Miss Stacy Franklin, 3358 Grovecrest Drive, Wenatchee, WA 98801

230 Mrs. Lori Brown, Director of Public Relations, Farmers' Cooperative, 353 Frost Street, Des Moines, IA 50318

231 Mr. Larry Sanders, 35 Justice Avenue, Salt Lake City, UT 84101

232 Mr. Harvey R. Simmons, 354 Windward Street, Lincoln, NE 68501

233 Mr. Fred Morgan, 691 Garfield Avenue, Hamilton, OH 45012

234 Mr. John Stone, 36 Skyview Drive, Kingsport, TN 37662

Lesson 40

235 Mr. Michael J. Trent, Ocean City Cannery, 990 Bay Harbor, Ocean City, WA 98569

236 Mrs. Cynthia Nettles, 853 North Cumberland Road, Lancaster, KS 66041

237 Mr. Dean Taylor, King Tractor Company, 63 Dover Street, Albuquerque, NM 87101

238 Mrs. Joyce Royal, 95 Victory Road, Ashley, ND 58413

239 Mr. Marc Mason, Tulsa Insurance Company, 802 Route 23, Tulsa, OK 74101

240 Mr. Charles S. Lee, 90 North Mayberry Lane, Springfield, IA 52336

CHAPTER 9

Lesson 41

241 Ms. Sally Brown, 1221 Avenue B, Reading, PA 19603

242 Mr. Kenneth Larson, Second National Bank, 602 Wilson Drive, Seattle, WA 98112

243 Professor Raymond O'Brien, State College, 1250 Main Street, Portland, OR 97520

244 Mrs. Margaret Johnson, 5340 West 49 Avenue, Denver, CO 80202

245 Miss Janet West, 525 East Grant Street, Temple, OK 73568

246 Ms. Sheryl Best, 122 Marion Lane, Williamstown, NJ 08094

Lesson 42

247 Mr. Kelley Smith, President, Smith and Company, 105 Twin Oaks Drive, Joliet, IL 60435

248 Ms. Marilyn Jason, 107 Novak Street, Mosinee, WI 54455

249 Mr. John L. Martin, Mutual Funding Corporation, 2111 Jefferson Avenue, Tacoma, WA 98402

250 Miss Mary T. Miller, 915 Sixth Avenue, Andover, MA 01810

251 Mr. John Davis, Madison Electronics, Inc., 3868 Steele Avenue, Albany, LA 70711

252 Mrs. Wanda Peters, Purchasing Agent, Stockton Department Store, 2407 Greenbay Drive, El Toro, CA 92630

Lesson 43

253 Mr. Glen Long, 1238 Oak Knoll Road, Barrington, IL 60010

254 Mr. Earl King, 782 East Hudson Avenue, San Jose, CA 95123

255 Memorandum from James Tate to W. F. Keith

256 Ms. Barbara Lee, 515 Pine Street, Iowa City, IA 52240

257 Mrs. Rose Edison, 2841 North Columbus, Tucson, AZ 85718

258 Mr. Harry Gates, 5310 Scofield Road, Springfield, MT 59082

Lesson 44

259 Mr. Edward Williams, 122 South Clarkson Street, San Diego, CA 92110

260 Mr. Edward Williams, 122 South Clarkson Street, San Diego, CA 92110

261 Mr. Peter Jackson, 855 Iris Avenue, Boulder, CO 80302

262 Mr. Walter Gates, 2100 South Third Avenue, Great Falls, MT 59401

263 Great Falls State Bank, 131 First Street, Great Falls, MT 59401

264 Resident, 1337 Oak Street, Springfield, MI 48205

Lesson 45

265 Mr. Andrew Simms, 2011 Jefferson Drive, Arlington, VA 22202

266 Mr. Scott Washington, 314 Howard Street, Midway, WI 54301

267 Mr. Nick Ray, 408 West Avenue, Columbus, NE 68601

268 Miss Virginia Harris, 315 Mountain View Lane, Portland, OR 97208

269 Mr. Wayne Bates, 1301 West Weldon Avenue, Austin, TX 78710

270 Mr. Adam Byers, 52 Pine Street, Pueblo, CO 81009

CHAPTER 10

Lesson 46

271 Mr. Sean Dix, Central Credit Association, 482 West 26 Street, Chicago, IL 60607

272 Mr. Michael Quinn, First National Bank, 217 North Fifth Avenue, Toledo, OH 45387

273 Mr. Frank A. Smith, 217 Independence Street, Dover, DE 19901

274 Mr. Ray Burton, Wheeler Publishing Company, 601 Walnut Avenue, Clearwater, FL 33515

275 Lincoln Production Company, 1215 Rose Street, Lincoln, NE 68501

276 Mr. Michael V. Thomas, East Side Savings and Loan Association, 118 Williams Street, Atlanta, GA 30304

Lesson 47

277 Mr. Gary Mathis, 31 Maiden Lane, Miami, FL 33175

278 Mr. Donald McCoy, 470 Monroe Street, Dallas, TX 75233

279 Miss Roberta Marsh, Credit Manager, Ray's Department Store, 60 Park Lane, Rapid City, SD 57701

280 Mrs. Donna Morris, 781 Clinton Avenue, Buffalo, NY 14240

281 Mrs. Wilma Thomas, 43 East Main Street, Central Point, OR 97501

282 Mr. Robert W. Smith, National Credit Service, 421 Pine Street, Providence, RI 02932

Lesson 48

283 Mr. Lawrence Dawson, 16 Peachtree Street, Atlanta, GA 30324

284 Mr. Raymond Mason, 613 Garden Avenue, Concord, NH 03301

285 Memorandum from Fred Smith to The Staff

286 Miss Suzanne Evans, 15 Main Street, St. Louis, MO 63146

287 Mr. Roy Edwards, 106 West Spruce, Ann Arbor, MI 48106

288 Mrs. Marla Gray, 1210 Court Avenue, Durham, NC 27701

Lesson 49

289 United Bank, 18 Dover Road, Baltimore, MD 21202

290 Mrs. Dorothy P. Morgan, Eastern National Bank, 118 Fir Street, Troy, NY 12180

291 Mr. Maxwell Gates, Boston Credit Bureau, 311 Hartford Avenue, Boston, MA 02109

292 Mr. Curtis Peterson, 415 Fairfield Avenue, Stockton, CA 95204

293 Mr. Carl B. Smith, 210 Spruce Street, Laramie, WY 82070

294 Memorandum from Mildred O'Connor to Robert Dennis

Lesson 50

295 Mr. Harold Worth, Mutual Bank of Cleveland, 118 Vermont Avenue, Cleveland, OH 44101

296 Ms. Joan White, Central Savings and Loan Association, 3112 East 16 Avenue, Aurora, CO 80010

297 Memorandum from M. C. Pryor to J. D. Norris

298 Resident, 18 Battery Place, Orangeburg, NY 10962

299 Miss Ada Mendez, Ace Furniture Company, P.O. Box 367, Detroit, MI 48233

300 Mr. Gregory Mason, 371 East Street, Cincinnati, OH 45227

CHAPTER 11

Lesson 51

301 Jennings Associates, 1100 Madison Lane, Burlington, VT 05401

302 Mr. Donald Davis, 64 Ward Street, Medford, NY 11763

303 Mrs. Helen Yates, Yates Associates, Inc., 13 Jefferson Drive, Modesto, CA 95350

304 Mr. George Dennis, 1224 Winchester Avenue, Allendale, NY 07401

305 Mr. Stephen Taylor, 747 Highland Drive, Woodburn, KY 42170

306 Mr. Martin Yale, Sports Clothes Manufacturing Company, 517 Oak Street, Stockton, CA 95204

Lesson 52

307 Mr. Robert T. Rogers, Keane Publishing Company, 916 King Avenue, Payne, OH 45880

308 Mr. Cecil Harris, 1041 Winchester Terrace, Omaha, NE 68108

309 Ms. Pamela Bates, 1124 West Eighth, Oakdale, LA 51560

310 Mrs. Edith Washington, 57 Oak Street, Madison, WI 53703

311 Memorandum from Jane White to David Jones

312 Professor Linda T. Mason, State College, 104 Campus Row, Biloxi, MS 39530

Lesson 53

313 Mr. Robert Morgan, 887 East Main, Concord, MA 01742

314 Mr. Ronald West, West's Emporium, 334 Harrison Road, Erie, PA 16501

315 Ms. Pamela Malone, President, National Philatelic Society, 200 K Street, Washington, DC 20013

316 Mrs. Estelle Lopez, 311 Washington Lane, Akron, OH 44309

317 Mr. Hugh Wilson, 2700 Falcon Avenue, Shreveport, LA 71102

318 Professor Matthew Chang, State College, 414 Lake Drive, Lincoln, NE 68501

Lesson 54

319 Mr. Paul Johnson, Johnson Luggage and Gift Shop, 262 West Clark Street, Boise, ID 83707

320 Mr. Richard Miles, P.O. Box 333, Anchorage, AK 99502

321 Mr. William Tate, Seattle Insurance Company, 300 East Pine Terrace, Seattle, WA 98101

322 Mr. Gerald B. Lee, Court Manufacturing Company, 43 Court Street, Columbia, SC 29201

323 Ms. Janet Morton, 3458 South Bend Street, Topeka, KS 66603

324 Memorandum from Jason Brown to All Department Heads

Lesson 55

325 Miss Francine Pace, Curtis Printing Corporation, 1815 Chester Avenue, Greensboro, NC 27420

326 Mr. Parker Woods, President, Parker Woods Fashions, 2390 West Grape Street, Spokane, WA 99210

327 Mr. Rodney Miller, 988 Wilson Way, Toledo, OH 43601

328 Memorandum from Ray Conway to Georgia Johnson

329 Mrs. Jeanne Kelley, 260 Walker Avenue, Arrington, TN 37014

330 Ms. Annette Price, 10 Orchid Lane, Waikiki, HI 96815

CHAPTER 12

Lesson 56

331 Mr. Thomas Lyons, Alumni Association, Bennington College, 237 West Burnside, Portland, OR 97208

332 Eastern State College, 275 East Main Avenue, Hamilton, OH 45012

333 Gardner Travel Agency, 334 West Madison Street, Boise, ID 83707

334 Mr. Joseph Williams, 560 Spruce Street, Green Bay, WI 54301

335 Miss Judy Washington, Swanson Publishing Company, 520 Cedar Street, Miami, FL 33101

336 Memorandum from James Cunningham to The Staff

Lesson 57

337 Atlas Travel Service, 320 East Seventh Avenue, Lincoln, NE 68501

338 Mr. Mark Taylor, Manager, Animal Kingdom, 27 Wildlife Road, Reedsport, OR 97467

339 Mr. Anthony Tatum, Tatum Travel Agency, 447 Forest Road, Cheyenne, WY 82001

340 Mr. Anthony Bronson, 140 Nutley Drive, Springfield, MA 01101

341 The Bayshore Real Estate Company, 26 Ocean Drive, Tampa, FL 33602

342 Memorandum from James Farmer to All Employees

Lesson 58

343 Miss Nora Moses, Suburban Bus Company, 22 West 11 Avenue, Portland, OR 97208

344 Lexington Motels, Inc., 23 Broadway, Dallas, TX 75221

345 Mr. Maxwell Stewart, 331 Lake Road, New Orleans, LA 70113

346 Memorandum from Helen Edwards to Fred Trent

347 Memorandum from Fred Trent to Helen Edwards

348 Memorandum from Max Tate to The Staff

Lesson 59

349 Miss Susan L. Jefferson, 27 West Prairie Lane, Erie, PA 16501

350 Miss Carole Miller, Manager, Nashville Motel, 1221 Edgewood Avenue, Nashville, TN 37202

351 Ms. Elisa Martinez, 800 State Street, Phoenix, AZ 85000

352 Resident, 989 Oak Drive, Los Angeles, CA 90052

353 Mr. Richard Case, Manager, The Eldon Hotel, 111 Woodland Avenue, Sioux Falls, SD 57101

354 Mr. and Mrs. Benjamin Broughton, 3200 Dover Shores, Orlando, FL 32806

Lesson 60

355 Mrs. Joan Bennington, President, International Travel Club, 345 State Street, Montgomery, AL 36100

356 Mr. Robert Gates, 87 Vine Avenue, Montgomery, AL 36104

357 Miss Stacy King, Manager, Tour-Time Travel Agency, 5789 Sunshine Street, Dallas, TX 75221

358 Mr. Kevin H. Tate, Tate Sporting Goods, Inc., 501 North Main, Peoria, IL 61601

359 Memorandum from Marsha Sloan to Vincent Davis

360 Memorandum from James Green to The Staff

CHAPTER 13

Lesson 61

361 Mr. Robert Wilson, Manager, Los Angeles Health Club, 439 Park Avenue, Los Angeles, CA 90052

362 Mrs. Jean Adams, 7903 Elm Street, Battle Creek, MI 49016

363 Home Television Theater, 24 Ridgeway Drive, St. Louis, MO 63155

364 Memorandum from Marlene West to Joan Chase

365 Memorandum from Paul Madison to Joseph Harrington

366 Resident, 751 Bayshore Drive, Pittsburgh, PA 15219

Lesson 62

367 Mr. Raymond Cunningham, 1319 Park Street, Chicago, IL 60010

368 Miss Roberta White, 971 Palm Street, Miami, FL 33101

369 Memorandum from Max Golden to The Staff

370 Memorandum from Martin Brown to The Staff

371 Mr. Ralph Lee, P.O. Box 425, Pueblo, CO 81001

372 Memorandum from Jeffrey Nelson to Elaine Gates

Lesson 63

373 Miss Stephanie Lee, 32 West Broadway, Brooklyn, NY 11212

374 Mr. Martin Stein, 13 River Road, San Diego, CA 92101

375 National Book Club, 903 Palisade, Englewood, NJ 07631

376 Cloverdale Tourist Center, 17 Lincoln Court, Cloverdale, OR 97112

377 Mr. Adam Keith, 6 Ford Road, Elm Grove, WV 26003

378 Mr. Adam Keith, 6 Ford Road, Elm Grove, WV 26003

Lesson 64

379 Memorandum to The Staff from James Burlington

380 Miss Regina Woods, Manager, River Tennis Club, 737 Country Club Drive, Del Norte, CO 81132

381 Mr. Jack Davis, Davis Company, 48 North Adams Street, Great Falls, MT 59401

382 Mr. Jeffrey Lloyd, 18 Estates Lane, Troy, NY 12180

383 Mrs. Wilma Madison, 87 Meade Avenue, San Francisco, CA 94101

384 Miss Freda Long, 562 West Ninth Street, Honolulu, HI 96800

Lesson 65

385 Miss Maureen Kelly, 118 East 46 Street, New York, NY 10019

386 Miss Diane Lexington, Lexington Tours, Inc., 302 Simmons Drive, San Antonio, TX 78205

387 Mr. Samuel Young, General Sporting Goods, Inc., 401 Butler Avenue, Crescent City, CA 95531

388 Mrs. Tina Lopez, 11 Wilson Drive, Lexington, KY 40507

389 Mrs. Anna Lee, 415 Fairfield Avenue, Jacksonville, FL 32201

390 Ms. Lena Poland, Piedmont Travel Agency, 3156 Clark Street, Piedmont, OH 43983

CHAPTER 14

Lesson 66

391 Professor Gary Lyons, President, Western Business Teachers Society, 319 56th Street, Portland, OR 97208

392 Mr. Brad Wheeler, President, National Office Machines Company, 7265 Fir Street, Albany, GA 31702

393 Mr. Christopher Brown, Interstate Business College, 725 Ash Street, Seattle, WA 98101

394 Miss Madeline Wilson, National Business Machines Manufacturing Company, 82 North Oak, Flint, MI 48502

395 Memorandum from Jane Tate to May White

396 Memorandum from May White to Jane Tate

Lesson 67

397 Mr. Robert Schultz, Bennington and Associates, P.O. Box 265, Atlanta, GA 30304

398 Ms. Marie Edwards, 28 First Street, Boston, MA 02109

399 Memorandum from Nora Carson to Mark Porter

400 Memorandum from A. C. Hughes to Marla Adams

401 Memorandum from Ellen James to All Department Heads

402 Memorandum from Anne Washington to Allen Moore

Lesson 68

403 Memorandum from J. D. Gomez to Jane Winters

404 Memorandum from Martin Trent to George Welsh

405 Mr. Rodney Mason, General Computer Company, 8641 East 27 Street, Cincinnati, OH 45202

406 Memorandum from Ellen Marks to Sean Kelly

407 Miss Alice Temple, The Mission Corporation, 8118 Water Street, Des Plaines, IL 60016

408 Mr. Frederic Morris, Morris and Associates, Inc., 616 Northwest 26 Street, Daytona Beach, FL 32014

Lesson 69

409 Mr. Raymond Edwards, 77 Sixth Street, Albany, GA 31702

410 Mr. Joseph Madison, National Music Company, 61 Center Street, Boston, MA 02109

411 Mr. Glen Carter, Manager, Nebraska Business Furniture, 3313 Main Street, Omaha, NE 68108

412 Memorandum from Jane Price to All Department Heads

413 Mrs. Gina Wilson, 1122 Tyler Boulevard, Federal, DE 19711

414 Memorandum from Marie Davis to All Department Heads

Lesson 70

415 Memorandum from A. M. Davis to Allen Case

416 Memorandum from Harry Simmons to The Staff

417 Memorandum from Ellen Ward to Cynthia Drake

418 Memorandum from Mary Stein to Ralph Jennings

419 Miss Elaine Day, Day and Associates, Inc., 127 Madison Avenue, New York, NY 10020

420 Mrs. Margaret Anderson, American Business Equipment Corporation, 12 Armstrong Drive, Albany, NY 12207

CHAPTER 15

Lesson 71

421 Memorandum from Max Hugo to All Department Heads

422 Mr. Ronald Harrington, Standard Sales Corporation, 56 Longview Drive, Toledo, OH 43601

423 Ms. Susan Long, Manager, Riverside Motel, 181 North Seventh, Kelso, MO 63758

424 Memorandum from Alvin Moore to Ruth Burns

425 Memorandum from May Stone to Lois Carter

426 Memorandum from James Clayton to Manuel Lopez

Lesson 72

427 Mr. David T. Lang, Editor, Gray Publishing Company, 55 Drake Street, Chicago, IL 60607

428 Miss Susan Wheeler, 79 West Pine, Miami, FL 33101

429 Memorandum from James Lexington to Dean Wilson

430 Memorandum from Paul Craft to Raymond Garcia

431 Memorandum from Henry Strong to The Members of the Executive Committee

432 Memorandum from L. C. Carpenter to Thomas Jackson

Lesson 73

433 Memorandum from James Reed to Janet Miller

434 Mr. Frank Powers, 823 Oak, Erie, MI 48133

435 Ms. Margaret Pierce, 789 West Tenth Street, Bridgeport, CT 06602

436 Mr. Robert Case, Manager, Stone's Department Store, 406 West 21 Street, Dover, DE 19901

437 Dr. Martin Reed, 135 North Pine Street, Montgomery, AL 36100

438 General Computer Corporation, 17 Grand Avenue, American Falls, ID 83211

Lesson 74

439 Memorandum from Frank Long to Bob Davidson

440 Smith's Hardware Store, 5511 Grape Street, Medford, MA 02155

441 Western Real Estate Association, 191 Spring Street, San Mateo, CA 94402

442 Mr. Norman Green, 3147 Geneva Street, Boise, ID 83707

443 Miss Barbara Adams, 81 Lincoln Boulevard, Framingham, MA 01701

444 Miss Sally Green, 75 Garden Way, Burwell, NE 68823

Lesson 75

445 Martin's Furniture Store, 1100 Wilson Turnpike, New Orleans, LA 70113

446 Ms. Marcia Chase, 655 Cloverdale Road, Eugene, OR 97401

447 Dr. Richard Weston, 197 Park Drive, Salt Lake City, UT 84101

448 Mr. James T. Lee, 1178 Broadway, Sacramento, CA 95814

449 Miss Suzanne Edwards, Edwards Emporium, 8822 Lakeside Drive, Duluth, MN 55801

450 Miss Madeline Peterson, 16 Ashley Drive, Lincoln, NE 68501

CHAPTER 16

Lesson 76

451 Miss Karen Lexington, Patterson Paint Company, 989 Monroe Street, Joliet, IL 60431

452 Ms. Carole Anderson, 117 Jefferson Street, Kansas City, MO 64108

453 Mr. Marvin Stern, General Hardware Corporation, 661 Grant Street, Dover, FL 33527

454 Mr. T. C. Mason, 317 Edgewood Drive, Albany, GA 31702

455 Memorandum from Leslie Yale to Edith Stern

456 Memorandum from James Davis to Nancy Adams

Lesson 77

457 Mr. Marvin Cunningham, 566 Rosewood Street, Denver, CO 80202

458 Jennings Supermarkets Corporation, 41 Bayside, Virginia Beach, VA 23458

459 Mr. R. T. Simmons, 8109 62d Street, Wheeling, WV 26003

460 Miss Louise Edwards, 67 Washington Street, Eugene, OR 97401

461 Mr. Samuel Kelly, Command Computer Corporation, 7781 Harmony Lane, St. Paul, MN 55101

462 Mr. Ronald Woodward, 751 Monticello Terrace, Little Rock, AR 72200

Lesson 78

463 Mr. William Reid, 2230 Catalina Drive, Nashville, TN 37202

464 Ms. Cheryl Martin, International Travel Agency, 45 State Street, Houston, TX 77002

465 Mr. Timothy Carson, 77 Granite Street, Minot, ND 58701

466 Ms. Patricia Lexington, 71 Clinton Street, Atlantic City, NJ 08401

467 Mr. Nathan Ryan, 14 Chestnut Drive, Tulsa, OK 74101

468 Miss Joan D. Lain, P.O. Box 442, Bonanza, OR 97623

Lesson 79

469 Memorandum to All Employees from Bill Adams

470 Mr. Frank Miller, Chamber of Commerce, 571 Elm Street, Springfield, MO 65801

471 Miss Alberta White, 134 Center Street, Charleston, WV 25301

472 Mr. Harold Yale, Jefferson Industries, 982 Avondale, Yakima, WA 98901

473 Miss Elaine Fleming, 3178 West Taylor Street, Phoenix, AZ 85000

474 Dr. Jacqueline Tate, 248 Morrison Street, Huntsville, AL 35800

Lesson 80

475 Professor Phyllis Sloan, Eastern College, 1380 Third Street, Newark, NJ 07102

476 Mr. Michael Cunningham, 975 Bush Street, Providence, RI 02904

477 Memorandum from Sam Jenkins to Annette Wilmington

478 Memorandum from Mary Tate to Calvin Mason

479 Memorandum from Charles O'Keefe to Leah Warden

480 Miss Lynda Lopez, 209 Lone Pine Road, Garden Grove, CA 92600

Index to Transcription Helps

The number next to each entry refers to the page in the text in which the entry appears.

ACCURACY PRACTICE

affect, effect 378
as, if 325
audit, order 178
fear, feel 178
get, gather 227
in the, at the 178
light, right 274
ought, should 274
pass, base 274
red, lead 378
say, see 325
test, text 378
theirs, ours 227
written, regular 227
your, this 325

COMMON PREFIXES

bi- 337
inter- 238
ir- 211
mis- 164
multi- 260
post- 362

GRAMMAR CHECKUP

already, all ready 299
common errors 252, 352, 406
fewer, less 299
one word or two 154, 202
preposition at the end of a sentence 309

LETTER PLACEMENT

Average letters 134
Hints 330
Long letters 230
Short letters 30

MODEL LETTERS

Average letter 123
Interoffice memorandum 405
Long letter 220
Short letter 22

OFFICE-STYLE DICTATION

Deletions 158
Extensive changes 412
Instructions during dictation 278, 304, 332, 357, 384
Long insertions 256

Long transpositions 206
Restorations 182
Short insertions 233
Short transpositions 206
Substitutions 182

PUNCTUATION PRACTICE

Apostrophe 67
—COLONS
Enumeration 129
Introducing long quote 140
—COMMAS
And omitted 16
Apposition 15
As clause 42
Conjunction 16
Geographical 42
If clause 42
In numbers 94
Introducing short quote 136
Introductory 42
Nonrestrictive 42
Parenthetical 15
Series 16
When clause 42
Courteous request 66
Dash 348
Exclamation point 400
Hyphens 67
Parentheses 373
—PUNCTUATION WITH QUOTATION MARKS
Colon introducing long quote 140
Comma inside quote 136
Comma introducing short quote 136
Period inside quote 136
Question mark inside quote 136
—SEMICOLONS
No conjunction 68

SIMILAR WORDS

adopt, adapt, adept 194
cents, sense, scents 266
course, coarse 389
formerly, formally 290
principal, principle 244
quite, quiet, quit 316
residents, residence 170
wear, ware 417
weight, wait 283

SPELLING FAMILIES

-an, -on, -en 150
-cal, -cle 174
-cede, -ceed, -sede 198
Forming -ed, -ing derivatives of words ending in *l* 248
Forming -ed, -ing derivatives of words ending in *r* 295
Forming -ed, -ing derivatives of words ending in *t* 270
-ize, -ise, -yze 187
-ly added to words ending in *e* 223
Words in which *l*, *m*, *s* are doubled 321

TRANSCRIPTION SUGGESTIONS

Accepting more responsibility 288
Arranging meetings and trips 216
Composing letters 264
Devising shortcuts 382
Future advancement 394
Looking for the job 12
Moving up 314
Organizing the work area 90
Preparing reports 192
Pretranscription procedures 144
Rough drafts 411
Sharpening skills 242
Supervising others 366
Taking dictation 118
The first day 64
The interview 40
The replacement 342
Transcribing 168

TYPING STYLE STUDIES

Addresses 92
Adjacent numbers 368
Ages and Anniversaries 344
Amounts 92
Capitalization 94
—CAPITALIZATION
Days, etc. 146
General classifications 218
Names 218
Personal titles 218
Dates 93
Expressions of time 93
Fractions and mixed numbers 396
Numbers 93
Titles of sections of published works 125
Titles of separate publications 120

Brief Forms of Gregg Shorthand

IN ALPHABETICAL ORDER

	A	B	C	D	E	F	G
1							
2							
3							
4							
5							
6							
7							
8							
9							
10							
11							
12							
13							
14							
15							
16							
17